Taxcafe.co.uk Tax Guides

How to Avoid Property Tax

By Carl Bayley BSc ACA

Important Legal Notices:

TAXCafe™
TAX GUIDE – "How to Avoid Property Tax"

Published by:
Taxcafe UK Limited
214 High St
Kirkcaldy KY1 1JT
United Kingdom
Tel: (01592) 560081

First Edition	March 2002
Second Edition	June 2002
Third Edition	September 2002
Fourth Edition	January 2003
Fifth Edition	April 2003
Sixth Edition	March 2004
Seventh Edition	March 2005
Eighth Edition	April 2006

ISBN 1 904608 39 6

About the Author

Carl Bayley is the author of a number of tax guides designed specifically for the layman. Carl's particular speciality is his ability to take the weird, complex and inexplicable world of taxation and set it out in the kind of clear, straightforward language that taxpayers themselves can understand. As he often says himself, "my job is to translate tax into English".

Carl takes the same approach when speaking on taxation, a role he has undertaken with some relish on a number of occasions, including his highly acclaimed series of seminars at the London Homebuyer Show and his annual 'Budget Breakfast' for the Institute of Chartered Accountants in England & Wales.

In addition to being a recognised author and speaker on the subject, Carl has also spoken on property taxation on BBC radio and television. Most recently, he has also appeared on Irish television too.

A Chartered Accountant by training, Carl began his professional life in 1983, in the Birmingham office of one of the 'Big 4' accountancy firms. He qualified as a double prize-winner and immediately began specialising in taxation.

After 17 years honing his skills with major firms, Carl began the new millennium in January 2000 by launching his own Edinburgh-based tax consultancy practice. The rapid growth of this practice led, in late 2005, to the formation of Bayley Miller Limited, through which Carl now provides advice on a wide variety of UK taxation issues, especially property taxation, Inheritance Tax planning and matters affecting small and medium-sized businesses.

Carl will shortly complete three years as Chairman of the Institute Members in Scotland group (2003-2006) and is also a former member of the governing Council of the Institute of Chartered Accountants in England and Wales (2003-2005).

When he isn't working, Carl takes on the equally taxing challenges of hill walking and writing poetry. Carl lives in Edinburgh with his partner Isabel and has four children.

Dedication

For the Past,

Firstly, I dedicate this book to the memory of those I have loved and lost:

To my beloved friend and companion, Dawson, who waited so patiently for me to come home every night and who left me in the middle of our last walk together;

To my dear grandparents, Arthur, Doris and Winifred;

And, most of all, to my beloved mother, Diana, who made it all possible.

They left me with nothing I could spend, but everything I need.

For the Present,

As usual, I would also like to dedicate this book to Isabel, my 'life support system', whose unflinching support has seen me through the best and the worst. Whether anyone will ever call me a 'great man' I do not know, but I do know that I have a great woman behind me.

Without her help, support and encouragement, this book, and the others I have written, could never have been.

For the Future,

Finally, I also dedicate this book to four very special young people: Michelle, Louise, James and Robert.

I can only hope that I, in turn, will also be able to leave them with everything that they need.

Thanks

Sincere thanks are due to my good friend, colleague and 'comrade-in-arms', Nick, who believed in me long before I did.

Thanks also to the rest of the Taxcafe team for their help in making these books far more successful than I could ever have dreamed.

And thanks to Ann for keeping us right!

C.B., Edinburgh, April 2006

Contents

Contents (cont ...)

Contents (cont ...)

Contents (cont ...)

Contents (cont ...)

Introduction

By the author

This guide was first produced in March 2002, as a response to the huge demand for advice on property taxation issues which we had been experiencing at Taxcafe.co.uk. That demand has continued to grow at a phenomenal pace and is responsible for the fact that this guide is already in its eighth edition, just four years later, and has expanded rapidly to the nine chapters which you have here.

People in the UK have invested in property for centuries. Substantial increases in personal wealth and disposable income over the last few decades, together with recent difficulties in other areas of investment and in the pensions industry, have however combined to make this an ever-increasingly important area of personal financial planning.

The last ten years, in particular, have seen a phenomenal growth in the property sector, not just in the amount of property development activity but also in the sheer numbers of people entering the property market as investors, developers and dealers. Where the big flotations of the 1980's acted to spread investment in stocks and shares into all sectors of society, the late 1990's and early years of this century have seen a similar spreading of property investment.

The word 'Landlord' used to sometimes conjure up images of a rather Dickensian, Fagin-like creature (especially to those of us who were in student accommodation twenty or more years ago), whereas now we more often tend to refer to a 'Property Investor', which seems to have an entirely different connotation. (Although there are some, I know, who are trying to reclaim the name of 'Landlord' without its Dickensian connotations.)

'Property Investment' itself is also a very wide term. A few years ago, the majority of new investors tended to be purely interested in the 'Buy-to-Let' market. As the property sector has grown larger and more sophisticated, however, many other types of activity have begun to proliferate more widely, including 'Buy-to-Sell', 'Let-to-Buy' and, of course, a great deal of renovation, conversion and development activity. Beyond these, there also lie the fields of property trading and management.

All of these different types of activity are subject to different tax regimes and establishing the correct tax classification for each property business can be quite tortuous. One of our first tasks in this guide is therefore to help you understand how your own business will be treated for tax purposes and this is something which we will consider in depth in chapter two.

There are also many different reasons for becoming a property investor. Some fall into it by accident, finding themselves with a second property through marriage, inheritance or other changes in personal circumstances.

Others move into the property sector quite deliberately, seeing it as a safe haven providing long-term security. Still others see the property market as a means to generate a second income.

More recently, a strong trend has emerged for people to enter the property business as a professional career. This 'new breed' of property investor is entering the market with a much higher degree of sophistication and is prepared to devote substantial time and resources to their business.

As increasing property prices have raised the barrier to entry and as the market in some parts of England appears to be reaching a state of maturity, people have found new ways to invest in property, such as investing in Northern England and Scotland, investing abroad (including the ten new states which joined the European Union on 1st May 2004), or clubbing together to invest through syndicates or special purpose vehicles (often called SPVs).

So, despite some recent concerns over the future of the UK property market, I personally believe that the property investment sector as we know it today is here to stay. Naturally, the sector will have its ups and downs, as any other business sector does, but the philosophy of property investment as a 'career move' is now so well entrenched that it has become impossible to imagine that it could ever disappear altogether.

Whatever reasons you may have for entering the property investment market and whatever type of property business you may have, my aim in this guide is to both give you a better understanding of how the UK tax system will affect you and also to provide you with some guidance on the techniques available to minimise or eliminate your potential tax liabilities.

In the first two chapters of the guide, we will set the scene by looking at the different UK taxes which you will meet as a property investor and then looking at how they apply to the various different kinds of property business.

Chapters three to seven are then devoted to explaining in detail how the UK tax rules apply to property investment and other types of property business.

There are plenty of **'Tax Tips'** along the way to help you minimise or delay your tax bills, as well as **'Wealth Warnings'** designed to keep you away from some of the more treacherous pitfalls awaiting the unwary taxpayer and **'Practical Pointers'** which will make the whole process of meeting your obligations as a taxpayer as painless as possible.

We will round off the guide, in chapters eight and nine, by examining some more advanced tax planning strategies which you, the investor, can employ to reduce your tax burden. Chapter eight is devoted to strategies available to individuals investing directly in property themselves. Chapter nine then goes on to cover some of the other main investment structures and techniques available.

I believe that this guide is now comprehensive enough to meet the needs of almost every property investor based or investing in the UK and I hope that, with its help, you will be able to enjoy a much larger proportion of the fruits of your endeavours.

Finally, I would just like to thank you for buying this guide and wish you every success with your property investments.

Scope of this Guide

In this guide, we aim to cover as much as possible of the UK tax implications of investing in property, or running some other kind of property business. There are three different types of property investor for whom UK tax will be an issue. These three types of investor may be summarised as follows:

(i) UK residents investing in UK property.
(ii) UK residents investing in overseas property.
(iii) Non-UK residents investing in UK property.

Obviously, the same person might have investments falling under both (i) and (ii) and we will cater for that situation also.

Non-UK residents may also have overseas property investments, but these should generally be outside the scope of UK taxation. (Why only "generally"? Well, if a German resident buys a house in France, it will generally be of no interest to Her Majesty's Revenue and Customs in the UK. But what if he buys it through a UK registered company?)

For tax purposes, the UK does not include the Channel Islands or the Isle of Man, but comprises only England, Scotland, Wales and Northern Ireland.

Wealth Warning

It is important to remember that both UK residents investing in property overseas and non-UK residents investing in UK property may also face foreign tax liabilities on their property income and capital gains.

Additionally, in some cases, citizens of another country who are resident in the UK for tax purposes, may nevertheless still have obligations and liabilities under their own country's tax system, even in respect of their business or investment activities in the UK (or, indeed, elsewhere in the world). The USA, for example, imposes this type of obligation on its expatriate citizens. Each country has its own tax system, and income or gains which are exempt in the UK may nevertheless still be liable to tax elsewhere.

It is only where we are talking about taxpayers who are both UK residents and UK citizens, and who are investing exclusively in UK property, that we can be absolutely certain that no other country has any right to tax the income or gains arising.

The tax-planning strategies outlined in this guide represent a reasonably comprehensive list of the main techniques available to all classes of property investor with UK tax obligations. Those who have the benefit of being non-UK resident or non-UK domiciled for tax purposes, however, are able to employ more specialised tax-planning techniques and these are covered in further detail in the Taxcafe.co.uk guide *Non-Resident & Offshore Tax Planning*.

Most of this guide is aimed primarily at those who are running a property business personally, jointly with another individual, or through a partnership. In the final chapter, however, we will be looking at some of the tax advantages, disadvantages and other implications of investing in property through other investment vehicles, such as limited companies, limited liability partnerships, property trusts or pension schemes. A great deal more detailed guidance on the implications of using a property company is contained in the Taxcafe.co.uk guide *Using a Property Company to Save Tax*.

Finally, the reader must bear in mind the general nature of this guide. Individual circumstances vary and the tax implications of an individual's actions will vary with them. For this reason, it is always vital to get professional advice before undertaking any tax planning or other transactions which may have tax implications. The author cannot accept any responsibility for any loss which may arise as a consequence of any action taken, or any decision to refrain from action taken, as a result of reading this guide.

Chapter 1

What is Property Tax?

1.1 KNOWING YOUR ENEMY

We will begin this guide with an explanation of how the UK tax system applies to property investment and other types of property business.

This is essential because you cannot begin to consider how to avoid property tax until you actually understand what property tax is. In other words, you must 'know your enemy' in order to be able to combat it most effectively.

The property investor needs to understand that there is no single 'property tax', but rather a whole range of taxes which can apply to property. There is no point in avoiding one of these taxes only to find yourself paying even more of another!

Horror stories of this nature happen all too frequently, such as the taxpayer who managed to avoid 1% Stamp Duty on part of his new house, only to find that he was stuck with a 17.5% VAT charge instead!

Worse still was the taxpayer who undertook some Inheritance Tax planning on the advice of his lawyer only to find himself stuck with a £20,000 Capital Gains Tax bill without any cash sale proceeds from which to pay it.

If only they'd spoken to a real tax expert first!

In this introductory chapter therefore, we will take a brief look at the taxes which can affect the property investor and give some consideration to the relative importance of each.

Later, when we begin to consider tax-planning strategies, it is vital to bear in mind that it is the overall outcome which matters most, not simply saving or deferring any single type of tax.

In fact, I would go even further than that....

Bayley's Law

The truly wise investor does not seek merely to minimise the amount of tax payable, but rather to maximise the amount of wealth remaining after all taxes have been accounted for.

If this seems like no more than simple common sense to you, then all well and good. However, in practice, I am constantly amazed at how often people lose sight of this simple fact and, in trying to save tax at any price, actually end up making themselves worse off in the long run!

1.2   WHAT TAXES FACE A PROPERTY INVESTOR?

Currently, the only UK taxes which are specific to property are council tax (for residential property) and business rates (for commercial property) and these, in any case, are levied on the occupiers of property and not necessarily on the owners or investors.

However, the investor should not for a moment think this means that property investment gets off lightly under the UK tax system.

Far from it! Without the existence of any specific national tax, property investment is left exposed to a huge range of UK taxes.
Tax is levied when property is purchased (Stamp Duty Land Tax), rented out (Income Tax) and sold (Capital Gains Tax). Property investors have to pay tax when they need to buy goods or services (VAT), when they make their investments through a company (Corporation Tax) and even when they die (Inheritance Tax).

Those who are classed as property developers or property traders will pay Income Tax and National Insurance Contributions on the profits derived from their property sales (or Corporation Tax if they use a company). Property developers must also operate and account for tax under the Construction Industry Scheme when using sub-contractors for even the most routine building work and may soon have to contend with the proposed Planning Gain Supplement as well.

When the successful investor needs to employ help in the business, he or she will have to pay PAYE and employer's National Insurance Contributions.

Doubtless, the investor will also be paying Insurance Premium Tax, as well as Road Tax and duty on the petrol they buy as they travel in their business. They may even be paying air passenger duty if their business takes them far.

Faced with this horrifying list, investors might be excused for turning to drink, only to find themselves paying yet more tax!

1.3   WHICH TAXES ARE MOST IMPORTANT?

For most property investors, two taxes comprise the vast majority of the actual or potential tax burden which they will face during their lifetime. These are Income Tax and Capital Gains Tax and they are covered in detail in Chapters three to six.

The exact way in which these two very important taxes will actually be applied to your property business will depend on exactly what type of property investor you are.

For tax purposes, there are a number of different categories into which a property business might fall and it is crucial that you understand how your business is likely to be classified before you can attempt to plan your tax affairs. I will return to this question in more detail in chapter two.

For some classes of investor, National Insurance Contributions will form what is effectively an additional layer of Income Tax and we will examine this extra tax burden in chapter five.

Other taxes which may also have a significant impact include Stamp Duty Land Tax, Inheritance Tax, VAT and, in future, perhaps also the proposed Planning Gain Supplement. These are covered in Chapter seven.

For those investors using a company, Corporation Tax will become of equal, if not greater, importance to the two main taxes.

1.4 HOW DOES PROPERTY TAX COMPARE WITH TAX ON OTHER TYPES OF INCOME?

At present, property <u>income</u> could reasonably be described as 'middle-ranking' in terms of the level of tax which is levied on it in the UK.

On the one hand, property income is treated less favourably than:

a) Dividends – basic rate taxpayers have no liability on UK dividends and higher rate taxpayers suffer an effective rate of only 25%.

b) Other savings income (primarily interest) – basic rate taxpayers pay 20% rather than 22%.

On the other hand, however, one saving grace is that property rental income is not regarded as 'earnings'. Many years ago, when we had the 'unearned income surcharge', this would have been quite disadvantageous.

Now though, as explained in section 1.4, it means that most property rental income does not generally give rise to any liability for National Insurance Contributions. This, in turn, means that the effective tax burden on rental income received is usually much less than for:

a) Self-employment or partnership trading income – most taxpayers have to pay an additional 8% in Class 4 National Insurance Contributions on the majority of their profits, plus £2.10 a week in Class 2 National Insurance Contributions. (The Class 4 rate drops to 1% for annual profits over £33,540, giving an overall effective 'top-rate' of 41% in combined Income Tax and National Insurance Contributions on this income.)

b) Employment income – the combined National Insurance Contributions burden for employers and employees on most earnings is 23.8%, giving an overall effective rate of 45.8% in combined Income Tax and National Insurance Contributions on most employment income. (The effective 'top-rate' of combined Income Tax and National Insurance here is 53.8%!)

One can therefore readily see the massive advantage which rental income has over employment income with a lesser, but still significant, advantage over other forms of self-employment. Consider the following by way of illustration:

For a basic rate taxpayer with annual income of less than £33,540 to get an extra £100 in his or her pocket net of all taxes will require:

- Their tenants to pay an extra £128.21 in rent (as a landlord),
- Their customers to pay an extra £142.86 (as a self-employed trader), or
- Their employer to pay an extra £168.36 in salary and National Insurance Contributions (as an employee).

Similarly, for a higher rate taxpayer to get an extra £100 in his or her pocket net of all taxes will require:

a) Their tenants to pay an extra £166.67 in rent (as a landlord),
b) Their customers to pay an extra £169.49 (as a self-employed trader), or
c) Their employer to pay an extra £191.19 in salary and National Insurance Contributions (as an employee).

Furthermore, most self-employed traders with gross annual income over £61,000 will also need to charge VAT on the figure given at (b) above, bringing the total extra charge required up to £199.15!

Naturally, however, the property market is not just about rental income and there are other forms of property income to be considered. The profit which property dealers or property developers make on the sale of their investments is treated as trading income and is subject to National Insurance Contributions as described above, just like any other trade.

Property management fees will also generally be treated as trading income subject to both Class 2 and 4 National Insurance Contributions.

1.5 WHAT ABOUT CAPITAL TAXES?

Unfortunately, this is where property investment really can suffer in comparison to other forms of investment.

10

The rates of Stamp Duty Land Tax on property are now quite prohibitive (see section 7.2), especially when compared with the single 0.5% rate of Stamp Duty which still applies to shares and securities.

Capital Gains Tax is extremely complex, as we will see in Chapter six. Whilst the tax has a highly complicated system of reliefs and exemptions, which can work well for the wiser and better prepared property investor, it is nevertheless somewhat disappointing to note that the most popular forms of property investment will fail to attract the more advantageous Business Asset Taper Relief.

Worse still, if you are classified as a property dealer or property developer, the profits arising on the sale of your properties will be taxed as income, rather than capital gains. Generally speaking, this will be quite disadvantageous, although, as with most things in tax, there are exceptions (as we shall see later in the guide).

Finally (in more ways than one), there is the fact that Inheritance Tax will most likely be payable in full on most property investments if the investor fails to plan effectively during his or her lifetime.

1.6   DEALING WITH REVENUE & CUSTOMS

At various points in this guide, you will see me refer to your 'Tax Office'. This is the Revenue & Customs office that sends you your tax return or, if you are not yet in the self-assessment system, the office that your employer deals with. Failing either of these, it will be the local Revenue & Customs office for the area where you live and can be found in the telephone directory under 'Revenue & Customs'. (With an older telephone directory try 'Inland Revenue' instead.)

Prior to their merger on 18th April 2005, the UK had two tax bodies. Some readers may be more familiar with these bodies' former names, the Inland Revenue and Customs & Excise. Whilst all UK taxes are now dealt with by HM Revenue & Customs, different departments within the organisation continue to deal with matters which previously concerned the Inland Revenue or Customs & Excise.

Chapter 2

What Kind of Property Investor Are You?

2.1 INTRODUCTION

Before we begin to look in detail at exactly how property businesses are taxed in the UK, we must first consider what type of property business we are looking at. This is an essential step, as the tax treatment of a property business will vary according to the type of business activities involved.

While it would be possible to come up with a very long list of different 'types' of property business, I would tend to regard the following four categories as the definitive list as far as UK taxation treatment is concerned:

a) Property investment (including property letting)
b) Property development
c) Property trading (or dealing)
d) Property management

Wealth Warning

Care must be taken here, because a great deal of what the layman would tend to call 'property investment' is, in fact, likely to be categorised as property development or property dealing for tax purposes.

Before we go on to look at the detailed tax treatment of these different types of property business, it is perhaps worth spending a little time to explain exactly what these different terms mean in a taxation context.

It is also important to understand that these different types of property business are not exclusive to individual property investors and that these different categorisations may also be applied to a property company, a partnership, or any other kind of property investment vehicle.

The reason that we need to consider these different types of property business here is the fact that an understanding of what type of property business you have is crucial in determining which taxes will apply to your business and when.

The most fundamental issue is whether you are carrying on a property investment business (type (a) above), or a property trade (types (b), (c) and (d) above).

Whilst each type of property business has its own quirks, the 'trading or investment' issue is by far the most important and I will be examining this in more detail in sections 2.8 and 2.9.

To complicate matters still further, however, there is also a strange 'no-man's land' lying somewhere between a property investment business and a property trade, which is not regarded as a business at all and is taxed neither as a capital investment nor as a trade. For want of a better term, I will refer to this as 'casual property income' and we will look at it further in section 2.7.

Further out, on the periphery of the property sector, there are other, property-based trades such as hotels, guest houses, nursing homes and hostels, as well as activities in the commercial property sector such as serviced offices and warehousing.

These trades involve the provision of services far beyond that which the normal property investor would provide. We will look briefly at the tax treatment of these property-based trades in section 2.11.

A property investor may, of course, be carrying on more than one type of property business, which could result in a mixture of tax treatments. I will spend a little time on the possible consequences of this in section 2.10.

You will see that there is no mention of Stamp Duty Land Tax in the remainder of this chapter. This is for the simple reason that this tax, uniquely, is unaffected by what kind of property business you have. The Stamp Duty Land Tax rules outlined in chapter seven apply equally to almost everyone.

2.2 DOES IT MATTER WHAT KIND OF PROPERTY YOU INVEST IN?

For tax purposes, there are two main types of property: residential and commercial.

Residential property, naturally, means people's homes, and covers flats, houses, apartments, bungalows, cottages, etc, etc. Also counted in this category are holiday homes, as we shall see later on in chapter four.

Commercial property covers a wide range of properties, including shops, offices, restaurants, pubs, doctors', dentists' and vets' surgeries, hotels, sports centres, warehouses, factories, workshops, garages, schools, hospitals, prisons … anything which isn't residential, basically.

Practical Pointer

It is important here to distinguish between:

a) Owning commercial property and renting it out to other businesses, (which is generally an investment activity), and,
b) Actually occupying and using the commercial property yourself, which is generally a trade.

Example

Basil owns a string of hotels which he does not run himself, but rents to a number of other businesses. Basil is therefore a property investor and is taxed as outlined in section 2.3.

Sybil rents one of Basil's hotels and runs it as her own business. Sybil is therefore operating a hotel trade, which is taxed as outlined in section 2.11. She is not a property investor.

Developing, or dealing in, commercial property is also a trade, but a very different one to occupying and using that property in your own trade. Naturally, it follows that the tax treatment of such trades is also very different.

How Does This Affect What Type of Business You Have?

Assuming that you are not actually occupying and operating a trade from your properties, the type of property in which you invest has absolutely no bearing on which of the four main types of property business you have.

The guidelines set out in the remainder of this chapter therefore apply equally to both residential and commercial property investors. The issue of what type of property business you have is based purely on the way in which you behave as an investor and not on the nature of your underlying properties.

Naturally, though, there are many other important differences between the tax treatment of residential property and commercial property and, indeed, in the tax treatment of different types of residential and commercial property. We will examine these differences as we progress through the following chapters. Note also that it is quite possible to have both commercial and residential property within the same property business.

2.3 PROPERTY INVESTMENT (OR PROPERTY LETTING)

These are businesses which predominantly hold properties as long-term investments. The properties are the business's fixed assets, which are held to produce income in the form of rental profit, long-term capital growth or, most commonly, a combination of both.

Whilst capital growth will be anticipated, and will form part of the investor's business plan, short-term property disposals should usually only take place where there is a strong commercial reason, such as an anticipated decline in value in that particular geographical location or a need to realise funds for other investments.

In general, properties will be held for a long period and rapid sales for short-term gain will be exceptional.

Having said that, where unexpected opportunities for short-term gains do arise, it would be unreasonable to suggest that the investor should not make the most of them.

Example

Fletcher purchases three properties 'off-plan' in September 2006, intending to hold them as long-term investments. On completion of the properties in January 2007, however, he sells one of them in order to provide funds for a new investment which he now wishes to make. Nevertheless, the other two properties are retained and rented out for a number of years.

Although Fletcher sold one of the properties very quickly, there was a good commercial reason for doing so. Hence, he may still be regarded as having a property investment business.

It is symptomatic of a pure property investment business that the investor has a minimal level of involvement in the day-to-day running of the business. Typically, the investor pays an agent to manage his or her property affairs. The majority of buy-to-let investors would be regarded as having this type of business.

There are, however, many other property letting businesses which are much more 'hands on' than the typical modern-style 'buy-to-let' business. The landlord/investor is much more involved in the management of the business on a day-to-day basis. For larger property letting businesses, the landlord's job even becomes a full-time one.

As long as the business still meets the overall long-term investment criterion outlined above, it remains a property investment business for tax purposes regardless of the level of the landlord's involvement on a day-to-day basis. Managing your own properties does not, in itself, mean that you have a property management trade.

Where the landlord begins to provide services way beyond mere management, the business could eventually become a property-based trade of the type examined in section 2.11. Generally, this does require some fairly extreme steps but we will return to this issue and, in particular, some instances in which it may be beneficial, later in the guide.

For tax purposes then, we can generally regard 'property investment businesses' and 'property letting businesses' as one and the same.

16

The only real difference lies in the level of administrative expenses which may justifiably be claimed, as we shall see in chapter four.

Tax Treatment

An investor with a property investment business must account for his rental profits under the specific rules applying to income from land and property (see chapter four).

Property disposals are dealt with as capital gains. Property held on death is fully liable to Inheritance Tax (subject to the 'nil rate band').

Is there any advantage to being regarded as having a property investment business rather than one of the other types of property business?

Yes, there is often quite an advantage for an individual property investor (or a partnership, trust, etc.) in having a property investment business instead of one of the other types of property business which are classified as trades for tax purposes.

The main reason for this is the fact that property disposals are treated as capital gains, taxed under the Capital Gains Tax regime and not income which is taxed under the Income Tax regime.

This, in turn, provides the investor with the opportunity to make the most of the many different reliefs available within the Capital Gains Tax regime (see Chapter six). However, this is far from the end of the story and we will return to the comparative advantages and disadvantages of property investment or property trading in section 2.8.

Wealth Warning

It is always important to remember that it is the way in which you carry on your business which determines the tax treatment, it is not a matter of choice!

In section 2.9 we will return to this issue and examine the borderline between investment and trading in greater detail.

2.4 PROPERTY DEVELOPMENT

These are businesses which predominantly acquire properties or land and carry out building or renovation work with a view to selling developed properties for profit.

The term 'property development' covers a very wide spectrum of activities, from major building companies that acquire vacant land and construct vast new property developments, to amateur property investors who acquire the occasional 'run-down' property to 'do up' for onward sale at a profit. No one would doubt that the former are correctly categorised as property developers, but not everyone realises that the latter type of activity will also lead to the investors being regarded as property developers.

It is vital to understand here that even the most minor of conversion or renovation projects can lead to the investor being treated as a property developer if the property concerned was clearly acquired with the sole or main intention of realising a quick profit. This is what many of the characters we see on morning television these days are actually doing.

Generally speaking with this type of business, a property will be disposed of as soon as possible after building or renovation work has been completed. It is the profit derived from this work which produces the business's income and the owners do not usually look to rent properties out other than as a matter of short-term expediency.

Example

Godber purchases three old barns in February 2006 and converts them into residential property. The work is completed in August 2006 and he then sells two of the former barns immediately.

The third barn, unfortunately, proves difficult to sell. In the meantime, in order to generate some income from the property, Godber lets it out on a short six-month lease. The property is never taken off the market during the period of the lease and a buyer is found in January 2007, with completion taking place in March.

Although Godber let one of the properties out for a short period, his main business activity remained property development. His intention was clearly to develop the properties for sale at a profit. This was reinforced by the fact that the property had remained on the market throughout the lease. Godber therefore has a property development business.

Tax Treatment

A property development business is regarded as a trade.

The profits from property development activities, i.e. the profits arising from development property sales, are taxed as trading profits. Trading profits are subject to both Income Tax and National Insurance Contributions (see further in chapter five).

Where, as in the example above, there is some incidental short-term rental income it should, strictly speaking, still be dealt with under the specific rules applying to income from land and property. In practice, however, it has sometimes been known for this to be accepted as incidental trading income. Whether this is beneficial to the taxpayer or not will depend on a great many factors, as we shall see in section 2.8.

The great disadvantage of being classified as a property developer is the fact that all profits are dealt with under the Income Tax regime and not the Capital Gains Tax regime. This means that reliefs such as the annual Capital Gains Tax exemption, principal private residence relief and private letting relief will not be available.

On the other hand, however, the business itself, if it has any value (e.g. Goodwill), will attract Business Asset Taper Relief and Business Property Relief for Inheritance Tax purposes. The latter relief would even apply to any properties held as 'trading stock' at the time of death.

Capital gains treatment would apply to any disposals of the business's long-term fixed assets, such as its own offices, for example.

Property developers who utilise the services of sub-contractors for any building work, including plumbing, decorating and electrical work, are required to operate the Construction Industry Scheme for tax purposes. This may involve having to deduct tax, at a special rate particular to the Construction Industry Scheme (currently 18%), from payments made to sub-contractors and then account for it to Revenue & Customs, rather like PAYE.

2.5 PROPERTY TRADING

This type of property business used to be fairly rare, but seems to have grown in popularity over the last few years. A property trader generally only holds properties for short-term gain. Properties are bought and sold frequently and are held as trading stock. Such traders may sometimes also be known as property dealers.

Properties will not usually be rented out, except for short-term financial expediency.

These investors derive their income simply by making a profit on the properties they sell.

Property traders differ from property developers in that no actual development takes place on the properties. Profits are made simply by ensuring a good margin between buying price and selling price.

To be a trade, however, there does need to be some degree of serious intent involved. The investor must be undertaking the property trading activity in a reasoned and methodical manner. There is an important distinction, therefore, between a professional property trader and a casual investor. To be 'professional' in this context does not, however, necessarily mean that it must be a full-time activity, merely that it is more than casual. I will explain the concept of 'casual property income' further in section 2.7.

Example

Over the last two years, Mr McKay has bought 30 different properties 'off-plan'. He has sold each property at a considerable profit within a few months of completion.

Since Mr McKay has neither developed any of the properties, nor held on to them as investments for any appreciable length of time, he is clearly neither a property developer nor running a property investment business. Furthermore, the frequency and scale of his activities clearly indicates that he is a professional property trader.

Tax Treatment

A property trader's profits from property sales should be taxed as trading profits within the Income Tax regime. Once again, these profits are also subject to National Insurance Contributions (see section 5.5).

As with a property developer, any incidental letting income which does arise should be dealt with under the specific rules applying to income from land and property.

The value of this type of business is specifically not eligible for Business Property Relief for Inheritance Tax purposes.

As for Capital Gains Tax taper relief, the theory is that a property trading business is still a 'trade' and hence the long-term assets of such a business (e.g. goodwill or office premises) should be eligible for the faster 'business asset' taper relief. In practice, however, I feel that there is a strong danger that some resistance will be encountered, with Revenue & Customs contending that the business is, in fact, a property investment business and hence its long-term assets do not qualify as 'business assets'. Time will tell on this one!

Wealth Warning

The major difference between property investment and property trading lies in the treatment of the profit arising on property disposals. In essence, the question is whether such 'profits' are capital gains or trading profits.

This is very much a 'grey area' and hence Revenue & Customs can be expected to examine borderline cases very carefully and to argue for the treatment that produces the most tax.

As explained above, Revenue & Customs may be inclined to deny the existence of a trading activity where taper relief is at stake.

Conversely, where an investor is potentially exempt from Capital Gains Tax (e.g. on a former principal private residence), Revenue & Customs may argue that there is a trading activity in order to be able to levy Income Tax on that investor instead. We will look at this further in chapter six.

2.6   PROPERTY MANAGEMENT

These businesses do not generally own properties at all (except, perhaps, their own offices). Instead, they provide management services to property owners. If you have a property letting agent taking care of the day-to-day running of your properties, the chances are that it is probably a property management company.

A property management business's income is derived from the management or service charges that it charges to the actual owners of the property.

Tax Treatment

A property management business is a trade for all tax purposes.

The long-term assets of a property management business are usually regarded as business assets for both Capital Gains Tax taper relief and Inheritance Tax purposes.

The profits arising from property management activities will be treated as trading profits, subject to both Income Tax and National Insurance Contributions.

Any incidental letting income should, as usual, be dealt with under the specific rules applying to income from land and property.

2.7   CASUAL PROPERTY INCOME

As I explained in the introduction to this chapter, somewhere between property investment and property trading there lies a 'no-man's land' (a 'twilight zone' if you like), which I will term 'casual property income'.

As we have seen already in previous sections, property investment businesses are treated as holding their properties as long-term capital assets, whereas property trades hold properties as short-term trading stock.

In this strange intermediate 'twilight zone' however, lie the property transactions which are neither long-term investments nor part of a trading activity.

The key features of this type of income are as follows:

i)   Investments are made with a high expectation of short-term profit.
ii) Profit is derived from a disposal of the investment, or an interest therein, rather than an income stream such as rent.
iii) The investor plays a passive role in the transactions.

Note that any property rental income, no matter how transient or casual, will always be subject to the special rules for 'income from land and property', as outlined in chapter four, and will never form 'casual property income'.

The best way to explain casual property income is by way of an example.

Example

Mr Barraclough is having a quiet drink in his local one night when he is approached by his friend Mr Grout.

Mr Grout explains that he has a fabulous property investment opportunity but is just £10,000 short of the capital he needs. He also reminds Mr Barraclough that he has just won that very sum of money on the National Lottery.

Groutie promises Barraclough a guaranteed return of at least 20% after just three months if he invests his £10,000 in the property deal.

After some persuasion, Mr Barraclough reluctantly agrees to invest £10,000 in Mr Grout's venture.

He hears nothing further about the matter for over four months and is beginning to get rather worried until Groutie turns up with a cheque for £12,000, as promised.

Clearly, Mr Barraclough's investment was made for short-term profit and would therefore appear to be income in nature, rather than a capital gain.

On the other hand, however, Mr Barraclough's role was totally passive. Mr Grout sought him out. Barraclough did not have to 'get his hands dirty' in any way and did not participate directly in either the purchase or the sale of the underlying property.

There is no way, therefore, that Mr Barraclough could be regarded as having a property trade and his £2,000 profit represents casual property income.

In reality, one would need to know a lot more about Mr Grout's proposition before being absolutely sure that Mr Barraclough's profit represented income rather than a capital gain, but this is certainly the sort of thing which would generally be regarded as casual property income. (I imagine also that Mr Barraclough would like to know a lot more about the proposed investment before he decided whether to invest at all in the first place!)

Most people in Mr Barraclough's position would tend to prefer this profit to be treated as a capital gain, rather than as income, as the first £8,800 of 'profit' would then be covered by their annual Capital Gains Tax exemption.

However, in the absence of any further information, I would tend to regard Mr Grout's proposal as being too short-term and having too certain an outcome to be regarded as a capital gain in Mr Barraclough's hands.

Tax Treatment

Casual property income is 'other income' for tax purposes. It is not treated under the special rules applying to income from land and property (as outlined in chapter four) and neither is it treated as trading income (as detailed in chapter five).

Any income of this nature should be entered in Boxes 13.1 to 13.3 of your Tax Return.

Any underlying assets held in the course of producing such casual property income will not be eligible for Business Property Relief for Inheritance Tax purposes and should not be held long enough to be eligible for any Capital Gains Tax taper relief.

Casual income should not generally give rise to any VAT liabilities or any obligation to register for VAT.

The best thing about casual property income though is the fact that, since it is not a trade, it does not attract National Insurance Contributions. For many people this means a saving of 8%. For most others there is still a saving of 1% - not much, but still better than a 'poke in the eye with a sharp stick'!

The only drawback, of course, is that to be 'casual income', there must be an absence of any serious trade-like intent. In other words, once you set out to make the income in any organised manner, it inevitably ceases to be casual and you will either have a property trade or, in tax terms, 'income from land and property'.

For this reason, this type of income is fairly rare. Nevertheless, if you do meet a 'Harry Grout' in the pub and do decide to participate in his venture, then you know now that there is a chance to save some National Insurance.

2.8   ADVANTAGES AND DISADVANTAGES OF INVESTMENT OR TRADING

As we have seen already, the most important issue is whether your property business is classed as investment or trading.

The major difference is in the treatment of profits arising on property disposals, but there are many other differences which need to be taken into account.

In this section, therefore, I thought it might be useful to set out a brief summary of the tax advantages and disadvantages of each type of property business.

Tax Advantages of Property Investment Businesses

- 'Profits' arising on property disposals are treated as capital gains. This means:
  - A maximum long-term tax rate of 24% (for properties held for ten years or more).
  - Ability to claim Capital Gains Tax exemptions and reliefs, including:
    - Annual Exemption
    - Taper Relief
    - Principal Private Residence relief
    - Private Letting relief
  - Total exemption for non-UK residents.

Tax Tip

For a non-UK Resident investor, capital gains are completely exempt from UK Capital Gains Tax. For these investors, treatment as a property investment business rather than any other type of property business is therefore an enormous advantage and they would be well advised to take care to arrange their affairs accordingly.

- No National Insurance is payable on rental income.
- No compulsory VAT registration of the business.

Tax Disadvantages of Property Investment Businesses

- All business assets are fully exposed to Inheritance Tax on death.

- Abortive expenditure on property purchases (e.g. surveys), or sales (e.g. advertising), may not be allowed for tax purposes.
- Very limited scope for loss relief (both for capital losses and for rental losses). Rental losses on furnished holiday lettings are, however, an exception to this rule (see section 4.11).
- Accounting periods ended 5th April each year are compulsory.
- Difficulty in transferring business without incurring tax charges.

Tax Advantages of Property Trades

- Greater scope for claiming indirect or abortive expenses relating to property purchases and sales.
- Long-term assets of the business attract the higher rate of taper relief for Capital Gains Tax purposes.
- Losses can be set off against any other income arising in the same tax year or the previous tax year.
- Any date may be chosen for the accounting year end.
- The value of a property development or property management business will be exempt from Inheritance Tax on death.
- Businesses may usually be transferred (e.g. to a company or to another individual) without any significant tax charges.

Tax Disadvantages of Property Trades

- Profits arising on property sales are subject to both Income Tax and National Insurance Contributions.
- Non-UK residents are fully taxable on all profits derived from a property trade based in the UK.
- VAT registration will become compulsory if annual turnover from taxable activities for VAT purposes exceeds £61,000.

2.9 THE BOUNDARY BETWEEN INVESTMENT AND TRADING

After reading the previous section, you've probably got a fair idea of how you would *like* your property business to be treated for tax purposes.

However, as I pointed out in section 2.3, it is not a question of choice, but is determined by how you conduct your business.

Furthermore, not only is it a matter of how you actually behave, very often it will hinge on what your intentions were at the beginning of any particular project.

There are two things which the examples I gave in sections 2.3, 2.4 and 2.5 had in common:

    i)   In each case the taxpayer's intentions were clear.
    ii) They were all chosen to illustrate a position which quite definitely fitted the type of business in question.

In reality, a taxpayer's intentions may not be so clear. When I ask my clients to tell me their plans for their property investments, I often hear answers like these:

> "I might sell it, or I might hang on to it for a while if I can't get a good price."

> "We think we'll rent it out for a few years, but we might sell if we get a good offer."

> "We'll probably sell a few and rent the rest out."

Naturally, any investor is going to do whatever produces the best result and if an unexpected opportunity comes along they would be foolish not to take it while they can.

For tax purposes though, what we have to do is establish what the investor's main intention was, at the outset, when the investment was made.

The trouble with intentions, of course, is that they can be very difficult to prove. Who but you can possibly know exactly what was in your mind when you purchased a property?

Looking at it from Revenue & Customs' point of view, the only evidence which they sometimes have to go on are the actual facts of what really transpired and this may be very different to what was intended.

Tax Tip

Document your intentions for your property business.

This could take many forms. Some of the most popular are a business plan, a diary note, a letter to your solicitor or a memo to a business partner.

Remember to date your documentary evidence.

Expect the Unexpected

A business plan which says "we will rent the properties out for five years and then sell them" may not ring true if you actually sell all the properties very quickly.

In other words, merely having a business plan (or other internal documentation) which purports to support your intention to hold properties as long-term investments may not be very persuasive if you actually start behaving blatantly like a property trader.

Example

McLaren buys 10 properties off-plan in August 2006. He financed the purchases through a loan obtained from a high street bank. To support his loan application he drew up a business plan which said "I intend to hold properties in prime rental sites for a period of five to ten years".

Despite his business plan, in May 2007, McLaren sells all of the properties, after having emigrated to Australia in March.

Any Tax Inspector worth his salt is going to question McLaren's motives here and it is highly likely that they would argue that he was, in fact, a property trader, despite his business plan.

But what if there's more to the story?

Example Part 2

McLaren protests that he had no intention of emigrating to Australia until the sudden and unexpected death of his great aunt Bunny in February 2007.

Bunny left McLaren a vast estate in Queensland and he had to move to Australia as quickly as possible in order to look after his new inheritance.

Running a UK property business now appeared impractical so McLaren sold the UK properties as soon as he could.

Now we can see that McLaren's behaviour was merely the result of an unexpected change in circumstances. His original business plan therefore regains more credence and might be sufficient to persuade Revenue & Customs that he did indeed have a property investment business and not a property dealing trade.

An occurrence as dramatic as the one in the example probably speaks for itself, but more often it is some more subtle shift in circumstances which causes an investor to change his mind.

Tax Tip

In such cases, documenting the reasons behind your change of plans is again the most sensible way to proceed. A diary note to the effect of "Johnny got a place at Glasgow University instead, so we sold the flat in St Andrews and bought one there", for example, could save you thousands of pounds one day!

Acceptable reasons for changing your mind could include:

- An unexpected shortage of funds.
- An unexpected and exceptionally good offer.
- Relocation due to work, family or other reasons.
- Divorce or separation.
- Bereavements and inheritance.
- Concerns over the property market in a particular location.
- Funds are required for an exceptional investment opportunity elsewhere.

But Life Isn't Always That Simple

The second common denominator in my examples was the fact that they each fell so obviously into one type of business or another.

Somewhere between these extremes though there is the 'grey area' where investment meets trading. It's not always so easy to be sure which side of the line you're on.

It is almost impossible for me to give you a definitive answer to explain exactly when investment becomes trading. Here, however, are some useful guidelines:

Renovation and Conversion Work

Activity such as building, conversion or renovation work may sometimes be indicative that there is a trading motive behind the purchase of land or property. However, the mere fact that this work takes place does not, in itself, necessarily make it a property development trade.

If you continue to hold the property for several years after the completion of your building work, it is likely that you still have an investment property.

On the other hand, however, if you sell the property immediately after completing the work, you may well be regarded as a property developer **unless** your original intention had been to keep the property and rent it out, but some change in circumstances led you to change your mind.

Frequency of Transactions

If you only sell a property once every few years, you are likely to be carrying on a property investment business.

If you make several sales every year, representing a high proportion of your portfolio, you may be a property trader or developer.

Number of Transactions

As well as their frequency, the number of property transactions which you have carried out can be a factor in deciding whether you are trading.

Many people like to buy a house, 'do it up', then sell it and move on. If you do this once then you're probably nothing other than a normal homeowner in the eyes of Revenue & Customs.

If you do it every six months for ten years, then I would suggest that somewhere along the way you have become a property developer.

Finance Arrangements

Long-term finance arrangements, such as mortgages or longer term personal loans are generally indicative of an investment activity.

Financing your business through short-term arrangements, such as bank overdrafts will be more indicative of a development or dealing trade. Short-term finance tends to indicate short-term assets.

Length of Ownership

There is no definitive rule as to how long you must hold a property for it to be an investment rather than potentially trading stock.

Naturally, however, the longer the period that you generally hold your properties, the more likely they are to be accepted as investment properties.

Renting the Properties Out

Renting properties out is usually definitive proof that they are being held as investments and not part of a property trade. Like everything else on this list though, it may not be conclusive on its own (see the example in section 2.4).

Living in a Property

Living in the property is another useful way to evidence your intention to hold it as a long-term asset. Once again though, this may not be enough if the other facts of the case prove to be contrary to this idea. We will explore this area of planning in a great deal more detail later in the guide.

'Hands On' Involvement

Being actively involved in the renovation or development of a property makes you look like a property developer. Contracting all of the work out looks more like property investment.

Property Management

As I mentioned in section 2.3, managing your own properties does not mean that you have a property management trade.

Managing other unconnected investors' properties would, however, almost always be a trade.

Managing a mixture of your own and other people's properties might, in some circumstances amount to a trade. To be more certain of this treatment, the property management activities are better carried out through a separate entity, such as a company or partnership.

Wealth Warning

Remember that everything that I have discussed in this section is merely one factor in determining what kind of property business you have.

Ultimately, it is the overall picture formed by your intentions, your behaviour and your investment pattern which will eventually decide whether you have a property investment business or a property trade.

In section 6.4, I have given some more detailed examples of cases which may, or may not be, regarded as investment or trading.

2.10 'MIXED' PROPERTY BUSINESSES

"What if my business doesn't happen to fit neatly into one of these categories?" you may be asking.

If you have a 'mixed' property business, involving more than one of the different types of property business described in this chapter, to a degree which is more than merely incidental, then, for tax purposes, each of the business types should be dealt with separately, in the usual manner applicable to that type.

However, having said that, there is a great danger that any property development or property trading may effectively 'taint' what would otherwise be a property investment business, with the result that Revenue & Customs might attempt to deny you Capital Gains Tax treatment on all of your property transactions.

(Property management will generally stand alone without too much difficulty, as it does not involve any property ownership.)

Tax Tip

To avoid the danger of a property investment business being 'tainted' by development or trading activities, you should take whatever steps you can to separate the businesses, such as:

    i)   Drawing up separate accounts for the different businesses.

    ii) Using a different business name for the different activities.

    iii) Reporting the non-investment activities as a different business in your Tax Return.

    iv) Consider a different legal ownership structure for the non-investment activities (e.g. put them in a company or a partnership with your spouse, partner or adult children).

2.11 OTHER PROPERTY-BASED TRADES

As discussed previously, there are a number of trades which are inextricably linked with the business's underlying property but which are quite distinct from simple property investment.

Such trades include:

- Hotels
- Guest houses
- Nursing homes
- Private hospitals
- Hostels
- Serviced Offices
- Warehouses
- Caravan parks

The key difference between these trades and the property businesses which we have examined previously in this chapter is the fact that the property's owners actually occupy the property for use in their own trade.

Tax Treatment

The profits derived from running these business activities are treated as trading profits subject to Income Tax and National Insurance Contributions.

Most of these businesses will need to be registered for VAT when their gross annual income exceeds £61,000.

Gains arising on disposal of the properties held by these businesses, however, will be subject to Capital Gains Tax, with the full range of attendant reliefs available to business property, including:

- Business Asset Taper Relief
- Rollover Relief

We will revisit the issue of rollover relief, in particular, in chapter eight.

Most properties used in these types of business will also be eligible for Business Property Relief for Inheritance Tax purposes. Dangers arise, however, where the business does confer some long-term rights of occupation to its customers, as is sometimes the case with nursing homes or caravan parks, for example.

2.12   HUSBANDS, WIVES AND CIVIL PARTNERS

Throughout this guide you will see me refer to 'married couples' and to 'husbands and wives' several times.

It is important to remember that, unless specified to the contrary, the tax treatment being outlined will be available to legally married couples only.

Civil Partnerships

Since 5th December 2005, same sex couples have been able to enter into a registered civil partnership affording them all of the same legal rights and obligations as a married couple. This equality of treatment also extends to all UK tax law from 5th December 2005 onwards.

Again, the couple will need to be in a legally registered civil partnership for this to apply. Otherwise, they will remain in the same position as any other unmarried couple. Wherever I use the term 'civil partner' in this guide I am referring to a legally registered civil partnership only.

If I use the terms 'spouse' or 'husband or wife' without mentioning civil partners then the tax treatment referred to should also still apply to civil partners from 5th December 2005 onwards.

Wealth Warning

Marriage, and now civil partnership, is usually advantageous for tax purposes. But not always!

It really is a case of 'for better or worse'.

2.13 JOINT OWNERSHIP & PROPERTY PARTNERSHIPS

Before we move on to look at the detailed tax treatment of property businesses, it is worth pausing to think about the potential impact of joint ownership.

The first point to note is that joint ownership itself does not alter the nature of your property business.

In England and Wales, joint ownership comes in two varieties:

• Joint Tenancy, and
• Tenancy in Common.

Do not be confused by the word 'tenancy' here, this is terminology only and does not affect the fact that you jointly own the freehold, leasehold, etc.

In Scotland, joint ownership of property comes predominantly in one major form called 'Pro Indivisio' ownership and, as far as the tax position is concerned, this is more or less the same as Tenancy in Common.

Joint Tenancy

Under a joint tenancy the ownership of each person's share passes automatically on death to the other joint tenant. This is known as 'survivorship'. Furthermore, neither joint owner is normally able to sell their share of the property without the consent of the other.

Each joint owner under a joint tenancy is treated as having an equal share in the property.

In effect, joint tenants are regarded as joint owners of the whole property.

Tenancy in Common

Under a tenancy in common the joint owners are each free to do as they wish with their own share of the property and there is no right of survivorship.

The joint owners' shares in the property under a tenancy in common need not necessarily be equal.

In effect, tenants in common each own their own separate share in the property.

The same considerations apply equally to joint 'Pro Indivisio' owners in Scotland.

Tax Tip

A tenancy in common provides far more scope for tax planning than a joint tenancy. We will see much more on the potential benefits of tenancies in common in the remaining chapters.

Property Investment & Joint Ownership

When it comes to a property investment business, all that joint ownership means is that each individual has their own property investment business and is taxed on their own share of rental profits and capital gains accordingly. The joint ownership does not affect the nature of the underlying business.

Joint owners carrying on a property investment business will not generally constitute a business partnership unless they have also formally created a business partnership.

Property Development

Joint owners engaged in property development will generally form a business partnership under basic legal principles. This is because two or more individuals engaged in the mutual pursuit of commercial trading profits are, in law, generally deemed to constitute a partnership.

Example

Ingrid and Lenny buy an old barn and some disused farm land as tenants in common.

They convert the barn into a pair of semi-detached dwellings and build two new houses on the disused land. They then sell all of the newly developed properties and share the profit equally.

Ingrid and Lenny are in a trading partnership.

It nevertheless does remain possible for joint owners of a property used in a property development trade to be engaged in a 'joint venture', rather than a business partnership, if the terms of the arrangements between the parties do not amount to the mutual pursuit of profit.

Example

Luke owns an old farm. At the edge of the farm there is a small field which Luke is no longer able to farm profitably.

Ives comes to Luke with a proposition which goes like this: "If you sell me a half interest in your small field for its current agricultural value, I'll get planning permission to build some houses and then, after I've built and sold them, I'll pay you the residential use value for your remaining half interest."

Whilst this proposition does involve joint ownership of some development land, it does not amount to a trading partnership as Luke is not participating in Ives' development profit.

A property trading partnership may also exist without joint ownership.

Example

Norman holds a piece of land on which he has planning permission to build ten houses. Unfortunately, however, he does not have the funds or the expertise to carry out the development.

Norman approaches Stanley, a wealthy property developer and suggests that they carry out the development jointly and share the profit equally.

Whilst Norman is the sole owner of the land, his arrangement with Stanley may constitute a trading partnership.

In practice, the boundary between a partnership and a joint venture can be quite blurred and this is a subject which could easily take up a whole book on its own. Usually, in reality, the issue is resolved by the nature of the agreements drawn up between the parties.

The best principle which I can provide is that a partnership usually exists where both parties share, whether equally or not, in the same risks and rewards. Where, however, one party's income is fixed or determined without reference to the other party's overall net profit then this is more akin to a joint venture.

Where a joint venture exists, each party has their own business and it is even possible for one of them to have a property investment business whilst the other has a property development business.

Property Partnerships

In England and Wales a partnership is not recognised as a separate person with its own legal status (like a company), except for new-style Limited Liability Partnerships, which were introduced in April 2000.

This means that traditional style partnerships in England and Wales cannot own property in their own name.

This is reflected in the fact that it is not the partnership which has any capital gain on the sale of a property, but the individual partners themselves.

The problem of legal ownership is generally circumvented through the use of nominees. Between two and four of the partners will usually own the partnership's property as nominees for the partnership. For legal reasons, it is wise to ensure that there are at least two nominee interests, as a single nominee could claim to own the property outright!

In Scotland, a partnership does have its own legal status and can own property in its own name. The tax position remains the same, however, with the partners themselves being taxed on any capital gains made by the partnership.

The nature of the business carried on by a property partnership is determined under exactly the same criteria as we have already examined earlier in this chapter.

For tax purposes, the partnership income is allocated to the individual partners in whatever shares have been established between them and continues to be treated as investment income or trading income, as appropriate.

Hence, a partner may be in receipt of partnership trading income subject to both Income Tax and National Insurance Contributions or partnership property rental income subject to Income Tax only. Or, indeed, both.

The way in which the amount of tax due on each partner's share of the partnership income is calculated remains exactly the same as if he or she had received an equal amount of that same type of income directly from their own individual business.

The way in which the income must be reported does, however, get a little more complicated and we will return to this in the next chapter.

Chapter 3

How to Avoid Income Tax

3.1   INTRODUCTION TO INCOME TAX

Income Tax will probably not be the first tax which you will encounter as a property investor. No, before you've even installed your first tenant or sold your first property you will most likely have had to pay some Stamp Duty Land Tax and some VAT on your legal and professional fees.

However, Income Tax is nevertheless still the first tax which causes the property investor any real concern and for this reason it seems appropriate to examine it first.

Income tax was originally introduced by William Pitt (the Younger) in 1799 as a "temporary measure" to enable the Government to raise the revenue required to fight the Napoleonic Wars. Bonaparte may have met his Waterloo in 1815, but it seems that the British taxpayer is still paying for it!

The tax was initially charged at a single rate of two shillings in the pound (10% in today's terms). The top rate rose to an all-time high of 95% under Harold Wilson's Labour Government of the 1960's. Rates remained fairly high (with a top rate of 60%) until Nigel Lawson's tax-cutting Budget of 1987 established the current higher rate of 40% as the top rate.

The long history of Income Tax may go some way towards explaining some of its quirks. Badly needed modernisation is often slow in coming. For example, it was only as recently as 1998 that 'the expense of keeping a horse for the purposes of travel to the taxpayer's place of work' ceased to be allowable.

The roots of how Income Tax affects the property investor lie in the so-called 'schedular' system of Income Tax introduced in the 19th Century. Under the schedular system, each type of income was classified separately and taxed under a different 'Schedule'.

From 1970, income derived from land and property investments was designated as Schedule A. This Schedule gave us the rules governing rental income and also some other property based income, such as premiums received on the grant of a short lease.

The rules governing rental income under Schedule A were, until relatively recently, somewhat archaic and hence rather restrictive. Fortunately, however, in 1995 the system underwent something of an overhaul producing the rather more sensible rules we have today which, quite rightly, treat property investment as a business. (But not as a trade, which does lead to some fundamental differences in tax treatment, as we will see to both our frustration and our delight later in this guide.)

From 6th April 2005, the old term 'Schedule A' is no longer applied for Income Tax purposes and, under the Income Tax (Trading and Other Income) Act 2005 we now refer simply to 'Property Income'.

The new tax act's rather lengthy name is often shortened to 'ITTOIA 2005', which, as a fan of Ms Wilcox, I refer to as 'I Toyah' – sounds like an early 1980's album doesn't it?

Anyway, despite the recent name changes, the basic principles of how property income is taxed in the UK have remained the same since 1995 and we will examine these in detail in chapter four.

Where the taxpayer is deemed to be trading, the income falls under a different set of rules which we will be looking at in chapter five.

Other major changes in recent years have included the introduction of 'separate taxation' for husbands and wives in 1990 (before which a wife's 'unearned' income was treated as her husband's for tax purposes); self assessment, which came into force from 6th April 1996, and the recognition of the legal status of registered civil partners on 5th December 2005.

However, despite recent reforms, Income Tax has passed its bicentenary with some of its greatest peculiarities still intact. Rumours of a possible merger of Income Tax and National Insurance Contributions have, thankfully for property investors, so far come to nothing. And the greatest oddity of all, the UK's peculiar tax year-end date of 5th April has survived into the 21st Century. But how long can it be before pressure from the European Union forces the UK, like the Irish Republic, to adopt a calendar year?

3.2   BASIC PRINCIPLES OF INCOME TAX

The UK tax year runs from 6th April each year to the following 5th April. The year ending 5th April 2007 is referred to as '2006/2007' and the tax return for this year is known as the '2007 Return'.

Since 1996/1997, individuals, partnerships and trusts have been subject to the self-assessment system for UK Income Tax.

Under this system, the taxpayer must complete and submit a tax return by 31st January following each tax year. The taxpayer must also calculate the amount of tax he or she is due to pay, although Revenue & Customs will do the calculation for you if the return reaches them by 30th September following the tax year.

Recent proposals may mean that all paper tax returns will have to be submitted by 30th September from 2008, with a two month extension given to those who file their returns electronically.

The Income Tax due under the self-assessment system is basically the taxpayer's total tax liability for the year less any amounts already deducted at source or under PAYE and less any applicable tax credits.

All Income Tax due under the self-assessment system, regardless of the source of the income or rate of tax applying, is payable as follows:

- A first instalment or 'payment on account' is due on 31st January during the tax year.

- A second payment on account is due on 31st July following the tax year.

- A balancing payment or, in some cases, a repayment, is due on 31st January following the tax year.

Each payment on account is usually equal to half of the previous tax year's self-assessment tax liability. However, payments on account need not be made when the previous year's self-assessment liability was either:

a) No more than £500, or

b) Less than 20% of the taxpayer's total tax liability for the year.

Additionally, applications to reduce payments on account may be made when there are reasonable grounds to believe that the following year's self-assessment tax liability will be at a lower level.

Taxpayers who are in employment or in receipt of a private pension may apply to have self-assessment tax liabilities which do not exceed £2,000 collected through their PAYE codes for the following tax year.

This produces a considerable cashflow advantage, where relevant.

Tax returns should be submitted by 30th September following the tax year if taxpayers wish to make such an application. *(E.g. submit your tax return for the year ending 5th April 2006 by 30th September 2006 to claim to have up to £2,000 collected through your PAYE coding for 2007/2008.)*

The self-assessment system, as described above, is also used to collect Class 4 National Insurance Contributions on self-employed or partnership trading income and certain student loan repayments.

3.3   INCOME TAX RATES

The current UK Income Tax rates and main allowances are set out in Appendix A. Property income forms part of the 'non-savings' or 'other' element of a taxpayer's income and is therefore currently taxed at three rates, namely 10%, 22% and 40%.

These same rates also apply to any trading income arising from property development, trading or management.

3.4 CALCULATING THE INCOME TAX DUE

The best way to explain how Income Tax due under self assessment is calculated is by way of an example.

In this example, we will look at the 'before' and 'after' scenarios applying to a taxpayer who begins to receive property profits.

For Income Tax purposes, the profits could equally be rental profits or property trading profits. Note, however, that property trading profits would also be subject to National Insurance Contributions which are not taken into account in this example, but will be examined later in chapter five.

The example will also demonstrate the impact that beginning to receive untaxed income, such as rental or trading profits, may have on the timing of an individual's tax liabilities.

Furthermore, this example will illustrate the effect of an anomaly which is caused by the way in which different types of income are now taxed at different rates.

As so-called 'other' income, property income is taxed before 'savings' income, such as interest or dividends.

This means that the ability to benefit from the lower rates applying to these types of income may be lost when the taxpayer begins to receive property income.

This, in turn, can sometimes create an effective Income Tax rate of 42% on the additional income. (Or even sometimes 50% in the case of trading income when National Insurance Contributions are also taken into account.)

Example – Part 1 (*Basic Income Tax Calculation, or 'Before'*)

In the tax year 2006/2007, Nick receives a gross salary of £20,000 and gross interest income of £20,000. He has already suffered Income Tax deductions totalling £3,034.30 under PAYE on his salary as well as Income Tax deducted at source on his interest of £4,000.

His self assessment tax liability for the year is calculated as follows:

Employment Income: £20,000
Less: Personal Allowance: (£5,035)
Total 'Other' Income Taxable: £14,965

Income Tax @ 10% on £2,150: £215.00
Income Tax @ 22% on balance (£12,815): £2,819.30

Interest Income: £20,000

Income Tax @ 20% on remainder of basic rate band
(£18,335 = £31,150 LESS £12,815 already used) £3,667.00
Income Tax @ 40% on balance (£1,665): £666.00

Total Tax For The Year: £7,367.30

Less: Tax paid under PAYE £3,034.30
Tax deducted at source from interest £4,000.00

  £7,034.30

Tax due under self assessment **£333.00**

Nick can either pay this tax directly to the Revenue & Customs in one single lump sum (due by 31ˢᵗ January 2008) or, if he submits his 2007 tax return by 30ᵗʰ September 2007, apply to have it collected through his PAYE coding for 2008/2009.

Nick's tax liability is too small for him to be required to make any payments on account in respect of his 2007/2008 tax liability.

Example – Part 2 *(Introducing Untaxed Property Income, or 'After')*

In addition to his salary and interest income, Nick also has profits of £10,000 from a property business. His Income Tax calculation for 2006/2007 now proceeds as follows:

Employment Income:	£20,000	
Income from Land and Property:	£10,000	
Less: Personal Allowance:	(£5,035)	
Total 'Other' Income Taxable:		£24,965

Income Tax @ 10% on £2,150:	£215.00
Income Tax @ 22% on balance (£22,815):	£5,019.30

Interest Income: £20,000

Income Tax @ 20% on remainder of basic rate band	
(£8,335 = £31,150 LESS £22,815 already used):	£1,667.00
Income Tax @ 40% on balance (£11,665):	£4,666.00

Total Tax For The Year: £11,567.30

Less: Tax paid under PAYE	£3,034.30
Tax deducted at source from interest	£4,000.00

                                                                          £7,034.30

Tax due under self assessment   **£4,533.00**

Immediately we can see that £10,000 of rental income has increased Nick's tax liability by £4,200 – hence producing the effective rate of 42% discussed above.

Although the rental income itself is only taxed at 22%, it also pushes an additional £10,000 of the interest income into the higher rate tax band, thus increasing the tax on that income from 20% to 40% - i.e. an extra 20%. The 42% effective rate is the sum of these two tax increases.

Not only does Nick have considerably more tax to pay, he is no longer eligible to pay his additional self-assessment tax liability through his PAYE coding and must also now make payments on account in respect of 2007/2008.

Hence, unless Nick has reasonable grounds for claiming that his 2007/2008 tax liability will be less than that for 2006/2007, he will have to make tax payments as follows:

By 31st January 2008:
    Tax due for 2006/2007:   £4,533.00
    First Instalment for 2007/2008: £2,266.50
    Total payment due: £6,799.50

By 31st July 2008:
    Second Instalment for 2007/2008:   £2,266.50

By 31st January 2009:
    Balancing payment (or repayment) for 2007/2008
    First Instalment for 2008/2009

And so on, every six months thereafter for as long as his self-assessment tax liability exceeds £500 per annum.

The example has also demonstrated another very important fact. When you begin to receive any significant level of income which is not taxed at source, such as property rental or trading profits, the tax liabilities arising in the first year can be quite severe. In effect, you will need to find the tax on two years' worth of profits within the space of only six months – most of it all on one single date. This is what I call the 'double whammy' effect of self assessment!

Of course, once you are 'in the system' and things settle down a bit, you should just be paying fairly similar levels of tax every six months. Nevertheless, every time your rental or trading income increases significantly, you will be hit by this 'double whammy' effect again!

Wealth Warning

Where a taxpayer is already paying tax under PAYE and also has other income which is not taxed at source, (e.g. a property investor who is also in employment or has a private pension), Revenue & Customs has the power to collect the tax due on the taxpayer's untaxed income (e.g. rental income) through the PAYE system.

Revenue & Customs could deduct as much as 50% of a taxpayer's earnings directly at source through this mechanism.

The effect of this would be to vastly accelerate the collection of the tax due on rental or trading income.

Whilst this power has existed for some time, it has very rarely been exercised in practice in recent years. Rumour has it, however, that Revenue & Customs may be looking to exercise this power more frequently in the near future.

Fortunately, at present, taxpayers have the right to appeal against any PAYE codings which attempt to include their rental or trading income in this way and hence continue to pay the tax on this income via the self-assessment system.

Turn to section 5.5 to see the example in this section revisited where Nick has a property trade and is thus also subject to National Insurance Contributions on his profits.

3.5 TAX RETURNS

Rental income from UK land and property should be detailed on pages L1 and L2 of the tax return. This is referred to as the 'Land and Property Supplement'.

Income from the commercial letting of furnished holiday accommodation in the UK is treated in a special way for a number of tax purposes and is returned on page L1. Other UK property rental income should be dealt with on page L2.

Income from land and property located overseas is treated as a different source of income and should be detailed on pages F4 and F5 which form part of the 'Foreign Supplement'.

Where your property business is deemed to be a trade for tax purposes, you will instead need to complete the 'Self-Employment Supplement', pages SE1 to SE4.

If you have both investment and trading activities then you will need to complete both the Land and Property Supplement (and/or the Foreign Supplement, as appropriate) and the Self-Employment Supplement.

Where property is held jointly, but not as a partnership (see section 2.13), each joint owner must include their own share of property income and expenses on their own tax return each year, as appropriate.

For any form of income received from a partnership, the Partnership Supplement should be used. The full version of this supplement will be required where there is partnership rental income but the short version can be used where there is only partnership trading income.

A separate partnership tax return must also be completed on behalf of the partnership in addition to each of the partners' own tax returns.

Details of how to obtain tax return supplements can be found in Appendix D.

Short Returns

In 2004, Revenue & Customs started issuing new-style short returns to selected taxpayers. These new short returns are only four pages long and may, in some circumstances, detail all of a taxpayer's sources of income rather more concisely than the usual full tax return of ten pages plus supplements.

Some property investors whose tax affairs are relatively simple will receive the new short return.

Wealth Warning

If you receive one of the new-style short returns, it remains your legal obligation to ensure that all of your income and capital gains are reported to Revenue & Customs, as appropriate.

In some cases, this will mean that you should revert to the normal full return and it is your responsibility to ascertain whether this is the case.

In particular, you cannot use the new short return if:

- Your gross business income exceeds £15,000 per annum, or
- You have any income from furnished holiday lettings.

It is anticipated that somewhere between 1,500,000 and 2,000,000 short returns will be issued in 2006. Completing a short return (if you are issued with one and remain eligible to use it) will make no difference whatsoever to your actual tax liability, nor its due date for payment.

3.6 NEW SOURCES OF INCOME

Strictly speaking, whenever a taxpayer begins to receive income from a new source, they should advise Revenue & Customs of this new source by 5th October following the tax year in which it is first received.

'New source' refers to the commencement of a property business, rather than a new property within an existing property business.

However, when someone with a UK property business purchases their first investment property overseas, this does amount to a new source (as explained in section 4.3). The same is true for anyone purchasing their first UK investment property, including non-Residents.

Furthermore, commencing a property trade when you already have a property investment business, or vice versa, will also constitute a new source of income for this purpose.

The commencement of a property trade also gives rise to some other reporting requirements, as detailed in section 5.5.

In practice, however, for property investment businesses, as long as the tax return includes the new source of income, and is completed and submitted by 31st January following the tax year, no penalties will arise.

3.7 NON-RESIDENTS, ETC

Non-UK residents remain liable for UK Income Tax on rental income receivable from property situated in the UK. Generally speaking, however, they are not liable for UK Income Tax on property situated abroad.

The UK Income Tax liability of non-residents may extend to both UK rental income and to other profits from UK-based property businesses, such as property developing, property management or property trading.

Tax Tip

Where a non-UK resident investor (who is therefore exempt from UK Capital Gains Tax on capital gains) is investing substantially in UK property, Revenue & Customs may argue that there is a trading activity, in order to be able to levy Income Tax on that investor instead.

A property company may be useful in this case, as there is less difference in the amount of tax payable *within* a company between a property 'trading' business or a property 'investment' business. Although this does effectively mean 'admitting defeat' and accepting that the business will be taxable in the UK, it is nevertheless a case of 'damage limitation', as the Corporation Tax rates applying will generally be lower than the Income Tax which is potentially at stake.

The taxation of non-residents will be subject to the terms of any double taxation agreement between the UK and their country of residence. Most treaties, however, still allow the UK to tax non-residents on income, profits or gains derived from property situated in the UK (although the UK does not impose Capital Gains Tax on non-residents).

Certain classes of non-resident individuals with taxable income in the UK are entitled to the same personal allowances as UK residents (see Appendix A), and may set these off against that income. These include British and Commonwealth citizens, nationals of states within the European Economic Area (see Appendix C), Crown servants and residents of the Isle of Man or the Channel Islands.

UK residents who are also UK domiciled are liable for UK Income Tax on all worldwide income as it arises. UK resident but non-UK domiciled individuals, however, are only subject to UK Income Tax on income from property situated abroad as and when they remit it back to the UK (known as the 'Remittance Basis').

The tax concepts of residence and domicile can sometimes be fairly complex and a full examination of them is beyond the scope of this guide. The only way to determine your residence or domicile for certain is to examine your own personal circumstances in detail. Broadly, though, in most cases:

- You are resident in the country in which you live.
- You are domiciled in the country where you were born or where your nationality lies.

Your residence can change throughout your life from year to year. Few people will ever change their domicile and, those that do, can do so only once.

For the vast majority of people, the situation is quite straightforward and it is safe to say that, if you have British parents and have lived in the UK all of your life, then you are most probably UK resident and domiciled.

The concept of domicile is examined further in section 7.4.

3.8 CLAIMING DEDUCTIONS

Whatever type of property business you have, there will usually be expenses which may be claimed as a deduction from your business profits.

Some deductions are very much dependent on the type of business which you have and we will therefore examine some of the specific types of deductible expenditure in the next two chapters.

Firstly, however, it is worth dealing with some of the basic principles which will apply to deductions claimed in any type of property business.

Wholly and Exclusively

All expenses must be incurred wholly and exclusively for the purposes of the business and, naturally, must actually be borne by the taxpayer themselves.

The term 'wholly and exclusively' is enshrined in tax law but it is not always interpreted quite as literally as you might think.

Example

Saleema pays £50 per week for gardening services. This covers the upkeep of her own garden and that of the house next door, which she also owns and rents out.

This is what we call 'mixed use'. The gardening costs are partly private expenditure and partly incurred for Saleema's property business. This does not mean that all of the gardening expenditure falls foul of the 'wholly and exclusively' rule. The correct interpretation is to say that part of the gardening expenses are incurred wholly and exclusively for business purposes and to claim an appropriate proportion.

Nevertheless, any expenditure incurred for the benefit of the taxpayer or their family will not be allowed as a business deduction. Where there is a 'dual purpose' to the same expenditure (i.e. both business and private elements exist), the strict position is that none of the expenditure is allowable.

This contrasts with 'mixed use' expenditure, as in our example above, where a reasonable apportionment between the business and private elements is possible so that the business element may still be claimed.

The distinction between 'dual purpose' and 'mixed use' is a difficult one. The best explanation I can give you is that with 'dual purpose' expenditure, the business and private elements generally take place simultaneously. This is why most office clothing is not allowable, since it performs the personal functions of providing warmth and decency at the same time as giving the wearer the appropriate appearance for their line of work.

The 'Revenue Versus Capital' Issue

As well as being incurred 'wholly and exclusively' for the purposes of the business, expenditure must also be 'revenue expenditure' if it is to be claimed for Income Tax purposes.

The term 'revenue expenditure' refers to expenditure which is incurred on an ongoing basis in order to earn revenue (i.e. income) in the business.

In the tax world, all business expenditure will be either 'revenue' or 'capital'. Capital expenditure may not be claimed for Income Tax purposes, but will often be deductible in Capital Gains Tax calculations (though not always!). Some Income Tax relief for certain types of capital expenditure is, however, given in the form of 'Capital Allowances' or the 'Wear and Tear Allowance'. We will examine these allowances further in sections 3.10 and 4.9 respectively.

Whether expenditure is capital or revenue depends not only on the nature of the expenditure itself, but also on the type of business which you have.

Capital expenditure is a particularly significant issue in a property investment or property letting business as a great many of your expenses will be deemed to be capital for tax purposes.

We will get on to some more specific examples relevant to property investment businesses in the next chapter.

Before that, however, let's look at a very simple example to illustrate the difference between capital and revenue expenditure.

Example

Willie runs a chain of sweet shops. As part of his expansion programme, he opens two new shops in Midchester and Normingham.

He buys the freehold of the Midchester shop, but only rents the premises in Normingham.

The Midchester shop is a long-term capital asset of Willie's business. The cost of buying the freehold is therefore a capital expense, deductible only for Capital Gains Tax purposes if and when Willie decides to sell the property. This extends to all costs incurred in the purchase, such as legal fees and Stamp Duty Land Tax. (But see section 4.4 for the treatment of interest and other finance costs.)

The Normingham shop, however, is only rented and Willie does not own any long-term asset. The rent paid is a direct cost of making sales of sweets in Normingham and thus represents a revenue cost which Willie may deduct against his profits for Income Tax purposes.

Practical Pointer

Many capital expenses which you incur will be deductible in the event of a sale of the underlying property. That sale may take place many years from now.

It is useful, therefore, if you keep the receipts and other documentary evidence of this expenditure in a safe and sensible place as it may save you a significant amount of Capital Gains Tax one day.

Grants & Insurance Claims

Any grants or insurance claims received should be deducted from the underlying expense.

Tax Tip

If you incur deductible expenditure which is also the subject of an insurance claim, you may .claim the expenditure as and when it is incurred and need only credit the insurance claim (as a 'negative expense') back into your accounts when it is actually received.

This could be in a later tax year, thus giving you a tax cashflow advantage to partly compensate you for the cashflow disadvantage you suffer whilst waiting for your insurance claim to be sorted out.

VAT On Expenses

If you are unable to recover the VAT on any expense then, as long as the underlying expense itself is deductible, you may also include your irrecoverable VAT cost in the deduction claimed. This is a simple reflection of the fact that, in such cases, the business expense incurred is the VAT-inclusive cost.

We will return in chapter seven to the question of when VAT may be recoverable.

Commencement & Pre-Trading Expenditure

You may incur some expenses for the purposes of your property business before it even starts. Such expenses incurred within seven years before the commencement of your business may still be allowable if they would otherwise qualify under normal principles. In such cases, the expenses may be claimed as if they were incurred on the first day of the business.

3.9   ADMINISTRATIVE EXPENSES

One category of expenses which is pretty common to any type of property business is administrative expenses. This heading is very broad, and can extend to the cost of running an office, motor and travel costs and support staff's wages. As usual, the rule is that any expenditure must be incurred wholly and exclusively for the purposes of the business. Sadly though, most entertaining expenditure is specifically excluded.

Motor Expenses

The cost of running any vehicles used in your business may be claimed as a business expense. Generally, the vehicle will also have some private non-business use, so an appropriate proportion only is claimed. (Or a proportion is disallowed, depending on how you look at it and how you want to draw up your accounts.)

The appropriate proportion to claim will vary from one taxpayer to the next. Typically, for a self-employed taxpayer with a property business, it will fall in the range 25% to 50%. The specific facts of your own case must, however, support your claim.

If, on the other hand, you were to buy a van, purely for use in your business, then, in such circumstances a 100% claim might be justifiable.

Home Office Costs

Many people with a new property business will begin by handling their business administration from a room in their own home, just like many other new small businesses.

In these cases, the taxpayer may claim an appropriate proportion of their household bills as a business expense.

Generally, the proportion to be used is based on the number of rooms in the house, excluding bathrooms, toilets, kitchens, landings and hallways.

Example

Shakira runs her property business from a small room in her house. The house also contains a living room, a kitchen, a bathroom and two bedrooms.

Shakira's house therefore has four rooms which count for the purposes of our calculation. She should therefore claim one quarter of her household bills as a business expense.

Strictly speaking, the claim should be further restricted where there is also some private use of the part of the house which is used in the business. In practice, however, where the private use is negligible, Revenue & Customs do not usually seek a further reduction in the proportion of household expenses which may be claimed.

The household expenses which may be included in the office cost calculation would generally comprise:

- Heating and lighting (electricity, gas, oil, coal, etc.)

- Council tax
- General repairs to the fabric of the building
- Insurance

In the case of repairs or insurance costs, Revenue & Customs take the view that these may only be claimed where there is exclusive business use of the relevant part of the property. Exclusive business use can, however, have a detrimental effect on the owner's Capital Gains Tax position, as we shall see in chapter six.

I have also known Revenue & Customs to dispute a proportionate claim for council tax where there is non-exclusive business use of part of the property. This should be resisted as their own manuals tell them to accept a proportion of council tax as a business expense under these circumstances.

The cost of telephone calls may also sometimes be allocated on the same basis, although it is preferable to attempt a more accurate allocation between the business and private elements where possible. Line rental and other service charges may only be claimed if incurred exclusively for business purposes (e.g. if you have a separate line for business).

The 'number of rooms' allocation method is not compulsory and any other method which produces a reasonable result may be applied instead. Some consistency in the allocation method used would generally be expected.

Business Premises

If your property business grows to the point where you need to rent premises from which to run it then, naturally, the rent, business rates and other running costs which you incur will generally be an allowable expense.

Expenditure on purchasing or improving your own business premises will always be treated as capital in nature, whatever type of business you have.

If you buy a property from which to run your business, you will be able to claim any interest and other finance charges incurred as a result in exactly the same way as if you'd bought a rental property (see section 4.4). The property's running costs, including business rates, may also be claimed as annual overheads.

Travel and Subsistence

Travel costs incurred for business purposes should generally be allowable. This might include the cost of:

- Visiting existing rental properties or development sites.
- Scouting for potential new properties or sites.
- Visiting your bank or your accountant.

Where your trip necessitates an overnight stay, you will additionally be able to claim accommodation costs and subsistence (meals, etc.).

Care needs to be taken here, however, in the case of any travel which has a 'dual purpose'. Travel, subsistence and accommodation costs will only be allowable if your trip was purely for business purposes, or if any other purpose was merely incidental.

If you travel to Brighton for a day to view some properties, for example, the fact that you spend a spare hour at lunchtime sunbathing on the beach will not alter the fact that this was a business trip.

If, on the other hand, you take your whole family to Brighton for a week and spend just one afternoon viewing properties, then the whole trip will be private and not allowable for tax purposes.

Strictly speaking, the taxpayer's own subsistence costs may only be claimed where connected with an overnight stay whilst travelling on business. However, in practice, reasonable expenditure incurred whilst some distance away from your own home and business base is usually accepted.

Staff Training

Any costs you pay to train your employees should be allowable. Different rules apply to the business owner's own training costs, however, and we will return to these in chapters four and five.

Staff Entertaining

At the beginning of this section, I pointed out that most entertaining expenditure is not allowable for Income Tax purposes. The only exception, for any business large enough to have employees, is staff entertaining.

Please don't take this as carte blanche to have continual parties and meals out 'on the business', as such expenditure represents a benefit in kind for the employees on which they will have to pay Income Tax and you will have to pay employer's National Insurance Contributions at 12.8%.

There is, however, an exemption for one or more annual staff parties or similar functions costing no more than £150 per head in total. For most businesses, this is sufficient to ensure that no-one gets taxed on the annual Xmas party.

Naturally, before you can make use of this exemption, you need to have some employees!

3.10 CAPITAL ALLOWANCES

As explained in section 3.8, capital expenditure is not eligible for an Income Tax deduction claim. Some capital expenditure is, however, eligible for a form of Income Tax relief known as 'capital allowances'.

Capital allowances on property expenditure are dependent on both the type of business and the type of property. We will therefore return to these in chapters four and five.

In this section, however, we will look at the basic principles of the capital allowances regime applying both to 'plant and machinery' and to motor vehicles used wholly or partly in a property business.

Plant and Machinery

The term 'plant and machinery' covers qualifying plant, machinery, furniture, fixtures, fittings, computers and other equipment used in a business.

What qualifies as 'plant and machinery' for capital allowances purposes depends on the nature of the business, so we will look at this in sections 4.8 and 5.8.

The First Year Allowance

For qualifying capital expenditure on plant and machinery, a first year allowance of either 40% or 50% of the expenditure is given in the year of the expenditure.

The allowance of 50% is only available for small businesses incurring capital expenditure during the tax year 2004/2005 or the tax year 2006/2007. For the tax year 2005/2006 and then again from 6th April 2007, this rate reverts back to 40%, in line with that available for 'medium-sized' businesses.

'Small' and 'Medium-Sized' for these purposes are as defined under Company Law. Broadly speaking, a business is 'Small' if it meets at least two of the following three tests:

i) Turnover (i.e. gross income) does not exceed £5,600,000 per annum.
ii) Total asset value does not exceed £2,800,000.
iii) It has no more than 50 employees.

Most property businesses will tend to qualify as 'Small' on the basis that they meet tests (i) and (iii).

A 'Medium-Sized' business is one which fails to meet the 'Small' business test but which does meet at least two out of the following three tests:

i) Turnover (i.e. gross income) does not exceed £22,800,000 per annum.
ii) Total asset value does not exceed £11,400,000.
iii) It has no more than 250 employees.

A 'Large' business which also fails to meet the 'Medium-Sized' business test is not entitled to any first year allowances, but still qualifies for writing down allowances.

Writing Down Allowances

The balance of qualifying capital expenditure which is left after claiming the first year allowance is carried forward to the taxpayer's next accounting period.

25% of this balance may be claimed in the next period. This is called the 'writing down allowance'. The remaining balance of expenditure is again carried forward and 25% of that balance may be claimed in the next again accounting period.

Example

On 3rd April 2007 Margaret buys a computer for her property business at a cost of £2,400. Her accounting period ends on 5th April.

For the year ended 5th April 2007, Margaret is able to claim a first year allowance of £1,200 (50%).

Her remaining 'unrelieved' expenditure of £1,200 is carried forward to the year ended 5th April 2008, when she is able to claim a 25% writing down allowance of £300.

A balance of £900 is then carried forward to the year ended 5th April 2009. Margaret will then claim £225, i.e. 25% of this remaining balance.

Note that, as I will explain below, it does not matter that Margaret only bought the computer two days before the end of her accounting period, the full first year allowance is still due.

The full first year allowance would also still be due for 2006/2007 even if Margaret's business had only just started.

Motor Vehicles

Capital allowances are also available on motor vehicles used in the business.

Vans will generally be eligible for the same allowances as plant and machinery, as described above.

The allowance on motor cars, however, is restricted to the lower of £3,000 or 25% of the unrelieved balance on a reducing balance basis.

I have included an example at the end of this section to illustrate how this works in practice.

Other Points on Capital Allowances

All capital allowances must be restricted to reflect any private use of the asset. This is most commonly encountered in the case of motor cars.

Writing down allowances, including allowances on motor cars, are restricted if the business starts or ends part-way through the year or, in the case of a trading business, if accounts are drawn up for a period of less than twelve months.

First year allowances are not available in the year that a business ceases, on assets acquired from connected persons (see section 6.8), or on used assets which the taxpayer introduces into the business.

Subject to the above points, the full allowance due is available on any business asset purchased part-way through the year.

First year allowances of 100% were available to 'small businesses' on the purchase of computer and certain qualifying communications equipment between 1st April 2000 and 31st March 2004.

Various qualifying energy-saving equipment continues to be eligible for a 100% allowance in the first year.

Capital allowances claimed previously may be reclaimed by Revenue & Customs, i.e. added back on to income (known as a 'balancing charge') when the assets on which the allowances have been claimed are sold or otherwise disposed of. The amount reclaimed is restricted when the asset is sold for less than its original cost.

A balancing allowance is also given on some assets if these are sold for an amount less than the unrelieved balance of expenditure at that time.

For plant and machinery which is wholly used in the business, a pooling system is operated. This has the result that no balancing charges or allowances can arise on these assets unless the business ceases or, rarely, one or more of the assets are sold for a sum in excess of the balance on the pool.

The following example serves to illustrate a number of these points:

Example

Damien starts a property business on 6th October 2006 and draws up accounts to 5th April each year.

He buys a new car for £13,000 in March 2007 and uses it partly for his property business. His total annual mileage is 10,000 miles and, of this, 2,900 miles are driven on business.

Damien's new car therefore has 29% business use.

If Damien had been in business throughout 2006/2007, the total allowance available on his car would have been £3,000, i.e. the lower of £3,000 and 25%). However, as he has only been in business for six months, this must be reduced to £1,500 (6/12 x £3,000).

As Damien only has 29% business use of the car, the amount which he can actually claim is 29% of £1,500, i.e. £435.

In 2007/2008, the 'unrelieved balance' on the car is £11,500 (£13,000 less £1,500) and the total allowance available is thus £2,875 (25% of £11,500, which is less than £3,000). This time, Damien's claim is therefore £834, (i.e. 29% of £2,875).

The unrelieved balance going forward to 2008/2009 is £8,625 and Damien will be able to claim 29% of 25% of this sum, which is £625.

In May 2009, Damien sells the car for £10,000. The unrelieved balance at this time is £6,469, so a balancing charge of £3,531 arises. However, as Damien was only ever able to claim 29% of the allowance, his balancing charge is also reduced to 29%, i.e. £1,024.

Had Damien sold the car for less than £6,469, he would have been entitled to a balancing allowance of 29% of the difference. E.g. if he sold it for £5,000, his balancing allowance would have been £426 (£1,469 x 29%).

On the other hand, if he had sold the car for more than £13,000, his balancing charge would have been restricted to £1,894, which is the total amount of allowances claimed on it.

Some important points to note from the example:

i) The total allowance available is deducted in arriving at the unrelieved balance for the next year, regardless of any private use restriction which reduces the amount actually claimed.
ii) Balancing charges or allowances are also restricted to take private use into account.

Capital Allowances Disclaimers

It is worth pointing out that capital allowances are not mandatory. The amount of allowance available is effectively a maximum which may be claimed and the taxpayer may claim any amount between zero and that maximum each year.

Why claim less than the maximum?

Tax Tip

If your taxable income is less than your personal allowance, any capital allowances which you claim will effectively be wasted.

Instead, you should claim a lower amount of allowances in order to fully utilise your personal allowance against your income (or as much as possible).

The unrelieved balance of expenditure carried forward will then be greater, giving you higher capital allowances next year when, hopefully, they will actually save you some tax!

Chapter 4

Avoiding Income Tax on a Property Investment Business

4.1 THE TAXATION OF RENTAL INCOME

In most respects, property letting is now treated very much like any other business for Income Tax purposes. You will need to draw up accounts which detail all your income as well as all relevant expenses.

If you are letting a number of UK properties on a commercial basis, this is treated as a single UK property business and one set of accounts will usually suffice (although many landlords prefer to have a separate set of accounts for each property).

Separate accounts, however, are required in the following cases:

- Furnished holiday lettings in the UK (see section 8.14).

- Overseas lettings (see section 4.14).

- Non-commercial lettings (see section 4.15).

All rental income must be included, no matter how modest the source, unless it is covered by the 'Rent-A-Room' scheme (see section 4.10 below).

Unlike other types of business, however, you are not free to choose which accounting period you wish to use and must, instead, draw up accounts for the tax year, which runs from 6th April to the following 5th April.

Generally, your accounts have to be drawn up on an 'accruals' basis.

This means that income and expenditure is recognised when it arises, or is incurred, rather than when it is received or paid (the latter being the 'cash basis' – see further below). For example, if you started renting out a property on 12th March 2007, at a monthly rent of £1,000, the income you need to recognise in your accounts for the year ended 5th April 2007 is:

$$£1,000 \times 12 \times 25/365 = £821.92$$

(You are renting it for 25 days in the 2006/2007 tax year.)

Expenses may similarly be recognised as they are incurred. For example, if you have some roof repairs carried out on a rented property in March 2006, you may deduct the cost in your accounts to 5th April 2006, even if the roofer doesn't invoice you until May.

Concessionary Use of Cash Basis

By concession, Revenue & Customs will still allow taxpayers whose gross annual receipts do not exceed £15,000 to use the old 'cash basis'. As stated above, this means that income and expenditure may be recognised when received or paid. The Revenue will only allow this method to be used where it is applied consistently and produces a reasonable result not substantially different from that produced on the usual accruals basis.

In most cases, since rent is usually received in advance and expenses are often paid in arrears, the cash basis will not be beneficial. Nevertheless, when you are starting out with a relatively modest level of rental income, it is an option to consider.

4.2   DEDUCTIBLE EXPENDITURE

The rules on what types of expenditure may be claimed as deductions in a property letting business are similar, but not quite the same, as for other types of business.

Some of the main deductions include:

- Interest and other finance costs
- Property maintenance and repair costs
- Heating and lighting costs, if borne by the landlord
- Insurance costs
- Letting agent's fees
- Advertising for tenants

- Accountancy fees
- Legal and professional fees
- The cost of cleaners, gardeners, etc, where relevant
- Ground rent, service charges, etc.
- Bad debts
- Pre-trading expenditure
- Landlord's administrative expenditure

If your tenant contributes part of the cost towards an otherwise allowable expense, you may claim only the net amount which you actually bear yourself.

In the next few sections, we will take a closer look at some of the more common areas of expenditure typically encountered in property letting businesses and examine what determines whether or not these expenses may be deducted for Income Tax purposes. Please note, however, that this is not an exhaustive list and other types of expenditure which meet the general principles outlined in section 3.8 will often also be allowable.

4.3   WHEN IS A PROPERTY A RENTAL PROPERTY?

Throughout this chapter you will see me refer to 'rental property'. Whether a property is a 'rental property' at any given time is often crucial in determining whether, or how much of, a particular piece of expenditure is allowable.

Quite obviously, a property is a rental property whilst it is actually being rented out.

For most tax purposes, a property is usually also a 'rental property' when:

- It is available for letting but is currently vacant.
- It is being prepared for letting.
- It is being renovated between lettings, with the intention of letting it out again thereafter.

In each case, however, the property's 'rental property' status would be lost if it was actually used for something else (e.g. a family holiday for the investor's own wife and children). Nevertheless, merely sleeping there overnight, whilst redecorating the property for subsequent rental, should not usually harm the property's status.

Strictly, for Income Tax purposes, a vacant property ceases to be a rental property immediately once a decision is taken to sell it. In practice, however, this rule will not usually be applied where the period between the decision and the sale is very brief.

Revenue & Customs generally regard the day on which your first rental property is let out for the first time as being the first day of your property letting business.

However, any eligible expenditure which is incurred within the seven year period before your first rental property is first let should remain claimable as 'pre-trading expenditure' (see section 3.8). This may sometimes mean that the expenditure has to be claimed in a later tax year.

Eligible expenses relating to your second, and subsequent, rental properties may generally be claimed as incurred, even if the relevant property is not let by the end of that tax year.

The exception to this last rule is that you have to treat UK properties and overseas properties as separate businesses. Hence, a first overseas rental gets treated as a 'first property' even if you already have a portfolio of UK properties. The same goes for your first UK rental when you have a portfolio of overseas properties.

4.4   INTEREST AND OTHER FINANCE COSTS

Interest is allowable if it is incurred for the purposes of the property business. Hence, the question of whether the interest on a loan is an allowable deduction is based on the use to which the funds borrowed were put. Generally, it does not, as many people seem to think, depend on which property the loan is secured on.

Interest will therefore be allowable if it arises on funds borrowed to purchase or improve rental properties or otherwise expended for the purposes of the property business.

Interest Example 1

Matthew takes out a buy-to-let mortgage on a house which he begins to let out. This is the most usual and simple situation and, naturally, Matthew may claim the interest on his buy-to-let mortgage against his rental income from the house.

Interest Example 2

Mark takes out a personal loan and spends the funds on making improvements to a flat which he subsequently lets out. The interest on his loan is deductible because it has been incurred for the purpose of his property business.

Interest Example 3

Luke re-finances one of his rental properties and obtains additional funds of £10,000 in the process. He spends this money by taking his partner on a luxury cruise.

*The interest on Luke's additional borrowings is **not** deductible against his rental income as the funds were not used for business purposes.*

Interest Example 4

John has a very large property rental business and employs several staff to assist him.

Whilst the business is generally buoyant, John runs into some cashflow difficulties in January 2007 and has to borrow an extra £5,000 to pay his staff's wages that month.

John's borrowings were used for business purposes and hence the interest he incurs will be an allowable deduction for tax purposes.

Interest Example 5

Adam borrows an extra £50,000 by re-mortgaging his own home. He uses these funds as the deposit on two new properties which he then lets out.

Adam may claim the interest on his extra £50,000 of borrowing as it has been used for business purposes.

Practical Pointer

In a case like Adam's in our last example here, there will usually be the practical difficulty of establishing just how much interest should be claimed.

Adam will already have an outstanding balance on his mortgage so it would not be right for him to claim all of his interest as a business expense.

In practice, we have to do an apportionment.

Example 5 Resumed

Prior to re-mortgaging, Adam had a balance of £120,000 on the mortgage on his own home. The extra £50,000 of borrowings took that balance up to £170,000. Adam should therefore claim 50/170ths of his mortgage interest as a business expense.

Repayment Mortgages

Interest calculations are fairly straightforward in the case of an interest-only mortgage, but what about repayment mortgages?

The first and most important point to note is that you can only ever claim the interest element of your loan or mortgage payments as an expense. The capital repayment element may not be deducted. Your mortgage provider will usually send you an annual statement detailing the amount of interest actually charged.

Where you have a repayment mortgage which is only partly allowable for business purposes, an apportionment must be made, as outlined above.

However, as you repay capital, the total outstanding balance on the account will reduce, so how do you do your apportionment then?

In my view, the answer is to stick with the apportionment ratio which you derived when you first did the re-mortgaging (e.g. 50/170ths in Adam's case above).

Some, more aggressive, accountants might, however, suggest that all repayments should be treated as repaying the original 'non-business' element of the loan. I do not believe this to be correct and suspect that Revenue & Customs would agree with my view.

Tax Tip

To maximise the business element within your interest payments, arrange for the new funds obtained on re-mortgaging to be allocated to a separate mortgage loan account with the bank.

Make the new account interest-only, whilst leaving the original mortgage account as a repayment account.

In this way, you can put beyond doubt the fact that the capital repayment element belongs exclusively to the 'non-business' part of your mortgage.

What Happens When Properties Are Sold Or Cease to Be Used In The Business?

An important point to note is that interest on borrowings used to finance the purchase or improvement of a property will generally cease to be allowable if that property ceases to be used in the rental business (e.g. if it is subsequently adopted as the taxpayer's own residence).

However, the eligibility of the interest for tax deduction will follow the use of the underlying funds. Consider this example:

Example

In 2006, Abel borrows £50,000 secured on his own home, Eden Cottage, and uses the money to buy a rental property, Babel Heights. At this stage, the interest on his £50,000 loan is clearly allowable.

A few years later, in 2009, Abel sells Babel Heights and uses the sale proceeds to buy a new rental property, Ark Villa. Abel's interest payments on the £50,000 loan continue to be allowable as the underlying funds have been reinvested in the business.

In 2011, Abel sells Eden Cottage and moves into a new house in Gomorrah. Abel's mortgage on the new Gomorrah property exceeds the balance on his Eden Cottage mortgage. The new mortgage therefore includes the original £50,000 borrowing used to acquire a business property and hence the appropriate proportion of Abel's interest payments should still be allowable.

In 2012, Abel sells Ark Villa in order to finance the costs of an extension he is building on his Gomorrah home. At this point, the interest on his £50,000 borrowings ceases to be allowable for Income Tax purposes.

Property Introduced Into The Business

Conversely, however, the interest on any mortgage over a property which is newly introduced into the rental business becomes allowable from that point onwards.

Hence, for example, the interest on the mortgage on your own former home may be claimed from the date on which you make it available for letting.

Tax Tip

If you intend to put your former home (or another non-business property) into your property letting business, consider re-mortgaging it before you do so.

As the entire value of the house represents capital which you have introduced into your business, the whole amount of any interest payable on loans secured on the property should be deductible for tax purposes.

Example Continued

By 2013, Abel's Gomorrah property is worth £500,000 and his outstanding mortgage is £300,000.

Abel re-mortgages the Gomorrah property, realising an additional £150,000 which he uses to buy a new home in neighbouring Sodom.

Abel now starts to rent out his Gomorrah property.

The entire interest payable on the whole of Abel's £450,000 mortgage will now be allowable against his rental income.

Loans In Joint Names, Etc.

Strictly, for interest to be claimed as a business expense it must be a liability of the owner of the business. This generally means that the underlying loan must be in the name of the property investor themselves.

By concession, however, Revenue & Customs will allow qualifying interest paid by a property investor to still be claimed when the underlying loan is:

i)   In joint names with their husband, wife or civil partner, or

ii)   In the sole name of their husband, wife or civil partner.

Under scenario (ii), it is vital that the interest is actually <u>paid</u> by the property investor themselves even though it is their spouse or partner's liability.

Naturally, the interest is still only allowable if incurred for the purposes of the business, as detailed above.

Other Finance Costs

The treatment of other finance costs, such as loan arrangement fees, will generally follow the same principles as that for interest. In other words, the key factor will always be the purpose to which the borrowed funds are put.

Difficulties may sometimes occur, however, over the timing of relief for such costs. Sometimes, general accounting principles may dictate that the cost should be spread over the life of the loan. In such cases, the tax treatment will follow the same principles.

Example

Eve has a large rental property portfolio and decides to consolidate her borrowings into one single 20-year loan.

The bank charges her an arrangement fee of £20,000 for this new finance.

Eve should therefore claim £1,000 each year over the 20-year life of the loan.

After 15 years, however, she decides to re-finance her business again and terminates the 20-year loan agreement.

At this stage she may claim the remaining £5,000 of the original fee which she has not yet claimed for tax purposes.

Early redemption fees will usually be regarded as a personal cost rather than a business cost and hence will neither be allowable for Income Tax nor for Capital Gains Tax.

This treatment does not extend to the unclaimed portion of the original arrangement fees, which, as we saw above, may now be claimed.

As for those early redemption fees, an Income Tax claim might sometimes still be possible under general principles where there is a good business reason for the early redemption.

4.5   LEGAL AND PROFESSIONAL FEES

Legal fees and other professional costs incurred for the purposes of the business may fall into one of three categories for tax purposes:

i)   Revenue expenditure

ii)   Capital expenditure
iii) Abortive capital expenditure

Revenue Expenditure

The first category, referred to by the technical name 'revenue expenditure', may be claimed as a deduction against rental income.

These are the costs which are incurred year in, year out, in earning the rental profits. They will include items such as the costs of preparing tenants' leases and, perhaps, debt collection expenses. This category will also include agent's fees and accountancy fees for the preparation of your annual accounts and the business part of your tax return.

Capital Expenses

Legal fees and other professional costs incurred on the purchase or sale of properties cannot be claimed for Income Tax purposes within a property letting or investment business.

As long as the purchase or sale in question goes through, however, all is not lost, as these items may then be claimed as allowable deductions for Capital Gains Tax purposes when the property is disposed of (see chapter six).

This category would include:

- Legal fees
- Estate agent's fees
- Stamp Duty Land Tax
- Survey fees
- Valuation fees
- Professional costs incurred on a successful application for planning permission

Note, however, that costs such as survey or valuation fees incurred when re-mortgaging a property (for business purposes) would be treated in the same way as loan arrangement fees, as detailed in the previous section.

Abortive Capital Expenditure

As we all know, sometimes a purchase or sale will not go through. In these cases, the investor will often have incurred costs such as survey fees, advertising or legal fees.

Unfortunately, when you have a property investment business, costs related to purchases or sales which do not proceed will not generally be allowable for Income Tax and neither will they be allowable for Capital Gains Tax purposes. These are what we sometimes call 'tax nothings'.

The same is true of professional costs incurred on an unsuccessful application for planning permission. (Although, if you can show that the same costs led to a later, successful, application they may still be regarded as part of the capital cost of the project for Capital Gains Tax purposes.)

This situation is a constant source of frustration to property investors and I would agree that it is very unfair.

> ### Tax Tip
>
> If you are incurring significant costs of this nature, you may be better off being treated as a property trader.
>
> Whilst, as explained in section 2.3, your tax status is not a matter of choice, if your situation is already pretty borderline, a small shift in your investment strategy may be enough to tip the balance.

'Pre-Decision' Expenditure

There is an argument that any costs incurred before making a decision to purchase or sell a property are part of the regular overhead costs of the property business and are therefore properly claimable as revenue expenditure of that business.

Example

Noah is considering buying an investment property in the Newcastle area. He spots a potential purchase in Gosforth and has a survey done on the property. However, he is unhappy with the results of this survey and decides not to pursue this purchase.

Noah may be able to claim that the cost of the Gosforth survey is an allowable business overhead expense.

Noah moves his attention to Durham and finds another potential investment property. He has a survey carried out and, happy with the results, this time he decides to proceed with the purchase. Things go well until the owner of the Durham property is made redundant and is forced to take it back off the market. By this time, Noah has incurred substantial legal fees.

Noah's legal fees were incurred after he decided to purchase the Durham property. These fees are therefore abortive capital expenditure which Noah is unable to claim.

Noah may, however, still be able to claim the cost of the survey fees for the Durham property as, once again, these were incurred before he made a decision whether to proceed with a purchase of the property.

To assist any claims for 'pre-decision' expenditure of this nature, it is useful to retain documentary evidence which shows that the decision to purchase or sell had not yet been taken.

Whilst I believe that claims for abortive 'pre-decision' expenditure incurred for the purposes of a property business are perfectly valid, this is a view which Revenue & Customs may not necessarily share. Some dispute over claims of this nature may therefore arise.

4.6   REPAIRS AND MAINTENANCE

Nowhere in the field of taxation is the question of 'capital or revenue' more difficult than in the area of repairs and maintenance and/or capital improvements.

In this section, we will concentrate on the general principles applying to this type of expenditure on all rental properties. Other aspects specific to commercial property and to furnished residential lettings are covered in more detail in sections 4.8 and 4.9 respectively.

Fundamental Principles

There are two main fundamental principles which we must consider in order to determine whether any expenditure represents a repair (i.e. revenue expenditure) or a capital improvement (capital expenditure):

i) When a property is first brought into the rental business, any expenditure which is necessary to make it fit for use in that business will be capital expenditure.

In most cases, a property will first be brought into use when it is purchased, but the same rule applies when the taxpayer's own former home becomes a rental property.

ii) Subject to (i) above, expenditure which merely restores the property to its previous condition (at a time earlier in the same ownership) will be a repair.

Conversely, any expenditure which enhances the property beyond its previous condition within the same ownership will be capital improvement expenditure.

The question of what constitutes an 'enhancement' to the property is determined as a question of fact, not opinion. Just because you think that a new extension on a building is hideous does not stop it from being classed as a capital improvement for tax purposes.

'Within the same ownership' may sometimes also apply to periods in a previous ownership, such as when a property has been transferred between husband and wife or civil partners.

Repairs are deductible for Income Tax purposes (as long as the property is a rental property at the time) whereas capital improvements *may* be deductible for Capital Gains Tax purposes (we will come back to this in chapter six).

81

Some Illustrative Examples

I could write an entire separate book covering umpteen different examples of repairs or capital improvements. Here, however, I have tried to set out a few cases which will hopefully serve to illustrate how the principles outlined above apply in practice.

Where a new principle emerges in the course of these examples, I have highlighted it for your attention as an 'Emerging Principle'.

Example 1

Melanie buys an old farmhouse intending to rent it out for furnished holiday lettings.

However, when she buys the property, it has no mains electricity, no mains sewerage and a large hole in the roof. She spends £75,000 getting the property into a fit state to let it out, including £5,000 on redecoration.

The whole of Melanie's expenditure of £75,000 will be treated as capital expenditure and no Income Tax deduction will be available. The fact that part of the expenditure was for decorating is likely to be regarded as merely incidental to the overall capital nature of the work in this case.

Emerging Principle

Expenditure which might normally be regarded as revenue in nature will be treated as capital where it forms an incidental part of a predominantly capital project. (We will look at some planning issues revolving around this principle in a later example.)

Prior to 6th April 2001, Revenue & Customs were prepared to allow some deduction for the 'notional repair' element within capital improvements, but sadly this is no longer the case.

Example 2

Geri has a small townhouse in Kensington which she rents out. She decides to have a conservatory built on the back of the house at a cost of £40,000, including £2,000 to redecorate the room adjoining the new conservatory.

Geri's conservatory is a capital improvement and no Income Tax deduction will be available for this expenditure. Once again, the capital nature of this work also extends to the cost of redecorating the adjoining room, as this was necessitated by the major building work.

Example 3

Emma owns a row of shops which she has been renting to a number of sole traders. A massive storm severely damages the roofs of the shops and Emma has these repaired at a cost of £50,000.

Emma's expenditure represents an allowable repair cost which she can quite correctly claim against her rental income.

Example 3A

The same storm also damaged several windows in Emma's shops.

The glazier advises her that it will actually be cheaper to replace the original wooden frames with new UPVC double glazing and she agrees to do this.

This expenditure remains revenue expenditure despite the fact that the new windows represent an improvement on the old ones.

Emerging Principle

When, due to changes in fashion, or technological advances, it becomes cheaper or more efficient to replace something with the more modern alternative, the fact that this represents an improvement may be disregarded and the expenditure may still be classed as a repair.

Replacing single-glazed windows with equivalent double-glazing has been specifically highlighted as meeting this criterion in Revenue & Customs' own publications.

Example 3B

At the same time, Emma also decides to have bay windows fitted in two of the shops.

This element of her expenditure is a capital improvement and will have to be added to the capital value of her shops rather than claimed as a repair.

Emerging Principle

Both capital improvements and repairs may sometimes be carried out simultaneously. In such cases, the expenditure must be apportioned between the two elements on a reasonable basis.

Readers may wonder why this apportionment is allowed here, when it was denied for both Melanie and Geri above. The key difference is that both Melanie and Geri **had to** do the redecoration at the same time as the other work, whereas Emma simply **chose** to install the bay windows. It is the element of choice which makes the difference.

Tax Tip

Where an apportionment of expenditure for tax purposes is necessary, it would be wise to obtain appropriate evidence of the allocation made in support of your claim. This can be achieved by asking the builder to separately itemise the repairs and capital improvement elements of the work on their invoices.

Example 4

Victoria has a flat which she has been renting to students for several years. She decides to upgrade the flat to make it more suitable for letting to the 'young professional' class (what we used to call 'yuppies'). She therefore incurs the following expenditure:

i) *£16,000 on a new kitchen, including £4,500 on new kitchen equipment.*
ii) *£7,000 redecorating the bathroom, including £2,000 to replace the existing fittings and £1,000 to install a shower (there was only a bath before).*
iii) *£5,000 redecorating the rest of the flat.*
iv) *£3,000 on rewiring.*

Kitchen Equipment

Victoria's new kitchen equipment falls under the heading of 'fixtures and fittings' and is not part of the fabric of the building for tax purposes.

Hence, if Victoria is claiming the 'Wear and Tear Allowance' (see section 4.9), she will not be able to claim anything in respect of this expenditure.

If she is not claiming Wear and Tear Allowance, she will be able to claim the cost of any equipment which is a direct replacement for the old equipment that she previously had in the flat, or its nearest modern equivalent.

Anything which is an entirely new item of equipment, or a major improvement on the old equipment (i.e. not just the modern equivalent) will be capital expenditure and not allowable for Income Tax purposes.

Hence, buying a new fridge to replace an old fridge of similar size may be allowable as a replacement (if the Wear and Tear Allowance is not being claimed). Buying a fridge-freezer to replace a fridge, however, would be a capital improvement and hence not allowed for Income Tax purposes.

Other Kitchen Expenditure

The treatment of the remaining expenditure on the new kitchen depends on two things:

- Whether there is any improvement element, and
- Whether the units are fitted or free-standing.

Free-standing units would be treated in the same way as the new kitchen equipment, as explained above.

The cost of a new fitted kitchen replacing a previous, broadly similar, set of units, work tops, sink, etc, would be accepted as a repair expense. This would extend to the necessary additional costs of re-tiling, re-plastering, plumbing, etc. The usual exemption for 'nearest modern equivalent' applies here also.

A fitted kitchen is treated as part of the fabric of the building, so the question of whether or not Victoria is claiming the Wear and Tear Allowance does not arise here.

If, however, Victoria's new fitted kitchen incorporates extra storage space or other extra features, such as an extractor fan where there had not been one before, for example, then an appropriate proportion of the expenditure will need to be treated as a capital improvement.

In an extreme case, where fairly standard units are replaced by expensive customised items using much higher quality materials, then the whole cost of the new kitchen will need to be regarded as a capital improvement.

Bathroom Fittings

Replacing the existing bathroom fittings should usually be allowable repairs expenditure. Toilets, baths and washbasins are all regarded as part of the fabric of the building, so repairing or replacing them is generally allowable for Income Tax purposes.

Once again, however, replacing the existing fittings with expensive customised items using much higher quality materials would amount to a capital improvement.

Fitting the new shower will definitely be a capital improvement as this is an item of equipment which had not been present before.

The remaining bathroom redecoration costs will need to be apportioned between the repair element and capital improvement element. Any expense arising due to the installation of the new shower would have to be treated as part of the capital element.

Redecorating The Flat

Most of the redecoration work, in the absence of any building work in the rooms concerned, should be fairly straightforward repairs expenditure.

As usual, we need to be on the lookout for any improvement element, but a great deal of redecorating cost will always fall into the 'nearest modern equivalent' category.

Carpets, curtains and other similar items need to be considered slightly separately. Once again, if Victoria is claiming Wear and Tear Allowance, the cost of these will not be allowable.

If Victoria is not claiming Wear and Tear Allowance, the cost of new carpets, curtains and similar items may be claimed if they represent direct replacements. New items and improvements will be capital expenditure.

In this context, it makes no difference if you are replacing carpets or curtains which you yourself fitted previously or which you acquired when you purchased the property.

Rewiring

The rewiring cost will be fully allowable if it is simply 'new for old'. If, on the other hand, Victoria took the opportunity to fit a few new sockets then there will be an improvement element and, as usual, an apportionment would be required.

Such an apportionment would probably also necessitate an apportionment of the redecorating costs, as some of these would also be incurred due to the electrical improvements.

Emerging Principles

Most moveable items, such as kitchen equipment, carpets and curtains are not regarded as part of the fabric of the building and will therefore be subject to slightly different rules.

In complex cases, the question of 'repairs or capital improvements' will need to be examined room by room, or even item by item.

The tax treatment of one item may have a knock-on effect on the tax treatment of another item.

Example 5

Mel buys a rather dilapidated house in Sunderland hoping to rent it out to a family or young couple. She gets the house at a very good price owing to its current state of repair but knows that safety regulations would bar her from letting it out to anyone in its current condition.

The house desperately needs rewiring and also some urgent plumbing work, which Mel carries out at a cost of £5,000. This expenditure will have to be treated as part of her capital cost.

At this point the house is basically habitable and will meet all necessary safety regulations, but it could really do with redecorating to make it attractive to the type of tenants that Mel is ideally looking for.

However, if Mel redecorates at this point then this expenditure too is also likely to be regarded as part of the capital cost of the property, especially since part of the redecorating will have been necessitated by the plumbing and rewiring work.

What Mel does instead, therefore, is to first let the house to a group of students for six months. After that, she is able to redecorate the property and to claim this as a revenue expense deductible for Income Tax purposes.

Tax Tip

Where there is a danger that repairs or maintenance expenditure might be regarded as an incidental part of a capital project, it will be beneficial to delay this element of the work, if possible, until after an intermediate period of letting.

In this way, the expenditure becomes an allowable revenue expense.

Naturally, any health and safety requirements will have to be observed before undertaking the initial letting period.

Example 6

Danni buys a flat from an elderly couple, intending to rent it out.

The elderly couple lived in the flat right up to the date of completion. Although it was a bit 'run down' and the decoration was very old-fashioned, it was perfectly habitable and met all applicable safety requirements for a rental property.

Immediately after completion, Danni redecorates the flat in a modern style and then begins to rent it out.

Danni's redecoration costs are an allowable maintenance cost for Income Tax purposes, even though she did the work straight away after buying the flat. The flat was already completely habitable and the redecoration work was purely a matter of choice or taste.

Emerging Principle

Where an expense is unequivocally revenue in nature, the timing of the expense should not, in itself, alter its treatment.

The Taxman's View on Expenditure on Newly Acquired Properties

In the case of any expenditure on newly acquired rental properties, Revenue & Customs' own manuals specifically state that any expenditure which is not allowed for Income Tax purposes on the grounds that it represents capital expenditure should then be allowed for Capital Gains Tax purposes on a disposal of that same property.

Accounting Treatment

Where there are no statutory rules to the contrary, Revenue & Customs will generally expect the tax treatment of an expense to mirror its treatment in the accounts.

Wealth Warning

It is therefore important to ensure that valid repairs expenditure is not treated as a capital item in your accounts, as this could prevent you from claiming that expenditure for Income Tax purposes.

Repair Cost Provisions

A 'provision' in accounting terms is a charge made in your accounts in respect of a future cost.

Provisions for future costs are not generally allowable until the costs have actually been incurred.

There are a few exceptions to this rule, however, and a provision for repair costs may be allowed for tax purposes if:

i)   There is a legal obligation to incur the expenditure.
ii) There is a specific programme of repair work to be undertaken.
iii) The accounting provision has been computed with a reasonable degree of accuracy.

Example 7

Kylie owns three flats in 'Hutchence Towers', a tenement block in Glasgow. In February 2007, she receives a statutory notice from the council requiring her (and the other owners in the same block) to carry our some urgent roof repairs.

The 'Hutchence Towers Owners and Residents Association' approaches Michael, a local builder, who provides them with a quotation for carrying out the necessary work.

On 4th April 2007, the Hutchence Towers Owners and Residents Association formally approves the quotation. Kylie's share of the cost will be £10,000.

Under these circumstances, Kylie may quite properly make a provision for her £10,000 share of the repair cost in her accounts for the year ended 5th April 2007, even though the work has not even started yet.

4.7   TRAINING AND RESEARCH

Many property investors these days spend a good deal of money on training and research. The first thing to note is the fact that this expenditure is often incurred before the business starts is not, in itself, a barrier to claiming it as a business expense. (Unless it was incurred more than seven years before the business started!)

As far as seminars, courses and even books (like this one) or videos are concerned, the rule is that expenses incurred in updating or expanding existing areas of knowledge may be claimed, but any costs relating to entirely new areas of knowledge are a personal capital expense.

This can be a difficult distinction to draw, especially in a field such as property investment, where a great deal of industry knowledge is simply a blend of common sense and experience. It's not like you're training to become a brain surgeon after all!

My personal view is that property investment is a field of knowledge which most adults already have (e.g. from buying their own house) and that any such expenses are really only updating or expanding that knowledge and are therefore allowable. However, this view is not shared by everyone, most especially Revenue & Customs, and hence such claims may well be challenged.

In the end, the decision over any expense claims in this area will inevitably require you to use your own judgement.

4.8   CAPITAL ALLOWANCES FOR LETTING BUSINESSES

As we have seen in the last few sections, the most significant types of disallowable expenditure in a property investment business are capital expenditure on property improvements and on furniture, fixtures and fittings.

Some capital expenditure is, however, eligible for a form of Income Tax relief known as 'capital allowances'.

There are various special rules for capital allowances, depending on the type of property being rented:

a)   So-called 'industrial property' attracts capital allowances on the cost of the building itself. These allowances are at the rate of 4% of cost per annum, but usually only apply to large structures, such as factories and warehouses, although they can also extend to garage workshops, for example.

b)   Other commercial property, such as shops, offices etc, do not attract any allowances on the structure. However, any fixtures and fittings provided by the landlord in non-residential property do attract 'plant and machinery' allowances, as detailed in section 3.10.

c)   Residential property does not usually attract any capital allowances at all. However, landlords may claim the 'wear and tear allowance' (see section 4.9 below) on furnished lettings. Alternatively, the cost of replacement furniture, equipment, etc, may sometimes be claimed, as we saw in section 4.6.

d)   Furnished holiday lettings (see section 8.14), however, are not eligible for the wear and tear allowance, but are eligible for 'plant and machinery' allowances in the same way as (b) above.

Landlord's Own Assets

As explained above, a landlord is unable to claim capital allowances on any assets, such as furniture and equipment, within his or her residential lettings.

Any landlord (residential or commercial), however, may claim 'plant and machinery' allowances (as detailed in section 3.10) on equipment purchased for their own business use, such as computers and office furniture.

Capital allowances are also available on motor vehicles used in the business as again detailed in section 3.10.

Landlord's Energy Saving Allowance

During the period from 6th April 2004 to 5th April 2009, residential landlords may claim an Income Tax deduction for up to £1,500 of qualifying energy saving expenditure per building per year.

The expenditure which qualifies is as follows:

- From 6th April 2004: new loft or cavity wall insulation.
- From 7th April 2005: solid wall insulation.
- From 6th April 2006: draught proofing and insulation for hot water systems.

Without this special relief, this expenditure would normally have been regarded as a capital item and hence disallowed.

The landlord must already own the property at the time that the relevant expenditure is incurred (and not merely be in the process of acquiring it, for example). Furthermore, the insulation must be installed in an existing building and must not be installed during construction of a new one.

The relief is not available if the property is treated as a furnished holiday letting or if rent-a-room relief is being claimed against rental income from it.

If the landlord has not yet commenced his letting business then, unlike most pre-trading expenditure, the insulation work must take place within a six-month period before commencement of the business.

Wealth Warning

This relief operates on a 'per building' basis. This has two very important consequences.

Firstly, if the property is held jointly, the amount which may be claimed is limited to £1,500 <u>in total</u> (e.g. £750 each for two equal joint owners).

Secondly, if the same landlord owns several dwellings in the same building, the relief is still limited to £1,500 for the whole building.

Amounts allowed under this relief do not, unfortunately, count as capital allowances for the purposes of loss relief (see section 4.11 below).

4.9 FURNISHED LETTINGS

Income from furnished lettings (other than qualifying furnished holiday lettings, as defined in section 8.14) is generally treated in much the same way as other rental income. The only differences, quite naturally, are related to the treatment of the furnishings.

No allowance is given for the initial expenditure in furnishing the property, nor for adding additional new furnishings which were not present before. Thereafter, the landlord may claim either:

a) Renewal and replacement expenditure, or
b) The 'wear and tear allowance'

To claim the wear and tear allowance, however, the property must be 'fully furnished' in the eyes of Revenue & Customs. In other words, it must have at least the bare minimum level of furnishings which an occupier would generally expect.

If the property is furnished to a lesser degree then only the renewals and replacements basis will be available.

The Wear & Tear Allowance

A 'Wear and Tear Allowance' of 10% of net rents receivable may be claimed each year against the rental income from furnished residential lettings. This allowance is given instead of Capital Allowances, which are not available for residential property, and as an alternative to the 'Replacements Basis'.

In calculating the allowance, we first need to establish the amount of 'net rents receivable' for the property in question.

'Net rents receivable' means the total rent receivable less any amounts borne by the landlord which would normally be a tenant's own responsibility (e.g. council tax, water rates or electricity charges).

Additionally, if the rental includes any material amount representing a payment for additional services which would normally be borne by the occupier, rather than the owner, of the property, then these amounts must also be deducted before calculating the 10% Allowance.

Example

Cherie owns a large flat in central Bristol which she lets out for £2,500 per month (£30,000 per annum). This includes a charge of £250 per month for the provision of a cleaner. Cherie also pays the water rates for the property, which amount to £1,000 per year, but the tenant pays their own council tax.

She is therefore able to claim a wear and tear allowance as follows:

Total Rent Received:	*£30,000*
Less:	
Cleaning charges:	*£3,000 (12 x £250)*
Water Rates	*£1,000*
Net rent receivable:	*£26,000*
Wear and Tear Allowance:	*£2,600 (10%)*

Note that whilst we only have to deduct the COST of the water rates, it is the amount which Cherie CHARGES for the provision of cleaning services which must be deducted in this calculation. (Although only the cost thereof can be deducted when arriving at Cherie's overall total rental profits.)

The Alternative: The 'Replacements Basis'

The Wear and Tear Allowance is not mandatory. Landlords may, instead, claim the cost of replacing or renewing furniture and fixtures. They may not, however, claim the costs of the original furnishings and fixtures when the property is first let out, nor the cost of improvements or additional items.

For example, replacing one Video Recorder with another (lucky tenants!) would be allowed under the Replacements Basis, but replacing a Video Recorder with a DVD Player (even luckier tenants!) would not, as it would represent an improvement.

Does Any Of This Affect Repair Costs?

Repair costs should continue to be allowable under both methods and this also extends to replacements of any items normally provided in an unfurnished residential property, such as sinks or toilets, for example.

Practical Pointer

Resistance is sometimes encountered from Tax Inspectors when claiming repairs to 'white goods' such as cookers and fridges. If you encounter this problem, point them at paragraph 134 of their own publication, IR150, which makes it clear that this expenditure is allowable.

If they tell you that IR150 is out of date then just answer "yes, but, Tax Bulletin Issue 59 makes it clear that it's only out of date regarding notional repairs."

The 'Catch'

The Wear and Tear Allowance and the Replacements Basis are alternatives. You may claim one OR the other, NOT both.

The 'BIG Catch'

Once you have chosen one method, you must stick with it, on ALL of your furnished lets of all properties!

Hence, once the wear and tear allowance has been claimed, no deductions can ever be claimed for any renewals or replacements of furniture, fixtures, etc.

Tax Tip

If you were considering acquiring two or more properties and had a clear idea that the wear and tear allowance was best for one (or more) of them, but the replacements basis would be better for the rest, you could consider acquiring the 'wear and tear' properties personally, whilst your spouse (or perhaps a trust or a partnership) could acquire the others and elect for the replacements basis.

So, Which Method Is Best?

Conventional wisdom states that the Wear and Tear Allowance is usually best. This is generally because this method provides some relief immediately, from the first year onwards.

Generally, it will take longer before replacement expenditure starts to come through, with the original capital cost of furnishings being unallowable.

In short, Wear and Tear generally provides faster relief.

However, it is worth bearing in mind that this will not always be the case.

Example 2

Tony rents out a number of small flats to students at the local Polytechnic (sorry, it's called a UNIVERSITY now).

He is constantly frustrated by the fact that they frequently wreck the furniture. However, he combats this by buying cheap furniture and keeping their security deposits.

As a result, his total rental income for 2006/2007 is £20,000. Out of this he has paid Council Tax and Water Rates totalling £2,000 and spent £3,000 on replacement furniture.

If Tony were to claim the Wear and Tear Allowance, he would only be able to deduct £1,800 from his rental income. Hence, he is much better off claiming £3,000 under the Replacement Basis.

(With apologies to all those students who treat their landlord's property with the utmost respect and to any student landlords who do not buy cheap furniture or look for any excuse to hang on to their security deposits.)

So How Do You Choose?

Despite Tony's example, most people are better off with the Wear and Tear Allowance. However, before you submit your first claim, I would suggest that you do a few quick calculations to see which method is likely to be better for you on average in the long run (and not just in the first year).

4.10 RENT-A-ROOM RELIEF

A special relief, called 'rent-a-room relief', applies to income from letting out a part of your own home. For this purpose, the property must be your only or main residence (see section 6.13) for at least part of the same tax year. The letting itself must also at least partially coincide with a period when the property is your main residence.

The relief covers not only income from lodgers, but also extends to the letting of a self-contained flat, provided that the division of the property is only temporary.

Complete Exemption

Complete exemption is automatically provided where the gross rent receivable from lettings in the property does not exceed the rent-a-room limit (currently £4,250). This limit is applied on an annual basis.

The gross rent receivable for this purpose must also include any contributions towards household expenses which you receive from your tenants.

The taxpayer may elect not to claim rent-a-room relief if desired. They might do this, for example, if the letting is actually producing a loss which, otherwise, could not be claimed (see section 4.11 below regarding losses).

This election must be made before the expiry of a period ending 12 months after the 31st January following the tax year. (E.g. for the tax year 2005/2006, such an election would need to be made by 31st January 2008.)

Partial Exemption

Where the gross rent receivable exceeds the rent-a-room limit the taxpayer may nevertheless elect (within the same time limit as outlined above) for a form of partial exemption.

The partial exemption operates by allowing the taxpayer to be assessed only on the amount of gross rents receivable in excess of the rent-a-room limit instead of under the normal basis for rental income.

Example

Duncan rents out a room in his house for an annual rent of £5,000. His rental profit for 2006/2007, calculated on the normal basis, is £1,800. He therefore elects to use the rent-a-room basis, thus reducing his assessable rental income to only £750.

Other Points on Rent-a-Room Relief

Where the letting income is being shared with another person, the rent-a-room limit must be halved. Where there is letting income from the same property during the same tax year which does not qualify for the relief, none of the income from the property that year may be exempted.

An election to claim rent-a-room relief is deemed to remain in place for future years unless withdrawn (the same time limit applies for a withdrawal).

Any balancing charges arising in the tax year (see section 3.8) must be added to gross rents receivable before considering the application of the rent-a-room relief limit.

A Final Point On Lodgers

Income from lodgers may sometimes be regarded as trading income where there are sufficient services being provided (cooking, cleaning, etc.). Rent-a-room relief still applies to this income in the same way, however. It is only the treatment of any excess which would differ.

4.11 RENTAL LOSSES

As explained in section 4.1, all your UK property lettings (including any furnished holiday lettings but excluding any non-commercial lettings) are treated as a single UK property business. Hence, the loss on any commercially let UK property is automatically set off against profits on other UK rental properties for the same period.

Any overall net losses arising from a UK property business may be carried forward and set off against future UK rental profits. Losses consisting of capital allowances may also be set off against the landlord's other income of the same tax year and the next one.

Example

In the tax year 2006/2007 Owain has employment income of £42,000, from which he suffers deduction of tax under PAYE totalling £8,534.

He also has a portfolio of rented commercial property on which he has made an overall loss of £10,000, including £2,000 of capital allowances.

Owain can claim to set his capital allowances off against his employment income, which will produce a tax repayment of £800.

Any losses from UK furnished holiday lettings will first be automatically set off against other UK rental profits. Any excess may then either be carried forward or may alternatively be set off against all of the taxpayer's other income of the same tax year and the previous one. Naturally, however, the same amount of loss can only be relieved once.

Had Owain's loss of £10,000 been from a furnished holiday letting business, he could have set the whole amount off against his employment income, producing a repayment of £2,859.70 instead of his measly £800.

The treatment of losses from overseas lettings is covered in section 4.14 below. Non-commercial lettings, which are effectively excluded from your UK property business, are covered in section 4.15.

How Long Can Rental Losses Be Carried Forward?

UK rental losses may be carried forward for as long as you continue to have a UK property rental business. There are two major pitfalls to watch out for here.

Firstly, rental losses are personal. They cannot be transferred to another person, not even your spouse or civil partner, and they do not transfer with the properties. If you die with rental losses, they die with you.

Secondly, if your UK property business ceases, you will lose your losses. It may therefore sometimes be vital to keep your UK property business going. Remember that as long as you continue to have at least one UK rental property, you still have a UK property business.

Example

Fergus has a large UK property portfolio. Despite having made some good profits in the past, by 2005/2006 he has rental losses of £1,000,000 carried forward.

Fergus decides he's had enough and begins to sell off his UK property empire. Before his rental income ceases, however, he buys one small lock-up garage in Argyllshire and starts to rent it out.

Fergus' lock-up garage is enough to ensure that he still has a UK property rental business. It doesn't matter that it is tiny by comparison with his previous ventures, this one small garage keeps his rental losses alive, with the possibility of saving him up to £400,000 one day.

The only absolutely safe way to ensure that you have a continuing UK property rental business is to ensure that you always have at least one UK rental property let out on a commercial basis.

However, Revenue & Customs will sometimes accept that a total cessation of all rental income is not necessarily the same as a cessation of your UK rental business, especially where the rental properties are still held.

They will usually accept that the rental business has not ceased:

- Where you can provide evidence that you have been attempting unsuccessfully to let out your property.

- Where rental has only ceased temporarily whilst repairs or alterations are carried out.

They will, however, generally regard the rental business as having ceased if there is a gap of more than three years between lettings and different properties are let before and after the gap.

They may sometimes accept a gap of less than three years as not being a cessation, but not if you have clearly employed all of your capital in some other type of business, or spent it for personal purposes, such as buying yourself a new home.

If in doubt though, rent out that garage!

Wealth Warning

Remember, an overseas property will not preserve your UK property business.

A non-commercial letting (e.g. to your aunt for £1 a year) will not do either.

4.12 OTHER PROPERTY INVESTMENT INCOME

Most forms of income derived from investments in land and property will be subject to Income Tax under the regime outlined in section 4.1.

This will include tenant's deposits retained at the end of a lease and usually also any dilapidation payments received.

Dilapidation payments may, however, sometimes be regarded as a capital receipt if the landlord does not rent the property out again (e.g. if the landlord sells it or adopts it as their own home).

Some items are specifically excluded from treatment as property income, however, including:

- Any amounts taxable as trading income.
- Farming and market gardening.
- Income from mineral extraction rights.

Wayleave (right of access) payments received are, however, sometimes included as property income.

Another important source of property income is lease premiums, which we shall examine in the next section.

4.13 LEASE PREMIUMS

Premiums received for the granting of short leases of no more than 50 years' duration are subject to Income Tax. The proportion of the premium subject to Income Tax is, however, reduced by 2% for each full year of the lease's duration in excess of one year.

The element of the lease not subject to Income Tax falls within the Capital Gains Tax regime (see section 6.43) and will be treated as a part disposal of the relevant property (or superior interest).

Example

Alexander, who owns the freehold to a property, grants a 12-year lease to Kenneth for a premium of £50,000. The lease exceeds one year by eleven years and hence 22% of this sum falls within the Capital Gains Tax regime. Alexander is therefore subject to Income Tax on the sum of £39,000 (i.e. £50,000 less 22%).

4.14 OVERSEAS LETTINGS

All of a taxpayer's commercially let overseas properties are treated as a single business in much the same way as, but separate from, a UK property business. A UK resident and domiciled taxpayer (see section 3.7) with overseas lettings is taxed on this income under exactly the same principles as for UK lettings except that:

   i)   Separate accounts will be required for properties in each overseas territory where any double tax relief claims are to be made.
   ii) Overseas furnished holiday lettings are not eligible for any of the extra reliefs accorded to UK furnished holiday lettings.

This second rule may be contrary to European law, but no-one seems to have taken a case to court on it yet.

Travelling expenses may be claimed when incurred wholly and exclusively for the purposes of the overseas letting business.

The UK treatment of losses arising from an overseas letting business is exactly the same as for a UK property business, except, of course, that this is treated as a separate business from any UK lettings which the taxpayer has. Hence, again, these losses are automatically set off against profits derived from other overseas lettings with the excess carried forward for set off against future overseas rental profits. The same rule as set out in section 4.11 applies to any capital allowances but the additional reliefs for furnished holiday lettings are not available.

Where there are substantial overseas rental losses carried forward it will be worthwhile ensuring that this business continues. The same principles as set out in section 4.11 will apply here, except that, to continue the business, it is necessary to continue to have overseas rental property.

Whilst the property must be let on a commercial basis and must be outside the UK, it can be in any other part of the world and need not be in the same country where the original rental losses arose. A loss made in Albania might conceivably be set off against a profit in Zanzibar!

4.15 NON-COMMERCIAL LETTINGS

Where lettings are not on a commercial or 'arm's length' basis, they cannot be regarded as part of the same UK or overseas property business as any commercial lettings which the taxpayer has. Profits remain taxable, but any losses arising may only be carried forward for set off against future profits from the same letting (i.e. the same property let to the same tenant).

Typically, this type of letting involves the lease of a property to a relative or friend of the landlord at a nominal rent, considerably less than the full market rent which the property could demand on the open market.

Where the tenant of such a non-commercial letting is a previous owner of the property (e.g. a parent of the landlord), the new 'Pre-Owned Assets' Income Tax benefit-in-kind charge may apply to the benefit so received by the tenant from 6th April 2005 onwards.

In many cases this will result in the tenant being charged Income Tax on the difference between the nominal rent which they pay and the full market rent.

Chapter 5

How to Avoid Tax on a Property Trade

5.1 THE TAXATION OF PROPERTY TRADING INCOME

Where your property business is deemed to be a trade, such as property development or property dealing, you will be taxed under a different set of principles to those outlined in the previous chapter.

In this section, we will take a brief look at the major differences which you need to be aware of before we proceed to look at these and other issues in more detail throughout the rest of the chapter.

In this section and most of the remainder of this chapter we will be concentrating mainly on the trades of property development and property dealing. Property management, which does not normally involve the ownership of any property, is treated slightly differently again and we will look at this briefly in section 5.9.

The major points to note are:

i) Properties held for development or sale are treated as trading stock rather than capital assets.

ii) Taxpayers with property trades may choose any calendar date as their accounting year end.

iii) Profits on property disposals are subject to both Income Tax and Class 4 National Insurance Contributions. Property traders must also pay Class 2 National Insurance Contributions.

iv) Most 'abortive' legal and professional fees should be allowed as incurred, as an Income Tax deduction.

v) A broader range of administrative expenditure will be claimable.

vi) Capital allowances will be available only on your own business's long-term assets.

vii) Trading losses may be set off against all of your other income and capital gains for the same tax year and the previous one.

viii) The same trade may involve both properties in the UK and properties overseas.

ix) Non-Resident individuals and non-domiciled individuals are taxed on a trade if it is managed in the UK. (For a UK Resident but non-domiciled individual, a foreign-based property trade is again taxed on the remittance basis.)

5.2   PROPERTIES AS TRADING STOCK

The properties which you hold in the business for development and/or sale are not regarded as long-term capital assets. They are, instead, regarded as trading stock.

For tax purposes, all of your expenditure in acquiring, improving, repairing or converting the properties becomes part of the cost of that trading stock.

Many of the issues which we examined in chapter four about the question of whether expenditure is revenue or capital therefore become completely academic. Most professional fees and repairs or improvement expenditure are treated as part of the cost of the trading stock in a property trade.

(As explained in section 3.8, the term 'revenue expenditure' means expenditure deductible from income, whereas capital expenditure is subject to different rules.) The way in which trading stock works for tax purposes can be illustrated by way of an example.

Example

In November 2006, Muhammad buys a property in Windsor for £260,000. He also pays Stamp Duty Land Tax of £7,800 and legal fees of £1,450. Previously, in October, he also paid a survey fee of £750.

Muhammad is a property developer and draws up accounts to 31st December each year. In his accounts to 31st December 2006, the

107

Windsor property will be included as trading stock with a value of £270,000, made up as follows:

	£
Property purchase	260,000
Stamp Duty Land Tax	7,800
Legal fees	1,450
Survey fee	750
	270,000

Points To Note

The important point to note here, is that whilst all of Muhammad's expenditure is regarded as revenue expenditure, because he is a property developer, he cannot yet claim any deduction for any of it, because he still holds the property.

Example Continued

Early in 2007, Muhammad incurs further professional fees of £10,000 obtaining planning permission to divide the property into two separate residences.

Permission is granted in July and by the end of the year, Muhammad has spent a further £40,000 on conversion work.

In his accounts to 31st December 2007 the property will still be shown in trading stock, as follows:

	£
Costs brought forward	270,000
Additional professional fees	10,000
Building work	40,000
	320,000

Muhammad still doesn't get any tax relief for any of this expenditure.

By March 2008, Muhammad has spent another £5,000 on the property and is ready to sell the two new houses that he has created.

One of them sells quickly for £185,000. Muhammad incurs a further £3,500 in estate agent's and legal fees in the process.

Muhammad's taxable profit on this sale is thus calculated as follows:

	£	£
Sale proceeds		*185,000*
Less Cost:		
Total cost brought forward:	*320,000*	
Additional building costs:	*5,000*	

Trading Stock prior to sale of first property	*325,000*	

Allocated to property sold (50%):	*162,500*	
Add additional costs:	*3,500*	

		166,000

Profit on sale		*19,000*
		======

This profit will form part of Muhammad's trading profit for the year ended 31ˢᵗ December 2008.

Points To Note

The additional building spend of £5,000 was allocated to trading stock as this still related to the whole property.

The legal and estate agent's fees incurred on the sale, however, were specific to the part which was sold and may thus be deducted in full against those sale proceeds.

In the example I have split the cost of trading stock equally between the two new houses. If the two new houses are, indeed, identical then this will be correct. Otherwise, the costs should be split between the two properties on a reasonable basis – e.g. total floor area, or in proportion to the market value of the finished properties.

The latter approach would be the required statutory basis if these were capital disposals. Although it is not mandatory here, it might still be a useful yardstick.

The most important point of all, however, is that even if Muhammad fails to sell the second new house before 31st December 2008, his profit on the first new house will still be taxable in full.

There is one exception to this, as we shall now examine.

Net Realisable Value

Trading stock is generally shown in the accounts at its cumulative cost to date.

On this basis, Muhammad's second house, if still unsold at 31st December 2008, would have a carrying value of £162,500 in his accounts.

If, however, for whatever reason, the market value of the property is less than its cumulative cost then, as trading stock, its carrying value in the accounts may be reduced appropriately.

Furthermore, since the act of selling the property itself will lead to further expenses, these may also be deducted from the property's reduced value in this situation. This gives us a value known in accounting terminology as the property's 'net realisable value'.

Practical Pointer

Trading stock should always be shown in the accounts at the lower of cost or net realisable value.

To see the effect of this in practice, let's return once more to our example.

Example

The second new house in Windsor doesn't sell so quickly, so, in September Muhammad decides to take it back off the market and build an extension on the back to make it a more attractive proposition to potential buyers.

Unfortunately, however, there are some problems with the foundations for the extension and the costs have more than doubled from what Muhammad had expected.

By 31st December, Muhammad has spent £27,500 on the extension work and it still isn't finished.

His total costs to date on the second new house are thus £190,000.

Muhammad's builder estimates that there will be further costs of £12,000 before the extension is complete and the property is ready to sell.

The estate agent reckons that the completed property will sell for around £200,000. The agent's own fees will amount to £3,000 and there will also be legal costs of around £750.

The net realisable value of the property at 31st December 2008 is thus:

	£	£
Market value of completed property		*200,000*
Less:		
Costs to complete	*12,000*	
Professional costs to sell	*3,750*	
		15,750
Net Realisable Value at 31/12/2008		*184,250*

Since this is less than Muhammad's costs to date on the property, this is the value to be shown as trading stock in his 2008 accounts.

The result of this is that Muhammad will show a loss of £5,750 (£190,000 less £184,250) on the second house in his 2008 accounts. This loss will automatically be set off against his £19,000 profit on the first house.

By March 2009, the second house is ready for sale.

Fortunately, there is an upturn in the market later in the year and Muhammad manages to sell the property for £215,000 in October 2009.

His actual additional expenditure on the extension work amounted to £11,800 and the professional fees incurred on the sale were actually £3,900.

Muhammad's taxable profit on this property in 2009 is thus:

	£	£
Sale proceeds		215,000
Less: Value of trading stock brought forward, as per accounts (i.e. net realisable value at 31/12/2008):	184,250	
Additional building cost	11,800	
Professional fees on sale	3,900	

		199,950

Taxable profit in year to 31/12/2009		15,050
		======

Points To Note

When Muhammad calculates his profit for 2009, he uses actual figures for everything which took place after 31st December 2008, his last accounting date (i.e. the sale price, the final part of the building work and the professional fees on the sale).

The property's net realisable value in the accounts at 31st December 2008 is, however, substituted for all of the costs which Muhammad incurred up until that date.

Hence, the apparent loss which Muhammad was able to claim in 2008 effectively reverses and becomes part of his profits in 2009.

In this example, some of the actual figures turned out to be different to the estimates previously available.

Taxpayers would generally be expected to use the most accurate figures available at the time that they are preparing their accounts.

In the case of sale price, however, this should be taken to mean an accurate estimate of the completed property's market value at the accounting date (i.e. 31st December 2008 in this example), rather than its actual eventual sale price.

5.3   WORK-IN-PROGRESS & SALES CONTRACTS

Generally, for speculative property developers, their trading stock, as we have seen, is valued at the lower of its cumulative cost to date or its net realisable value.

However, if a contract for the sale of the property exists, the developer has to follow a different set of rules.

This is a complex area of accounting but, broadly speaking, the developer is required to value properties under development, for which a sale contract already exists, at an appropriate percentage of their contractual sale value. This is done by treating the completed proportion of the property as having already been sold.

The same proportion of the expected final costs of the development can be deducted from the sale. Any remaining balance of development costs is included in the accounts as 'Work-in-Progress', which is simply a term for trading stock which is only partly completed.

Example

Aayan is building a new house on a plot of land and has already contracted to sell it for £500,000.

Aayan draws up accounts to 31ˢᵗ March each year and, at 31ˢᵗ March 2007, the new house is 75% complete. Aayan's total costs to date are £320,000, but he expects to incur a further £80,000 in order to complete the house.

Aayan will need to show a sale of £375,000 (75% of £500,000) in his accounts to 31ˢᵗ March 2007. He will, however, be able to deduct costs of £300,000, which equates to 75% of his anticipated final total costs of £400,000 (£320,000 + £80,000).

In other words, Aayan will show a profit of £75,000 in his accounts to 31ˢᵗ March 2007, which is equal to 75% of his expected final profit of £100,000.

The remaining £20,000 of Aayan's costs to date will be shown in his accounts at 31ˢᵗ March 2007 as Work-in-Progress.

During the following year, Aayan completes the property at an actual cost of £77,000.

His accounts for the year ending 31ˢᵗ March 2008 will show a sale of £125,000, i.e. the remaining 25% of his total sale proceeds of £500,000.

From this, Aayan can deduct total costs of £97,000, which is made up of his £20,000 of Work-in-Progress brought forward and his actual costs in the year of £77,000.

This gives Aayan a development profit of £28,000 for the year ended 31ˢᵗ March 2008.

As we can see from the example, the effect of this accounting treatment is to accelerate part of the profit on the development. As there is no specific rule to the contrary, the tax position will also follow the accounting treatment, so that the developer is taxed on part of his property sale in advance.

It follows that the whole profit on a property for which a sales contract exists will need to be included in the developer's accounts once the property is fully completed.

Where this accounting treatment applies, the developer may nevertheless claim deductions to reflect:

- Any doubt over the purchaser's ability, or willingness, to pay.
- Rectification work which is still to be carried out.
- Administration and other costs relating to completion of the sale.

5.4   ACCOUNTING DATE

As you will have noted from Muhammad's position in section 5.2, as a property developer or dealer, you may choose any accounting date you like and do not have to stick with a 5th April year end. This provides some very useful tax-planning opportunities.

For example, if you feel that you are generally likely to make more sales in the late Spring and Summer, a 30th April accounting date may be very useful.

Profits made on sales in May or June 2006 would therefore form part of your accounting profit for the year ended 30th April 2007. For tax purposes, this accounting period falls into the 2007/2008 tax year, as it is generally the accounts year end date which determines when profits are taxable.

Under self-assessment, the Income Tax and National Insurance Contributions due on these profits therefore would not be payable until 31st January 2009, almost *three years* after you made the sales!

Note that there are special rules which apply in the first two or three years of a trading business which would lead to a different effect, sometimes more beneficial and sometimes less so.

Generally, in these early years, if your profit is static, or increasing, you will benefit from an accounting date early in the tax year, such as 30th April.

If, however, you are starting on high profits and expect them to fall thereafter, then a 31st March or 5th April accounting date will generally be preferable.

5.5 NATIONAL INSURANCE CONTRIBUTIONS

Unlike a property investment business, the profits of a property trade are regarded as 'earnings' for National Insurance purposes.

This means that property dealers or developers operating on their own as sole traders, jointly with one or more other people, or in a more formal partnership structure, will be liable for Class 2 and Class 4 National Insurance Contributions.

Class 2

Most self-employed traders will be liable to pay Class 2 National Insurance Contributions at the rate of £2.10 per week for 2006/2007. In practice, it will usually be collected via monthly direct debits. These direct debits will be either £8.40 or £10.50 each month, depending on the number of Sundays in the month.

Property trades are no exception, but there are other exceptions. Taxpayers are exempt from Class 2 National Insurance Contributions if they:

- Have reached state retirement age (65 for men or 60 for women) on or before the first day of the tax year.
- Are aged under 16.
- Have profits below the 'small earnings exception' limit (£4,465 for 2006/2007).

The last exemption must be applied for.

Your Class 2 liability as a property trader will therefore amount to a mere £109.20 per year.

"Big deal", I hear you say. Well, yes, it's true that Class 2 National Insurance is not exactly the most important tax issue which you are going to face.

In many cases, however, it is the first, and for this reason Revenue & Customs now use it as a means to police new unincorporated trading businesses. Registering for Class 2 National Insurance Contributions gets you into the tax system and from then onwards Revenue & Customs become your silent partner every step of the way!

Hence, unless you fall within one of the first two exceptions described above, you will need to register for payment of Class 2 National Insurance Contributions within three months from the end of the calendar month in which you commence your property trade.

Wealth Warning

Failure to register for Class 2 National Insurance Contributions within three months of the commencement of trading is now subject to a penalty of £100. (A hefty penalty indeed for an annual tax bill of only £109.20 – equivalent to 91.6%!)

In the case of a partnership or joint owners, each individual must register for Class 2 National Insurance Contributions.

However, if any person is already paying Class 2 contributions due to some other existing source of self-employment trading income, there is no need to register again.

Class 4

Class 4 National Insurance Contributions are payable on trading profits. The profits on which the National Insurance Contributions are based are exactly the same trading profits as those calculated for Income Tax purposes.

The rates of National Insurance Contributions payable are set out in Appendix A.

For profits falling to be taxed in the tax year 2006/2007, this has the result of giving most property traders with no other sources of income the following overall effective tax rates, combining Income Tax and Class 4 National Insurance Contributions:

Profits up to £5,035:   Nil
Profits between £5,035 and £7,185:   18%
Profits between £7,185 and £33,540:   30%
Profits between £33,540 and £38,335:   23%
Profits over £38,335:   41%

Plus, in most cases, an additional £109.20 in Class 2 National Insurance Contributions.

To see the impact of this in practice, let's revisit an earlier example.

Example

In section 3.4 we saw that Nick was paying a total of £4,533 in Income Tax under self-assessment for 2006/2007.

Let us now assume that Nick is, in fact, a property developer and his £10,000 of property income is actually a property trading profit. In addition to his Income Tax bill, therefore, Nick will also be liable for Class 4 National Insurance Contributions of £397.20 (8% of £10,000 less £5,035), bringing his total self-assessment tax liability up to £4,930.20, an overall effective tax rate on his property trading profits of 46%! (Remember that he already had tax of £333 to pay on his investment income before we took his property income into account.)

In fact, adding in Nick's £109.20 of Class 2 National Insurance Contributions will give him a total tax bill on his property profits of £4,706.40, or 47.1%!

Taxpayers like Nick with both employment and self-employed trading income may end up paying more in National Insurance Contributions than the law actually demands.

This can arise where there is more than one source of earned income and the total income from all such sources exceeds the upper threshold for the main rate of National Insurance Contributions (currently £33,540).

118

In such cases, taxpayers may apply for a refund of the excess National Insurance paid or, if they are able to foresee in advance that this situation is likely to arise, apply for a deferment of their Class 2 or Class 4 contributions.

Tax Tip

> If you are already in receipt of other earnings and anticipate that your property trading profits will result in your total earnings for the tax year exceeding £33,540 you should consider applying for deferment of National Insurance Contributions.

Remember that 'earnings' is generally restricted to employment income and self-employed or partnership trading income. It does not include pensions, rental income or other investment income.

5.6   TRADING DEDUCTIONS: GENERAL

The basic principles outlined in sections 3.8 and 3.9 continue to apply to the deduction of business expenditure from trading profits. Many of the points discussed in chapter four will also remain relevant.

On the other hand, however, the different treatment of the profits arising on property sales in a trading scenario naturally creates some differences too!

As we already know, expenditure must be 'revenue expenditure' if it is to be claimed for Income Tax purposes. As we have seen, however, this rule operates quite differently in the context of a property trade. Expenditure on long-term assets for use in the trade will nevertheless continue to be capital in nature. Such assets might include:

- Office premises from which to run the trade.
- Motor vehicles for use in the trade.
- Computers.
- Building tools and equipment.

Capital allowances will be available on much of this expenditure as we shall see in section 5.8.

Expenses incurred which are ancillary to the purchase of capital assets continue to be treated as capital expenditure also. Hence, whilst the legal fees incurred on the purchase of trading stock are a revenue expense, similar fees incurred on the purchase of the business's own trading premises will be capital in nature.

5.7   TRADING DEDUCTIONS: SPECIFIC AREAS

Most forms of business expenditure which meet the criteria outlined in section 3.8 should be allowable as deductions from trading income. These will include the items which we covered in section 3.9.

There are a few exceptions which are specifically disallowed, such as business entertaining and gifts. (Even here there can be exceptions to the exceptions.)

In this section, we will quickly look at some of the other main trading deductions to be considered in the specific context of a property trade. As in chapter four, however, this is certainly not meant to be an exhaustive list of potential trading expenses.

Interest and Other Finance Costs

Interest is allowable if it is incurred on funds used for the purposes of the trade. The question of where the borrowings are secured is completely irrelevant.

The treatment of other finance costs, such as loan arrangement fees, will generally follow the same principles.

However, where accounting principles dictate that a cost should be spread over the life of the loan, the tax relief will have to be spread over the same period.

Legal and Professional Fees

Legal fees and other professional costs incurred on the successful purchase or sale of properties classed as trading stock will be allowed as part of the cost of those properties in the computation of the profits arising on sale.

As explained previously, however, costs relating to the purchase or sale of the business's long-term assets remain capital expenses.

Other professional costs incurred year in, year out, in earning trading profits may include items such as debt collection expenses and accountancy fees. These costs are deductible as general overheads of the business.

Abortive Expenditure

In a property development or dealing trade, abortive costs such as survey fees, advertising or legal fees relating to unsuccessful transactions should be allowed as a trading expense.

This should also extend to the costs of any unsuccessful planning applications attempted in the course of the trade.

Training and Research

The rule here is that expenses incurred in updating or expanding existing areas of knowledge may be claimed, but any costs relating to entirely new areas of knowledge are a personal capital expense.

Hence, if you are already a competent plumber but go on a plumbing course to learn the latest techniques in the industry then the cost of this course should be allowable.

The cost of the same course would, however, not be allowable if you knew nothing about plumbing.

Health & Safety

Notwithstanding the general rules given in section 3.8, any expenditure on safety boots, hard hats and other protective clothing or equipment will be allowable.

This may sometimes extend to 'all-weather' clothing if the taxpayer spends all or part of their working life outdoors and does not use that clothing for any non-business purposes.

5.8   CAPITAL ALLOWANCES FOR PROPERTY TRADES

Most of the basic principles governing the claiming of capital allowances are explained in section 3.10.

Items typically qualifying for 'plant and machinery' allowances, as detailed in section 3.10, would include the following:

- Building equipment and tools.
- Computers.
- Office furniture, fixtures and fittings.
- Vans.

In general terms, property developers are likely to have greater scope for claiming capital allowances than those with property investment businesses.

Property dealers and those with property management businesses will not usually be able to claim quite as many allowances, although the same principles continue to apply.

Capital allowances cannot be claimed on any expenditure which is included within trading stock.

Capital allowances are available on motor cars used in a property trade, as again detailed in section 3.10.

5.9   PROPERTY MANAGEMENT TRADES

Most of the principles outlined in this chapter will apply equally to property management trades when they are relevant.

The biggest difference is the fact that these trades are unlikely to hold properties as trading stock.

Other than their own office premises, any properties held are likely to be investment properties and dealt with in accordance with chapter four for tax purposes.

Staff costs will often be a significant issue in a property management trade. The National Insurance consequences of this are examined in section 7.10.

Chapter 6

How to Avoid Capital Gains Tax

6.1 THE IMPORTANCE OF CAPITAL GAINS TAX

Although its impact is not as immediate as that of Income Tax, nevertheless Capital Gains Tax is perhaps the most significant tax from a property investor's perspective (though not those who are classed as property developers or property dealers, as we have already seen in chapter five).

Most property investments will eventually lead to a disposal and every property disposal presents the risk of a Capital Gains Tax liability arising and reducing the investor's after-tax return drastically, sometimes by as much as 40%.

Paradoxically, however, Capital Gains Tax is also the tax which presents the greatest number and variety of tax-planning opportunities. We will be examining some of these further in chapter eight.

First, however, it is worth recalling how this tax developed and looking at how it affects property investors today.

6.2 THE DEVELOPMENT OF CAPITAL GAINS TAX

Capital Gains Tax was introduced by Harold Wilson's first Labour Government in 1965.

The new tax was designed to combat a growing trend for avoiding Income Tax by realising capital gains, which at that time were mostly tax free, rather than taxable income.

Because the tax was only introduced on 6th April 1965, gains arising before that date remained exempt from Capital Gains Tax. Thus for many years it was necessary to make detailed, and often complicated, calculations designed to remove these 'pre-1965' gains from the amount to be taxed. In theory, such calculations could still be relevant even today, although their incidence is now extremely rare.

The high inflation of the late 1970's and early 1980's brought about a significant change after 31st March 1982, with the introduction of Indexation Relief. This new relief was designed to exempt gains which arose purely through the effects of inflation. Ironically, and somewhat frustratingly, however, it was only post-March 1982 inflation which was exempted and, by then, the highest rates of inflation lay in the past.

The next major change came in 1988 with so-called 're-basing'. The Government finally recognised the unfairness of not exempting pre-1982 inflationary gains. However, rather than merely combating this oversight with an improved Indexation Relief, instead they decided to exempt all pre-31st March 1982 gains. Hence Capital Gains Tax was 'rebased' from 6th April 1965 to 31st March 1982.

Naturally, however, since nothing in the tax world is ever simple, the new 31st March 1982 base did not operate in the same way as the old 6th April 1965 base and phrases like the 'kink test' entered the tax adviser's vocabulary, as even more complex calculations became necessary. Only the subsequent passage of time has rendered most of these complexities irrelevant in most cases today.

The Conservative Governments of the late 1980's and early 1990's continued to introduce a number of Capital Gains Tax exemptions and reliefs, including some very generous holdover reliefs for reinvestment of gains, as well as substantial increases in the annual exemption.

By the time of the 1997 General Election, the Conservatives were set well on a path towards the abolition of Capital Gains Tax and a return to the pre-1965 situation.

However, as we all know, the Election on 3rd May 1997 brought an historic victory for 'New Labour'. Those with potential capital gains awaited the seemingly inevitable crackdown.

But when the changes came, they were very far from the draconian measures which some rather hysterical commentators had predicted. In fact, the new Capital Gains Tax regime ushered in by Chancellor Gordon Brown's second Budget in 1998 is quite possibly the most generous we have seen since 1965.

Clearly, 'New Labour' had recognised that the immense changes in British society over nearly two decades of Conservative Government meant that capital gains were no longer the perquisite of the privileged few, but were now very much a part of life for a significant proportion of the population in the modern economy of investment and enterprise.

The cornerstone of Labour's new Capital Gains Tax regime, Taper Relief, has, from the outset, come in two different tiers, Business Asset Taper Relief and Non-Business Asset Taper Relief.

Since 1998, the rate and availability of Business Asset Taper Relief has been improved significantly, with the maximum relief now reached after just two years, as opposed to the ten-year period introduced initially.

Best of all, from 6th April 2004, most commercial (i.e. non-residential) properties are classified as 'Business Assets' for Taper Relief purposes.

Non-Business Asset Taper Relief, which is far more relevant to residential property investment, has, however, remained unchanged since its introduction.

6.3   WHO PAYS CAPITAL GAINS TAX?

Capital Gains Tax is payable in the UK by:

i)   Individuals who are UK resident or UK ordinarily resident.
ii)   UK resident trusts.
iii) Non-resident persons trading in the UK through a branch, agency or other permanent establishment.

Except for persons falling under (iii) above, non-UK Residents are generally exempt from UK Capital Gains Tax. Some do, however, get caught out by the 'ordinarily resident' rule and we will return to this in section 8.18.

In this chapter, we will be concentrating mainly on category (i) above, i.e. UK resident or UK ordinarily resident individuals investing in property.

Individuals who are UK resident or UK ordinarily resident and also UK domiciled are liable for Capital Gains Tax on their worldwide capital gains.

Individuals who are UK resident or UK ordinarily resident but not UK domiciled are always liable for Capital Gains Tax on capital gains arising from the disposal of UK property but only liable for Capital Gains Tax on 'foreign' capital gains if and when they remit their disposal proceeds back to the UK.

The tax concepts of residence and domicile were examined in section 3.7 above. Domicile is also covered further in section 7.4.

6.4 WHAT IS A CAPITAL GAIN?

A capital gain is the profit arising on the disposal, in whole or in part, of an asset, or an interest in an asset.

Put simply, the gain is the excess obtained on the sale of the asset over the price paid to buy it. (However, as we will see in the sections that follow, matters rarely remain that simple.)

Sometimes, however, assets are held in such a way that their disposal gives rise to an Income Tax charge instead. The same amount of gain cannot be subject to both Income Tax and Capital Gains Tax.

Where both taxes might apply, Income Tax will take precedence, so that no Capital Gains Tax arises. (There is little comfort in this, as the regime of reliefs available under Capital Gains Tax is far more generous than under Income Tax and the latter tax therefore usually produces a higher charge where it applies.)

The most common type of asset sale which gives rise to an Income Tax charge, rather than Capital Gains Tax, is, of course, a sale in the course of a trade. In other words, where the asset is, or is deemed to be, trading stock.

If a man buys sweets to sell in his sweet shop they are quite clearly trading stock and his profits on their sale must be subject to Income Tax and not Capital Gains Tax. This is pretty obvious because there are usually only two things you can do with sweets, eat them or sell them.

Properties, however, have a number of possible uses. A property purchaser may intend one or more of several objectives:

a) To keep the property for personal use, either as a main residence or otherwise.
b) To provide a home for the use of family or friends.
c) To use the property in a business.
d) To let the property out for profit.
e) To hold the property as an investment.
f) To develop the property for profit.
g) To sell the property on at a profit.

Where objectives (f) and/or (g) are the sole purpose behind the purchase of the property, this will render the ultimate gain on the property's sale a trading profit subject to Income Tax. The taxation of property development and dealing profits has been dealt with in detail in chapter five.

All of the other objectives listed above make the property a capital investment subject only to Capital Gains Tax.

This is simple enough where the objectives described in (f) and (g) above are either completely absent or the sole purpose of the purchase.

Naturally though, in the majority of cases, objective (g) is present to some degree. This does not necessarily render the gain on the property's sale a trading profit subject to Income Tax. This would only be the case where (g) is the sole or overwhelmingly dominant objective behind the purchase.

In practice, there is often more than one objective present when a property is purchased and objectives (f) and (g) may exist to a lesser or greater extent. In many cases, the correct position is obvious but, in borderline situations, each case has to be decided on its own merits.

Some of the key factors to consider are described in section 2.9. Here though, it is perhaps worth looking at a few more detailed examples.

Example 1

James bought a house in 1990 which he used as his main residence throughout his ownership. In 1995 he built an extension, which substantially increased the value of the house. He continued to live in the house until eventually selling it in 2006.

This is clearly a capital gain because James carried on using the house for his personal enjoyment for several years after building the extension. (Furthermore, the house will be exempt from Capital Gains Tax, as it was James' main residence throughout his ownership.)

Example 2

Charles bought a house in 1990 and used it as his main residence for five years. In 1995, he moved into a new house and converted the first one into a number of flats. Following the conversion, Charles let the flats out until he eventually sold the whole property in 2006.

Charles' situation is less clear-cut. Nevertheless, he has still realised a capital gain as the conversion work was clearly intended as a longer-term investment. (Charles would have a partial exemption under the main residence rules.)

Example 3

William, a wealthy man with three other properties, bought a derelict barn in 2005. He developed it into a luxury home. Immediately after the development work was complete he put the property on the market and sold it in 2007.

This is clearly a trading profit subject to Income Tax. William simply developed the property for profit and never put it to any other use.

Example 4

Anne bought an old farmhouse in 2006. She lived in the property for three months and then moved out while substantial renovation work took place. After the work was completed, she let it out for six months.

Halfway through the period of the lease she put the property on the market and sold it with completion taking place the day the lease expired.

This is what one would call 'borderline'. Anne has had some personal use of the property, and has let it out, but she has also developed it and sold it after only a short period of ownership. This case would warrant a much closer look at all of the circumstances. It should be decided on the basis of Anne's intentions but who, apart from Anne herself, would ever know what these truly were?

Such a case could go either way. The more Anne can do to demonstrate that her intention had been to hold the property as a long-term investment, the better her chances of success will be. Her personal and financial circumstances will be crucial. For example, if she had got married around the time of the sale, or had got into unexpected financial difficulties, which had forced her to make the sale, then she might successfully argue for Capital Gains Tax treatment.

Note that, just because the profit arising on the sale of an asset is a capital gain, this does not necessarily mean that it is subject to Capital Gains Tax.

A number of assets may be exempt from Capital Gains Tax, including motor cars, medals and Government securities.

Most importantly for property investors though, the taxpayer's only or main residence is also exempt and we will return to this in section 6.13.

The bad news though is that capital losses derived from exempt assets are also not allowable.

6.5   WHEN DOES A CAPITAL GAIN ARISE?

For Capital Gains Tax purposes, a disposal is treated as taking place as soon as there is an unconditional contract for the sale of an asset.

The effective disposal date may therefore often be somewhat earlier than the date of completion of the sale.

130

This is an absolutely vital point to remember when undertaking any Capital Gains Tax planning.

Example

Aidan completes the sale of an investment property on 8th April 2007. However, the unconditional sale contract was signed on 1st April 2007.

Aidan's sale therefore falls into the tax year ended on 5th April 2007 and any Capital Gains Tax due will be payable by 31st January 2008.

The effective acceleration of Aidan's Capital Gains Tax bill is bad enough, but what if he had also emigrated on 3rd April 2007?

Where the contract remains conditional on some event beyond the control of the parties to it, then the sale is not yet deemed to have taken place for Capital Gains Tax purposes. The most common scenarios here are for the sale to be conditional on:

- The granting of planning permission.
- Completion of a satisfactory survey.
- Approval of finance arrangements.

Many English investors who have travelled North get caught out by the Scottish system where the exchange of missives generally creates an unconditional binding contract.

6.6   HUSBANDS, WIVES AND CIVIL PARTNERS

There are a number of cases where, although an asset is held as a capital investment, there is deemed to be no gain and no loss arising on a disposal.

The most important instance of this is that of transfers between husband and wife or registered civil partners. The effect of this is that these transfers are ***totally exempt*** from Capital Gains Tax.

The exemption comes into force on the date of marriage or registration and thereafter continues to apply for the whole of any tax year during any part of which the couple are living together as husband and wife or civil partners.

Separated couples remain 'connected persons' (see section 6.8) even after the exemption has been lost. Divorced couples only become unconnected persons for tax purposes once more following the grant of a decree absolute.

Wealth Warning

If the couple separate, the exemption ceases to apply at the end of the tax year of separation.

6.7   THE AMOUNT OF THE GAIN

Having established that a gain is subject to Capital Gains Tax, it is next necessary to work out how much the gain is.

As stated in section 6.4 above, the essence of this is that the gain should be the excess obtained on the sale of the asset over the price paid to buy it. This is a reasonable statement of the underlying principle. However, in practice, thanks to the many complexities introduced by tax legislation over more than 40 years, there are a large number of other factors to be taken into account.

Hence, one has to slightly amend the definition of a capital gain to the following:

'A capital gain is the excess of the actual or deemed proceeds arising on the disposal of an asset over that same asset's base cost.'

A shorter version of this is: Gain = Proceeds Less Base Cost

The derivation of 'Proceeds' is examined in section 6.8 below and 'Base Cost' is covered in sections 6.9 and 6.10. Note that, for the majority of this chapter, we will be looking at the rules governing capital gains. Slightly different rules apply to capital losses, which are covered in section 6.42.

6.8 PROCEEDS

In most cases, the amount of 'Proceeds' to be used in the calculation of a capital gain will be the actual sum received on the disposal of the asset. However, from this, the taxpayer may deduct incidental costs in order to arrive at 'net proceeds', which is the relevant sum for the purposes of calculating the capital gain.

Example

In July 2006, George sells a house for £375,000. In order to make this sale, he spent £1,500 advertising the property, paid £3,750 in estate agents' fees and paid £800 in legal fees. His net proceeds are therefore £368,950 (£375,000 LESS £1,500, £3,750 and £800).

Remember George – we will be seeing him again!

Now this sounds very simple, but it is not always this easy.

Exceptions

There are a number of cases where the proceeds we must use in the calculation of a capital gain are not simply the actual cash sum received. Three of the most common types of such exceptions are set out below.

Exception 1 – Connected persons

Where the person selling or disposing of the asset is 'connected' with the person buying or acquiring it, the open market value of the asset at the time of sale must be used in place of the actual price paid (if any).

Connected persons include:

- Husband, wife or registered civil partner (but note that no gain usually arises in such transfers)
- Mother, father or remoter ancestor
- Son, daughter or remoter descendant
- Brother or sister

- Mother-in-law, father-in-law, son-in-law, daughter-in-law, brother-in-law or sister-in-law
- Business partners
- Companies under the control of the other party to the transaction or of any of his/her relatives as above
- Trustees of a trust where the other party to the transaction, or any of his/her relatives as above, is a beneficiary.

Example

Victoria sells a property to her son Edward for £500,000, at a time when its market value is £800,000. She pays legal fees of £475.

Victoria will be deemed to have received net sale proceeds of £800,000 (the market value). The legal fees she has borne are irrelevant, as this was not an 'arm's-length' transaction.

Exception 2 – Transactions not at 'arms-length'

Where a transaction takes place between 'connected persons' as above, there is an automatic assumption that the transaction is not at 'arm's-length' and hence market value must always be substituted for the actual proceeds.

There are, however, other instances where the transaction may not be at 'arm's-length', such as:

- The transfer of an asset from one partner in an unmarried couple to the other
- A sale of an asset to an employee
- A transaction which is part of a larger transaction
- A transaction which is part of a series of transactions

The effect of these is much the same as before – the asset's market value must be used in place of the actual proceeds, if any.

The key difference from Exception 1 above is that the onus of proof that this is not an 'arm's-length' transaction is on Revenue & Customs, rather than there being an automatic assumption that this is the case.

Example

John has a house worth £200,000. If he sold it for this amount, he would have a capital gain of £80,000.

Not wishing to incur a Capital Gains Tax liability, John decides instead to sell the house to his friend Richard for £120,000. However, John only does this on condition that Richard gives him an interest-free loan of £80,000 for an indefinite period.

The condition imposed by John means that this transaction is not at 'arm's-length'. The correct position is therefore that John should be deemed to have sold the house for £200,000 and still have a capital gain of £80,000.

Wealth Warning

Where a person has disposed of an asset at less than an 'arm's length' value, whether to a connected person or not, there is a danger of Income Tax charges arising under the new 'pre-owned asset' regime if the original owner ever makes any use, or derives any benefit, from the transferred asset at any time after 5th April 2005.

Exception 3 – Non-cash proceeds

Sometimes all or part of the sale consideration will take a form other than cash.

The sale proceeds to be taken into account in these cases will be the market value of the assets or rights received in exchange for the asset sold.

Example

Matilda is an elderly widow with a large house. She no longer needs such a large house, so she offers it to Stephen, who lives nearby with his wife and young children. Rather than pay the whole amount in cash, Stephen offers £100,000 plus his own much smaller house, which is worth £150,000.

Matilda incurs legal fees of £2,400 on the transaction and also pays Stamp Duty Land Tax of £1,500 to acquire Stephen's house. 75% of the legal fees are for the sale of her old house and the remainder for the purchase of Stephen's house.

Matilda's total sale proceeds are £250,000. This is made up of the cash received plus the market value of the non-cash consideration received, i.e. Stephen's house. Matilda may deduct her incidental costs of disposal from her proceeds in her Capital Gains Tax calculation. This is unaltered by the existence of non-cash consideration; the transaction has still taken place on 'arm's-length' terms.

However, as far as her legal fees are concerned, it is only the element which relates to the disposal of her old house (£1,800) which may be deducted. The element relating to the purchase of Stephen's house will be treated as an acquisition cost of that house, as will the Stamp Duty Land Tax Matilda has paid (see section 7.2 below).

Hence, the net sale proceeds to be used in Matilda's Capital Gains Tax calculation are £248,200 (£250,000 LESS £1,800).

6.9   BASE COST

The 'Base Cost' is the amount which may be deducted in the Capital Gains Tax calculation in respect of the cost of the asset being disposed of. The higher the base cost, the less Capital Gains Tax payable!

As before, in most cases, the basic starting point will be the actual amount paid.

To this may be added:

- Incidental costs of acquisition (e.g. legal fees, Stamp Duty Land Tax, etc).
- Enhancement expenditure (e.g. the cost of building an extension to a property).
- Expenditure incurred in establishing, preserving or defending title to, or rights over, the asset (e.g. legal fees incurred as a result of a boundary dispute).

Example

George (remember him from section 6.8?) bought a house in July 1984 for £60,000. He paid Stamp Duty of £600, legal fees of £400 and removal expenses of £800.

Shortly after moving into the house, George spent £3,000 on redecorating it. £1,800 of this related to one of the bedrooms, which was in such a bad state of repair that it was unusable. The remainder of the redecorating expenditure merely covered repainting and wallpapering the other rooms in the house.

In March 1985, George's neighbour erected a new fence a foot inside George's back garden, claiming this was the correct boundary. George had to take legal advice to resolve this problem, which cost him £250, but managed eventually to get the fence moved back to its original position.

In October 1987, the house's roof was badly damaged by hurricane-force winds. The repairs cost £20,000, which, unfortunately, George's insurance company refused to pay, claiming he was not covered for an 'Act of God'.

In May 1995, George did a loft conversion at a cost of £15,000, putting in new windows and creating an extra bedroom. Unfortunately, however, he had not obtained planning permission and, when his neighbour filed a complaint with the council, George was forced to restore the loft to its original condition at a further cost of £8,000.

In August 1998, George had the property extended at a cost of £80,000. He also incurred professional fees of £2,000 obtaining planning permission, etc.

When George eventually sold the property in July 2006 for £375,000, his base cost for the house for Capital Gains Tax purposes was made up as follows:

- *Original cost - £60,000.*
- *Incidental costs of acquisition - £1,000 (legal fees and Stamp Duty, but not the removal expenses, which were a personal cost and not part of the capital cost of the property).*
- *Enhancement expenditure - £1,800 (restoration of the 'unusable' bedroom; the remaining redecoration costs are not allowable, however, as the other rooms were already in a fit state for*

habitation and George's expenditure was merely due to personal taste, rather than being a capital improvement.).

- *Expenditure incurred in defending title to the property - £250 (the legal fees relating to his neighbour's new fence).*
- *Further enhancement expenditure - £82,000 (the cost of the new extension, including the legal fees incurred to obtain planning permission).*

Total base cost: £145,050.

Notes to the example

i. If the house were George's only or main residence throughout his ownership, his gain would, in any case, be exempt from Capital Gains Tax. However, we are assuming that this is not the case here for the purposes of illustration.

ii. The cost of George's roof repairs do not form part of his base cost. This is not a capital improvement, but rather repairs and maintenance expenditure of a revenue nature.

iii. Neither the cost of George's loft conversion, nor the cost of returning the loft to its original condition, form part of his base cost. This is because enhancement or improvement expenditure can only be allowed in the capital gains calculation if the relevant 'improvements' are reflected in the state of the property at the time of the sale.

iv. Based on net proceeds of £368,950 (see section 6.8), George has a capital gain of £223,900 before indexation (see section 6.11) and other reliefs.

Wealth Warning

An additional point to note under (iii) above is that enhancement or improvement expenditure is only deductible if still reflected in the state of the property at the date of <u>completion</u> of the sale.

6.10 BASE COST – SPECIAL SITUATIONS

As before with 'Proceeds', there are a number of special situations where base cost is determined by reference to something other than the actual amount paid for the asset.

The major exceptions fall into two main categories:

- The asset was not acquired by way of a 'bargain at arm's length'.
- The asset was acquired before 31st March 1982.

Inherited assets

All assets are 'rebased' for Capital Gains Tax purposes on death. Hence, the base cost of any inherited assets is determined by reference to their market value at the date of the previous owner's death.

Note that, whilst transfers on death are exempt from Capital Gains Tax, they are, of course, subject to Inheritance Tax. See the Taxcafe.co.uk guide *How To Avoid Inheritance Tax* for further details.

Example 1

Albert died on 1st January 1996, leaving his holiday home, a cottage on the Isle of Wight, to his son Edward. The property was valued at £150,000 for probate purposes. In August 2000, Edward has a swimming pool built at the cottage at a cost of £40,000. He then sells the cottage for £287,000 in March 2007.

Edward's base cost is £190,000. His own improvement expenditure (£40,000) is added to the market value of the property when he inherited it. Any expenditure incurred by Albert is, however, completely irrelevant.

Assets acquired from husband, wife or registered civil partner

As explained in section 6.6, when an asset is transferred between spouses or registered civil partners, that transfer is treated as taking place on a no gain/no loss basis.

Furthermore, in the case of a subsequent disposal, the transferee spouse or partner effectively inherits the transferor spouse or partner's base cost.

Example 2

Henry bought a house for £350,000 in November 1999. He spent £100,000 on capital improvements and then gave the house to his wife Katherine in March 2000. Katherine had the house extended in May 2006 at a cost of £115,000 and then sold it the following February for £750,000.

Katherine's base cost for the house is £565,000. This includes both her own expenditure and her husband's.

The 'no gain/no loss' rule does not, however, apply in the case of a transfer on death, when the inheritance rules explained above take precedence.

Assets acquired from connected persons

As explained in section 6.8 above, the transfer of an asset to a connected person is deemed to take place at market value. Hence, for the person acquiring an asset by way of such a transfer, the market value at that date becomes their base cost.

Other assets acquired by way of a transaction not at 'arm's-length'

Again, for the person acquiring the asset, the market value at the date of acquisition becomes their base cost. (See 'Exception 2', in section 6.8 above, for further guidance on circumstances where this might arise.)

Assets with 'held-over gains'

From 6th April 1980 to 13th March 1989, it was possible to elect to hold over the gain arising on the transfer of any asset by way of gift. Since then, it has only been possible to hold over gains arising on transfers by way of gift which are:

- Transfers of business assets, or
- Chargeable transfers for Inheritance Tax purposes.

Furthermore, even in these cases, the ability to hold over a gain was blocked for transfers into a 'self-interested trust' on or after 10th December 2003. A 'self-interested' trust means a trust which includes the transferor, their spouse or civil partner or, from 6th April 2006, a dependent minor child of the transferor, as one of its beneficiaries.

The base cost of an asset which was subject to a hold-over election when it was acquired, will be reduced as follows:

- For assets acquired between 1st April 1982 and 5th April 1988: half the amount of the held over gain,
- For other assets acquired with held over gains: the full amount of the held over gain.

Example 3

Arthur owned two properties, 'Camelot' and 'Elsinore'. On 3rd January 1982, he gave Camelot to his son Lancelot. Camelot's market value at that date was £100,000 and Arthur and Lancelot jointly elected to hold over Arthur's gain of £70,000. In 1990 Lancelot had the property extended at a cost of £55,000.

On 12th May 1982, Arthur gave Elsinore to his other son, Merlin. Elsinore's market value at that date was £90,000 and Arthur and Merlin jointly elected to hold over Arthur's gain of £48,000.

Lancelot's base cost for Camelot is £85,000 (£100,000 LESS £70,000 PLUS £55,000 – his own enhancement expenditure is still added on, as normal).

Merlin's base cost for Elsinore is £66,000 (£90,000 LESS HALF OF £48,000).

Assets acquired for non-cash consideration

Where an asset was acquired for non-cash consideration, its base cost will be determined by reference to the market value of the consideration given.

Example 4

Julius bought a house in Chester from his friend Brutus. Instead of paying Brutus in cash, Julius gave him his ancient sword collection, which he had recently had valued at £125,000. Julius' base cost in the Chester house will therefore be £125,000.

Assets acquired before 31st March 1982

Due to the 'rebasing' of Capital Gains Tax, gains arising due to an asset's increase in value prior to 31st March 1982 are exempt.

Generally speaking, the way that this is achieved is by substituting the asset's market value on 31st March 1982 for its original cost.

Example 5

Alfred bought a house for £20,000 in April 1980. Its market value on 31st March 1982 was £28,000. He sold the house for £200,000 in July 2006.

Alfred should substitute the March 1982 value of £28,000 for his original cost in the calculation of his capital gain.

However, the strict rule is that it is actually the sum which produces the lower gain which should be used. Naturally, this will usually mean using the higher sum out of March 1982 value and original cost.

Where March 1982 value is being used in the calculation of base cost, however, any enhancement or improvement expenditure may only be included where it was incurred after 31st March 1982. This might mean that it remains more beneficial to continue to use the original cost basis in some cases.

Example 6

Ethelred bought a house for £14,500 in June 1980. In September 1981, he had an extension built at a cost of £4,000. The market value of the house on 31st March 1982 was £17,800. He sold the house for £135,000 in July 2006.

In this case, Ethelred should continue to use his total original cost of £18,500 (£14,500 + £4,000) as his base cost, as it produces the smaller gain.

Further rules apply to assets held before 6th April 1965. However, these are seldom needed in practice nowadays.

6.11 INDEXATION RELIEF

From March 1982 to April 1998, taxpayers were given a form of relief known as 'Indexation Relief', designed to eliminate the purely inflationary element of their capital gains. Indexation relief is still given now to taxpayers disposing of assets held since before April 1998 and hence it remains relevant to many Capital Gains Tax calculations.

The relief is based on the increase in the retail prices index (RPI) over the period of the asset's ownership up to April 1998.

Where the base cost of the asset is made up of original cost and later enhancement expenditure, each element of the base cost which arose before April 1998 will attract indexation relief at its own appropriate rate.

Example ('George the Third')

In section 6.8, we saw that George received net proceeds of £368,950 for the sale of his house in July 2006. In section 6.9, we saw how his base cost for the house came to £145,050, leaving him with a gain of £223,900.

George is due indexation relief as follows:

a) *From July 1984 to April 1998 on £62,800 (purchase price of £60,000 PLUS acquisition costs of £1,000 PLUS enhancement expenditure of £1,800).*

The RPI for July 1984 is 89.1 and the RPI for April 1998 is 162.6. The increase in the RPI over the relevant period is therefore 82.4916%. However, for Capital Gains Tax calculation purposes, the increase in the RPI is always taken to the nearest tenth of a percentage point, i.e. 82.5% in this case.

The indexation relief due on this expenditure is thus £51,810 (82.5% of £62,800).

b) *From March 1985 to April 1998 on £250 (the legal fees relating to his neighbour's new fence).*

The RPI for March 1985 is 92.8, making the increase to April 1998 75.2%. The indexation relief due on this expenditure is thus £188 (75.2% of £250).

George is therefore due indexation relief totalling £51,998, reducing his gain to £171,902 (£223,900 LESS £51,988).

Note to the example

Note that George is not entitled to any indexation relief on his further enhancement expenditure of £82,000 in August 1998. This is because the relief only applies to expenditure before April 1998.

Some terminology

Sometimes, the asset's base cost plus the indexation relief due is known as the 'indexed base cost'. In George's case this would amount to £197,048.

This can be a slightly misleading concept, however, due to the different treatment of indexation where capital losses arise. (See section 6.42 below.)

The remaining gain after indexation (i.e. £171,902 in George's case) is also sometimes known as the 'indexed gain'.

The maximum relief

The maximum rate of indexation relief applies to assets held throughout the period since the relief's commencement in March 1982. This maximum relief amounts to 104.7%. For example, an asset held on 31st March 1982, which has a base cost of £10,000, would attract indexation relief of £10,470.

A useful list of the applicable indexation relief rates for all disposals by individuals, partnerships or trusts after 5th April 1998 is given in Appendix B at the end of this guide.

Companies and Indexation Relief

Companies continue to be eligible for indexation relief and will attract higher levels of relief than those shown in Appendix B.

6.12 OTHER RELIEFS

It is at this point in the Capital Gains Tax calculation, after indexation relief, that other reliefs and exemptions may be claimed, where appropriate. These include:

- The Principal Private Residence exemption (for taxpayers selling their current or former only or main residence). This is covered in detail from section 6.13 below onwards.
- The Private Letting exemption (where a property which is eligible for the principal private residence exemption has also been let out as private residential accommodation at some point during the taxpayer's ownership). Again, this is covered in detail in section 6.14 below.
- Relief for reinvestment of gains in Enterprise Investment Scheme shares (see section 8.16 below for further details).
- Holdover relief on gifts of business assets.
- Holdover relief in respect of chargeable transfers for Inheritance Tax purposes.
- Holdover relief on transfer of a business to a limited company.
- Rollover relief on replacement of business assets.
- Relief for capital losses (see section 6.42 below).

It is important to note that all these reliefs must be claimed BEFORE Taper Relief (see section 6.30 below). In many cases, this effectively devalues these reliefs, especially where the assets concerned are business assets for Taper Relief purposes.

Only the annual exemption (see section 6.37 below) is applied after Taper Relief.

6.13 THE PRINCIPAL PRIVATE RESIDENCE EXEMPTION

Most people are well aware that the sale of their own home is exempt from Capital Gains Tax. In technical terms, this is known as the Principal Private Residence exemption. What is less well known is just how far the principal private residence exemption can extend, especially when combined with other available exemptions and reliefs.

Each unmarried individual, and each legally married couple or registered civil partnership, is entitled to the principal private residence exemption in respect of their only or main residence. The principal private residence exemption covers the period during which the property was their main residence PLUS, in every case, their last three years of ownership.

Example

Elizabeth Windsor bought a flat for £80,000 in January 1995. In January 1999, she married Philip and moved out of her flat. In January 2002, she received an offer to sell the flat for £120,000, but was concerned about her potential tax liability.

Elizabeth didn't need to worry. If she had made this sale, her gain on the flat would have been exempted under principal private residence. The first four years of her ownership were exempt because it was then her main residence and the last three years because it was a former main residence.

But what if the property has been let out?

Because the principal private residence exemption always extends to the final three years of ownership of a former main residence, letting the property out for up to three years after you have moved out of it will make no difference to your Capital Gains Tax position if you then go ahead and sell the property. (Income Tax is, of course, due on the rental profits.)

If you retain the property for more than three years after it ceased to be your main residence, you will no longer be fully covered by the principal private residence exemption alone. However, at this point, as long as the property is being let out as private residential accommodation, another relief will come into play: Private Letting Relief. We will examine this further in the next section.

Does The Property Have to Be Your Main Residence Immediately on Purchase to Qualify?

To be *fully* exempt from Capital Gains Tax under the principal private residence exemption alone, the property will need to fit one of the following circumstances:

- It became your only or main residence immediately on purchase.
- It was acquired with the intention of it becoming your only or main residence but required renovation work which took no more than a year to complete, after which you did move into it as your only or main residence immediately.
- You acquired a plot of land with the intention of building a property to become your only or main residence thereon. The building work took no more than a year to complete, after which you moved into the property as your only or main residence immediately.
- It was your only or main residence at some point and you sold it no more than three years after purchase.

The second and third points here are examined further in sections 6.17 and 6.18 respectively.

If you don't fit one of the situations above, you won't be fully covered by principal private residence relief alone.

However, you will still get a proportional relief based on your period of occupation of the property as your main residence, plus last three years of ownership.

When combined with other reliefs, this will often be enough to prevent any Capital Gains Tax from arising, although you will probably have to report the gain on your tax return.

Example

Alexander buys a house in June 2000 as an investment and lets it out for two years.

In June 2002, he sells his own home and moves into the new house.

Alexander sells the new house in June 2006.

Alexander has used the house as his own main residence for four years out of six and hence he will be exempt on four sixths of his capital gain by virtue of principal private residence relief.

Notes to the Example

Alexander cannot benefit from the additional 'last three years of ownership' rule because he was, in any case, living there at the time anyway. The extra three-year period is not given in addition to an exemption for actual occupation during the same period.

This is why when people ask me "do you need to live in the house at the beginning to get principal private residence relief?" I always answer "no, but it works best that way".

Tax Tip

Occupying a property as your only or main residence will produce the best result if this is not within the last three years of your ownership.

Alexander will, however, still be eligible for some private letting relief, as we shall see in the next section.

What If Part Of The Property Is Unused?

The principal private residence exemption is not restricted merely because part of the house is left vacant and unused. Restrictions will apply, however, where part of the house is used for some purpose other than the owner's own private residential occupation.

6.14   PRIVATE LETTING RELIEF

In the previous section, we saw how the principal private residence exemption often extends to cover the capital gain on a former only or main residence for a further three years after it ceases to be your own home.

Additionally, however, any property which qualifies as your only or main residence at any time during your period of ownership, and which you have, at some time, let out as private residential accommodation will also qualify for private letting relief.

Private letting relief will also apply where you let out a part of your home.

Private Letting Relief is given as the lowest of:

  i) The amount of gain already exempted under principal private residence relief,
  ii) The gain arising as a consequence of the letting period, and
  iii) £40,000.

Usually, it is the lower of (i) and (iii), especially if the property has been let out ever since the owner ceased to reside in it.

Example

Since marrying Philip in January 1999, Elizabeth has been renting her flat out. She turned down the January 2002 offer but in January 2009 she receives an offer of £160,000. Again, she is concerned about her potential tax liability.

Elizabeth still has nothing to worry about. As before, a total of seven years of her ownership is exempt under principal private residence relief. Her total gain over 14 years is £80,000 (ignoring indexation for the time being). 7/14ths (or half) of this is covered by principal private residence relief, leaving £40,000, which is covered by Private Letting Relief.

Hence, Elizabeth still has no Capital Gains Tax liability on her flat!

Bayley's Principal Private Residence Relief Law

The general rule here is that a gain of up to £80,000 is covered until at least two times (N + 3) years after you first bought the property. 'N' is the number of years that it was your own main residence, not counting the last three years of ownership.

In Elizabeth's case 'N' was 4, so 2 x (N + 3) becomes 2 x 7 = 14 years of exemption!

Multiple Sales of Former Homes

The £40,000 private letting relief limit described above applies to every property which has been your only or main residence at any time during your ownership. Hence, even if you were to sell two or more former homes during the same tax year, you would still be entitled to up to £40,000 of private letting relief on each property.

What if the property was let out <u>before</u> it became your main residence?

Any property which qualifies for partial exemption under principal private residence relief, and which has also been let out as private residential accommodation at <u>any time</u> during the taxpayer's ownership, is also eligible for Private Letting Relief.

Hence, although in our example we have been looking at a <u>former</u> main residence, which is subsequently let out, Private Letting

150

Relief will apply equally in a case where a property is let out first and then subsequently becomes the owner's main residence.

If, in the latest example, Elizabeth had instead rented her flat out from 1995 to 1997, then lived in it as her main residence for four years before continuing to rent it out again, the result would have been exactly the same.

(Note that Elizabeth's flat would have had to be Philip's main residence too after they got married, as a married couple or registered civil partnership is only allowed one main residence for principal private residence relief purposes.)

As we have already seen though, there is no additional benefit to be derived from the extension to the principal private residence exemption for a former main residence's last three years of ownership if, in fact, it is still your main residence throughout that time in any case.

We left Alexander in just this sort of situation in section 6.13. How will private letting relief operate in his case?

Example

Alexander, as we know had a rented property from 2000 to 2002 which he then lived in as his own main residence from 2002 to 2006.

His total capital gain was £180,000 and four sixths of this was covered by the principal private residence exemption.

This leaves him with a gain of £60,000. He will be able to claim private letting relief of £40,000, leaving a taxable gain of £20,000.

Even this won't be the end of the story for Alexander, as we shall see in the next section.

6.15   THE IMPACT OF OTHER RELIEFS

Three other reliefs will have a major impact where part of a gain is already exempted under principal private residence relief:

- Indexation relief,
- Taper relief, and
- The annual exemption.

Example

Elizabeth turns down the January 2009 offer and continues to rent the flat out. In January 2012 she receives an offer of £180,000. Once more, she is concerned about her potential tax liability.

This time it is necessary to carry out a full calculation of Elizabeth's capital gain.

Her total gain is £100,000. She is, however, entitled to indexation relief of £9,120, producing an indexed gain of £90,880.

As before, seven years of her ownership is exempt under principal private residence relief. This now represents 7/17ths of her total period of ownership, so £37,422 of her indexed gain is exempt, leaving £53,458 chargeable. Of this, a further £37,422 is exempted by Private Letting Relief, leaving only £16,036.

Having owned the property for more than ten years, Elizabeth gets taper relief of 40%, leaving a tapered gain of £9,621, which, by 2012, is very likely to be covered by her annual exemption (£8,800 indexed up for five years), hopefully leaving her with no Capital Gains Tax to pay!

Notes to the Example

If you are checking these calculations, you may notice that the principal private residence exemption actually works out at £37,421.18. This brings out a very minor, but nevertheless beneficial, principle – i.e.: you are always allowed to **round up** reliefs and exemptions to the nearest £1.

Private Letting Relief has been restricted to the lowest of the three items detailed above. In this case, this is the amount already exempted under principal private residence relief.

Now let's see how Alexander is getting on.

Example

After private letting relief, Alexander still had a capital gain of £20,000.

As he bought the property in 2000, he is not entitled to any indexation relief. Having owned it for six years prior to his sale in June 2006, however, he will be entitled to 20% taper relief (see section 6.31), reducing his gain to £16,000.

We can then deduct Alexander's annual exemption of £8,800 from the remaining gain, leaving him a taxable gain of just £7,200. This will result in a Capital Gains Tax bill of between £1,225 and £2,880, depending on the level of Alexander's taxable income for 2006/2007.

We will come back to the principles behind the calculation of Alexander's Capital Gains Tax bill later in this chapter.

Summary of Principal Private Residence Examples

In our first example, Elizabeth has managed to make a tax-free capital gain of £100,000 despite living in her flat for only four years out of a total of seventeen. This remarkable result arises due to the impact of a number of reliefs which each build onto the basic exemption already available for a former main residence.

These reliefs are invaluable to both those with a former home they now wish to sell and those who wish to plan for future tax-free capital growth.

Things were not quite so rosy for Alexander and he did end up with a tax bill after only six years of ownership, despite also living in the property for four years.

To some extent, this shows how much better the principal private residence exemption works if you move into the property as your only or main residence immediately on purchase.

Planning Ahead

Nevertheless, despite Alexander's small tax bill, the principal private residence exemption and its associated reliefs can be used to great effect to allow a taxpayer to invest in property with little or no exposure to Capital Gains Tax. This subject is covered in depth in chapter eight later in the guide.

6.16   GARDENS AND GROUNDS

There have been a large number of cases before the Courts over the question of whether the 'grounds' of a house, including some of the subsidiary outbuildings, are covered by the principal private residence exemption.

In the usual situation, where a house has a reasonably normal sized garden and perhaps a shed, a garage or other small outbuildings, there is no doubt that the entire property is covered by the principal private residence exemption.

Naturally, we are talking here only of the situation where there is no use of any of the property other than private residential occupation.

Where the whole property is let out at some point, so that private letting relief also applies, the garden and 'modest' grounds continue to be covered by the relevant reliefs in the same way as already outlined in the previous sections.

The general rule of thumb for grounds is that Revenue & Customs will usually accept them as being a normal part of the property where they do not exceed half a hectare (1.235 acres) in area. Beyond this, it is necessary to argue that the additional space is required 'for the reasonable enjoyment of the dwelling-house as a residence'.

What does this mean? Well, unfortunately, this is one of those rather enigmatic answers which judges love to give and which can only be decided on an individual case-by-case basis.

The whole situation changes once any part of the property is used for any other purpose. Here the position differs for buildings or gardens and grounds.

For gardens and grounds, they will obtain the same exemptions that are due on the house itself as long as they are part of the 'private residence' at the time of sale.

For subsidiary buildings, it becomes necessary to apportion any gain arising between the periods of residential occupation and the periods of non-residential use.

Example

Lady Jane has a large house with grounds having a total area of half a hectare. Her property lies next to a major amusement park and, for several years, she leased half her grounds to the park for use as a car park.

Within the half of her grounds let to the amusement park there is a small outbuilding. Whilst she was letting the space to the amusement park, this outbuilding was used as the parking attendant's hut.

In 1999, the amusement park gave up its lease over Lady Jane's grounds and she hired a landscape gardener to restore them.

The outbuilding reverted to its previous use as a storage shed for garden equipment.

In 2006, Lady Jane sold the entire property. Apart from the lease of the car park, the whole property had been used as her main residence throughout her ownership.

Lady Jane's main house and her entire grounds will be fully covered by the principal private residence exemption. However, the element of her gain relating to the outbuilding must be apportioned between the periods of private use and the period of non-residential use. The non-residential element of the gain will be chargeable to Capital Gains Tax.

Tax Tip

Lady Jane may have been better off if she had demolished the outbuilding prior to the sale of her house. No part of her gain would then have related to this building and her entire gain would have been covered by the principal private residence exemption.

Naturally, it is only worth doing this if demolishing the building does not impact on the whole property's sale price by more than the amount of the potential tax saving.

Wealth Warning

Note that, unlike the house itself, the principal private residence exemption does not extend to unused outbuildings or gardens and grounds and <u>actual use</u> for private residential purposes is required.

6.17 RENOVATIONS ON A NEW HOME

Many people buy a 'run-down' property and then embark on substantial renovation works before occupying it as their own main residence.

The tax rules cater for this situation and the principal private residence exemption specifically extends to cover any period of up to one year during which the taxpayer is unable to occupy a newly acquired house due to either:

i) An unavoidable delay in selling their old property, or
ii) The need to await the finalisation of renovation or construction work on the new property.

During this period, it is possible for both the old and new properties to simultaneously be covered by the principal private residence exemption. Of course, the scope for claiming this exemption is lost if the new property is being used for some other purpose between purchase and initial occupation as the taxpayer's main residence. (Although the private letting exemption could apply to this period in appropriate circumstances.)

Under exceptional circumstances, Revenue & Customs may allow this initial period to be extended to up to two years. This extension is not granted lightly, however, and is reserved for genuine cases of delay caused by factors beyond the taxpayer's control. You would also be expected to have done everything in your power to facilitate the property being ready for your occupation within the original one year period.

If the delay in occupation extends beyond the first year or beyond any additional period which Revenue & Customs permit, then the principal private residence exemption is lost for the whole of the period prior to occupation of the property.

6.18   BUILDING YOUR OWN HOME

The initial period allowed for the renovation of property, as outlined in the previous section, also applies to a house which you have built on a vacant plot of land.

In both cases, the property, or land, must be bought with the intention of adopting it as your only or main residence and must not be used for any other purpose prior to occupation.

6.19   TEMPORARY ABSENCES

The principal private residence exemption will remain available in full for certain temporary periods of absence, as follows:

   i) Any single period of up to three years or shorter periods totalling no more than three years, regardless of the reason,
  ii) A period of up to four years when the taxpayer, their spouse or civil partner, is required to work elsewhere by reason of their employment or their place of work, and
 iii) A period of any length when the taxpayer, their spouse or civil partner is working in an office or employment whose duties are all performed outside the UK.

These temporary absences are only covered by the principal private residence exemption if:

  a) The taxpayer occupies the property as their main residence for both a period before the absence period <u>and</u> a period following the absence period, and
  b) Neither the taxpayer nor their spouse or civil partner have any interest in any other property capable of being treated as their main residence under the principal private residence exemption.

In the case of absences under (ii) or (iii) above, the Revenue may, by concession, sometimes accept that the taxpayer was unable to resume occupation of the property following their absence if they are then required to work elsewhere on their return.

6.20 DEPENDENT RELATIVES

A property occupied before 6th April 1988 by a 'dependent relative', as their main residence, may be covered by the principal private residence exemption. This is a rare exception to the general rule that each individual taxpayer, married couple or civil partnership may only have one property exempted as their main residence at any given time.

For this purpose, a 'dependent relative' must be either

    a) The taxpayer's widowed, separated or divorced mother or mother-in-law, or
    b) Another relative who is either elderly or dependent on them by reason of ill-health or disability.

(Rather insultingly, Revenue & Customs class anyone over the male state retirement age of 65 as 'elderly'!)

Where the qualifying 'dependent relative' was in occupation of the property as their main residence prior to 6th April 1988, their period of occupation provides principal private residence relief in exactly the same way as if it had been the taxpayer's main residence for that same period. This includes relief for the last three years of occupation.

If the dependent relative moves out of the property after 6th April 1988, however, any subsequent re-occupation of the property will not be counted.

Example

In May 1980, Edward buys a house for his widowed mother, Isabella.

Isabella lives in the house from May 1980 to May 1985, then again from January 1988 to January 1995 and from June 1999 until her death in August 2001.

In May 2006 Edward sells the house realising a substantial capital gain.

Edward will be entitled to the principal private residence exemption for a total of 15 years out of his total ownership period of 26 years.

The qualifying period is made up of his mother's first two periods of residence plus his last three years of ownership. Isabella's final period of residence does not qualify, as it commenced after 6th April 1988.

Occupation of a property by a dependent relative would not usually qualify for private letting relief.

6.21 PROPERTIES HELD IN TRUST

A trust is a separate legal entity in its own right for tax purposes and here the principal private residence exemption is no exception. The exemption extends to a property held by a trust when the property is the only or main residence of one or more of the trust's beneficiaries.

However, from 10th December 2003, the principal private residence exemption is not available on a property held by a trust if a hold-over relief claim was made on the transfer of that property into the trust.

In some cases this may lead to a difficult decision:

- Decline to make a hold-over relief claim at the outset and pay some Capital Gains Tax immediately, or

- Make the hold-over relief claim and risk paying a great deal more Capital Gains Tax on the eventual sale of the property.

In essence, one has to weigh up the prospective current tax bill against the ultimate tax potentially arising in the future.

Properties with held over gains which were already held in trust before 10th December 2003 are still eligible for principal private residence relief in respect of any periods of occupation by a beneficiary as their only or main residence prior to that date. The additional three-year period of relief at the end of the trust's ownership does not, however, apply in these circumstances.

6.22 WHAT IS A RESIDENCE?

Before we go any further, it is worth pausing to consider what we mean when we refer to a property as a taxpayer's residence.

As we will see in the next section, we are sometimes concerned with situations where a taxpayer has more than one residence. One of these will be their main residence and will qualify for principal private residence relief.

But no property can be a **_main_** residence until it is **_a_** private residence of that individual taxpayer, married couple or registered civil partnership.

A residence is a dwelling in which the owner habitually lives. Whilst it needs to be habitual, however, their occupation of the property might still be occasional and short.

Example

Constantine owns a small cottage in Pembrokeshire but lives and works in London. Constantine bought the Pembrokeshire cottage as a holiday home, but he only manages to visit it about two or three times each year, when he will typically stay for the weekend.

Despite the rarity of Constantine's visits to his cottage, it nevertheless qualifies as his private residence.

Some actual physical occupation of the property (including overnight stays) is necessary before it can be a residence. Constantine's situation is probably just about the minimum level of occupation which will qualify.

'Dwelling' means a property suitable for occupation as your home and can include a caravan or a houseboat. It will not, however, include a plainly unsuitable property such as an office, a shop or a factory. (But there are flats over shops and offices which are dwellings!)

To 'live' in a property means to adopt it as the place where you are based and where you sleep, shelter and have your home.

The Capital Gains Tax regime does not make any distinction between property in the UK and property overseas, so a foreign property may also be classed as the owner's residence where appropriate.

Some other use of a property at other times, when not occupied as the taxpayer's private residence, does not necessarily prevent it from qualifying as a residence. If such a property were to be treated as your main residence though, there would be a proportionate reduction in the amount of principal private residence relief available.

Example

In 2006, Bonnie buys a small cottage on Skye for £100,000. For the next twelve years she rents the cottage out as furnished holiday accommodation for 48 weeks each year and occupies it herself for the remaining four weeks.

Bonnie's regular occupation of her Skye house is enough to make it a residence. In this example we are also going to assume that it is her main residence throughout her ownership.

In 2018, Bonnie sells the cottage for £204,000, realising a total capital gain of £104,000.

For the nine year period from 2006 to 2015, Bonnie is only entitled to principal private residence relief on 4/52nds of her capital gain, reflecting her own private use of the property.

However, as usual, Bonnie is entitled to full relief for the last three years of her ownership.

Her total principal private residence relief therefore amounts to:

£104,000 x 9/12 x 4/52 =   £6,000
£104,000 x 3/12 =   £26,000
*   -----------*
Total relief: £32,000
*   ======*

Note that Bonnie is also entitled to several other reliefs and we will return to this example in section 8.14.

A residence for Capital Gains Tax purposes must also be a property in which the taxpayer has a legal or equitable interest. A legal interest in a property means any form of ownership, sole or joint, including freehold, leasehold and the tenancy of a property rented under a lease.

An equitable interest in a property is less easy to define. Generally it must mean some sort of right over the property itself and not merely an ability to reside in it.

Hence, for example, if an individual stays rent free with family or friends, they are occupying the property under a gratuitous licence and they clearly have no equitable interest.

Occupation of property may also be under contractual licence, such as staying in a hotel, hostel, guest house or private club. This also does not give the guest any equitable interest in the property.

An unmarried partner in a co-habiting couple may perhaps have an 'equitable interest' in the couple's home when it is owned wholly by the other partner, although this particular point has not yet been tested in the courts in connection with Capital Gains Tax.

For married couples and registered civil partners, all of the principles regarding residences and main residences must be applied to the couple as a single unit.

Hence, for example, if William owns a property in Brixham which he has never visited, but his wife Mary stays there regularly, then that property must be counted as a private residence of the couple.

If an individual, married couple or registered civil partnership has only one property which qualifies as a private residence, as outlined above, then that property must be their main residence for Capital Gains Tax purposes. Indeed, Revenue & Customs' own Capital Gains manual sets out the principle that where an individual's main home is occupied under licence, but they also own another residence, the residence which that individual owns must be regarded as their main residence for Capital Gains Tax purposes.

However, once an individual, a married couple or a registered civil partnership has more than one eligible private residence, we will need to work out which one is their main residence. This is what we will look at in the next section.

6.23 SECOND HOMES

As already stated, each unmarried individual and each legally married couple or registered civil partnership can (generally) only have one main residence covered by the principal private residence exemption at any given time. Many people, however, have more than one private residence.

When someone acquires a second (or subsequent) private residence they may, at any time within two years of the date that the new property first becomes available to them as a residence, elect which of their properties is to be regarded as their main residence for the purpose of the principal private residence exemption.

The election must be made in writing, addressed to 'Her Majesty's Inspector of Taxes' and sent to the taxpayer's tax office (see section 1.6). An unmarried individual must sign the election personally in order for it to be effective. A married couple must both sign the election, as must both members of a registered civil partnership.

There is no particular prescribed form for the election, although the following example wording would be suitable for inclusion:

> 'In accordance with section 222(5) Taxation of Chargeable Gains Act 1992, [I/We] hereby nominate [Property] as [my/our] main residence with effect from [Date*].'

* - The first such election which an individual, a married couple or a registered civil partnership makes in respect of any new combination of residences will automatically be treated as coming into effect from the beginning of the period to which it relates – i.e. from the date on which they first held that new combination of residences. It is this first election for the new combination of residences to which the two-year time limit applies.

However, once an election is in place, it may subsequently be changed, by a further written notice given to the Inspector under the same procedure, at any time. Such a new election may be given retrospective effect, if desired, by up to two years. We will look at the possible benefits of this further in chapter eight.

Example

Alfred lives in a small flat in Southampton where he works. In September 2006 he also buys a house on the Isle of Wight and starts spending his weekends there. In August 2008, Alfred realises that his Isle of Wight house has appreciated in value significantly since he bought it. His small mainland flat has not increased in value quite so significantly. He therefore elects, before the expiry of the two-year time limit, that his island house is his main residence.

In 2010 Alfred sells the Isle of Wight house at a substantial gain, which is fully exempted by the principal private residence exemption.

Note in this example that Alfred's flat will not be counted as his main residence from September 2006 until the time of sale of his island house. However, should he sell the flat, his final three years of ownership will be covered by the principal private residence exemption.

Tax Tip

As soon as Alfred decided to sell his Isle of Wight house, he should have submitted a new main residence election nominating the Southampton flat as his main residence once more, with effect from a date two years previously. This would give an extra two years of principal private residence exemption on the flat, whilst leaving the Isle of Wight house fully exempt as long as he sold it within one year after making the new election (i.e. within three years after the date that it was now deemed to cease to be his main residence).

Regardless of any election, however, a property may only be a main residence for principal private residence purposes if it is, in fact, the taxpayer's own private residence. Hence, a property being let out cannot be covered by the principal private residence exemption whilst it is being let. (It could nevertheless still attract the private letting exemption if it were the taxpayer's main residence at some other time.)

In the absence of any election, the question of which property is the taxpayer's main residence has to be determined on the facts of the case. Often the answer to this will be obvious but, in borderline cases, Revenue & Customs may determine the position to the taxpayer's detriment. Clearly then, it is <u>always</u> wise to make the election!

The factors to be considered when determining which property was a taxpayer's main residence for any given period not covered by an election, include:

- The address given on the taxpayer's Tax Return.
- The address shown on other correspondence, utility bills, bank statements, etc.
- Where a mortgage was obtained over a property before 6th April 2000, whether mortgage interest relief (MIRAS) was claimed.
- Whether the mortgage over a property was obtained on the basis that it was the taxpayer's main home.
- What security of tenure (leasehold, freehold, etc) is held over each residence.
- How is each residence furnished.
- Where do the taxpayer's family spend the majority of their time.
- Where is the taxpayer registered to vote.
- Where is the taxpayer's place of work.

As always, a married couple or a registered civil partnership have to be considered as a single unit for this purpose.

Each factor above is not conclusive in its own right but will contribute to the overall picture of which property may properly be regarded as the main residence.

In the previous section we considered the issue of whether a property was occupied under licence or whether an equitable interest existed.

Where a taxpayer has only one residence in which they have a legal or equitable interest, a main residence election will not be valid. (Although, in certain limited circumstances, Revenue & Customs may still honour such an election made before 16th October 1994.)

My advice, however, is that whenever there is any possibility that a taxpayer may have two eligible private residences they should make a main residence election.

If this election proves to be invalid, no harm is done and the property in which the taxpayer has a legal or equitable interest will automatically be treated as their main residence.

If a third residence is acquired, however, it will be important to make a new election within two years.

6.24   HOMES ABROAD

Note that the principal private residence exemption applies in exactly the same way to any private residence which the taxpayer has overseas. The exemption applies to the taxpayer's main residence, not, as some people have mistakenly thought (to their cost) their main UK residence.

6.25   JOB-RELATED ACCOMMODATION

In many occupations, it is sometimes necessary, or desirable, for the taxpayer to live in accommodation specifically provided for the purpose. Examples include:

- Caretakers
- Police officers
- Pub landlords
- Members of the clergy
- Members of the armed services
- Teachers at boarding schools
- The Prime Minister and the Chancellor of the Exchequer

For people in this type of situation, the principal private residence exemption may be extended to a property which they own and which they eventually intend to adopt as their main residence.

In these circumstances, the principal private residence exemption will thus cover their own property during the period that they are living in 'job-related accommodation', despite the fact that their own property is not their residence at that time.

This provides an exception to the general rule that there must be some actual physical occupation of a property for it to be eligible for principal private residence relief.

This treatment can also be extended to a property owned by the spouse or registered civil partner of a person living in job-related accommodation, which the couple eventually intend to adopt as their main residence.

If a taxpayer in job-related accommodation has a property which might qualify as a main residence under these rules but also has another residence, such as a holiday home, for example, they can use a main residence election to determine which property is given the principal private residence exemption.

The election will also be appropriate where the taxpayer has some legal or equitable interest in the job-related accommodation itself.

6.26 WHAT IF PART OF YOUR HOME IS NOT PRIVATE?

Whenever any part of your home is put to some use other than your own private residential occupation, you are inevitably putting your principal private residence exemption at risk. In the next few sections, we will look at some of the most common types of 'other use' and their tax implications.

One fundamental principle to note, however, is that if any part of your home is used for purposes other than your own private residential occupation throughout the period when that property qualifies as your main residence, then that part will not be eligible for any principal private residence relief at all.

6.27 LETTING OUT PART OF YOUR HOME

Taking A Lodger

Revenue & Customs generally accept that taking in one individual lodger does not necessitate any restriction to the principal private residence exemption. In this context, a 'lodger' is someone who, whilst having their own bedroom, will otherwise live as a member of the taxpayer's household.

As a general rule, where 'rent-a-room' relief is available for Income Tax purposes (or would be if the level of rent were lower – see section 4.10), then the principal private residence exemption is unlikely to be affected.

Other lettings – within the same 'dwelling'

Where a part of the house is let out under other circumstances, the principal private residence exemption will be restricted. However, Private Letting Relief is available to cover this restriction in very much the same way as it applies to the letting out of the whole property.

Example

Robert bought his five-storey house for £200,000 in 1990. From 1998 to 2004 he let the top two floors out as a flat. He then resumed occupation of the whole house, before selling it in May 2006 for £650,000.

Robert's total gain is £450,000 (we are ignoring indexation relief in this example, although, in reality, it would apply). This gain is covered by the principal private residence exemption as follows:

Lower three floors – The gain of £270,000 (three fifths of the total) is fully covered by the principal private residence exemption.

Upper two floors – The gain of £180,000 is covered by the principal private residence exemption from 1990 to 1998 AND for the last three years of Robert's ownership, a total of 11 years out of 16. Hence, £123,750 of this gain is exempt, leaving £56,250 chargeable.

Robert can then claim Private Letting Relief of the lowest of:

i)   The amount of principal private residence exemption on the <u>*whole*</u> *property: £393,750 (i.e. £270,000 PLUS £123,750),*
ii) The gain arising by reason of the letting (£56,250), or
iii) £40,000.

The relief is thus £40,000, leaving Robert with a gain of only £16,250 before taper relief (35%) and the annual exemption (£8,800). Hence, his maximum Capital Gains Tax liability (at 40%) works out at a mere £705 – even despite us ignoring indexation relief!

Now, all that Robert probably did was to fit a few locks to a few doors in order to separate the flat from his own home. As a result, re-occupying the whole property was a simple matter and when he came to sell it, it remained a single 'dwelling' for tax purposes. The situation would have been quite different, however, if he had carried out extensive conversion work in order to create a number of separate dwellings.

6.28   CONVERSIONS

Where a property has undergone extensive conversion work, it no longer remains a single dwelling for tax purposes. This is what Revenue & Customs refer to as a 'Change of Use' and it has a wider-ranging impact than merely letting out part of your home.

Example

David bought a large detached house for £160,000 in 1993. He lived in the whole house for one year and then converted it into two separate, semi-detached, houses. He continued to live in one of these, but rented the other one out. The conversion work cost £40,000, bringing his total costs up to £200,000.

In 2006, David sold both houses for £300,000 each, making a total gain of £400,000 (again, we are ignoring indexation relief in order to simplify the example).

David's gain will be treated as arising equally on each house (assuming that they are of equal size, etc – see section 5.2 for other allocation methods which might be used in more complex cases). The £200,000 gain on the house which he retained as his own home will be fully covered by the principal private residence exemption.

However, David's £200,000 gain on the other house will only be covered by the principal private residence exemption for one year out of his 12 years of ownership. His principal private residence exemption on this house thus amounts to only £16,667, leaving a taxable gain of £183,333 (before taper relief and annual exemption and ignoring indexation relief).

Note the two very important differences here to the previous example, both of which occur because the rented house was no longer a part of the same dwelling, namely:

i)   The principal private residence exemption is not available for the last three years of ownership.
ii) No private letting relief is available.

Tax Tip

David would have improved his position dramatically if he had spent some time living in the other semi-detached property after the conversion.

6.29   USING PART OF YOUR HOME FOR BUSINESS PURPOSES

Where any part of the property is used **exclusively** for business purposes, the principal private residence exemption is not available for that part of the property for the relevant period.

Where the exclusive business use covers the entire period that the property is the taxpayer's main residence, the exemption for the final three years of ownership will also be withdrawn for this part of the property.

The effect on the principal private residence exemption is the same whether part of the property is being used exclusively in the taxpayer's own business or is being rented out for use in someone else's. However, where it is the taxpayer's own business which is concerned, then this part of the property becomes 'business property' for the purposes of a number of tax reliefs, including rollover relief and holdover relief for gifts.

The 'business' part of the property may also become a 'business asset' for taper relief purposes (see section 6.32).

Property rented out for use in someone else's business will, in most cases, be treated as 'business property' for Taper Relief purposes from 6th April 2004. Property rented to an unquoted trading company has been eligible for Business Asset Taper relief since 6th April 2000.

As in section 6.27 above, where the 'business use' of part of the property requires extensive conversion work, that part of the property will no longer be part of the original 'dwelling' and hence the principal private residence exemption will not be available for the last three years of ownership.

Non-Exclusive Business Use ('The Home Office')

Where part of the home is used non-exclusively for business purposes, there is no restriction on the principal private residence exemption. This is a fairly common situation amongst professionals who work from an office or study within their home. To safeguard the principal private residence exemption in such situations, it is wise to restrict the taxpayer's Income Tax claim in respect of the office's running costs (as a proportion of household expenses) to, say, 99%, in order to reflect the room's occasional private use.

Hence, if the office is one of four rooms in the house (excluding hallways, kitchen, bathrooms and lavatories), one would claim 99% of one quarter of the household running costs.

For this purpose, just about any kind of private use will suffice, such as:

- A guest bedroom.
- Additional storage space for personal belongings.
- A music room.
- A library.

Naturally, it makes sense to adopt some form of private use which will only lead to a small reduction in the Income Tax claim.

Tax Tip

Whilst restricting one room to, say, 99% business use, you may also be able to argue for 1% business use in another room, thus effectively reversing the effect of the restriction without affecting your Capital Gains Tax position on the house.

See section 3.8 for details of how to claim an expense deduction for Income Tax purposes when using part of your own home as an office from which to run your business.

6.30 TAPER RELIEF – INTRODUCTION

Taper relief was introduced by Chancellor Gordon Brown's second Budget on 17th March 1998 and applies to all asset disposals after 5th April 1998. The new relief was designed to replace two existing reliefs:

- Indexation relief (which, for individuals, partnerships and trusts, ceased to accumulate any further after April 1998).

- Retirement relief (which was gradually phased out and finally abolished altogether on 6th April 2003).

Taper relief applies at two rates, as follows:

- Business Asset Taper Relief, and

- Non-Business Asset Taper Relief.

In either case, the relief is given as a percentage of the gain remaining after all other reliefs, except for the annual exemption, have been claimed.

172

Example

John has a gain of £30,000 after indexation and any other relevant reliefs, but before Taper Relief. He is eligible for Taper Relief at 10%. His gain after Taper Relief, or 'Tapered Gain', is therefore £27,000.

Quick Overview

Business asset taper relief will exempt 75% of your gain after only two years of ownership.

Non-business asset taper relief takes three years to give you anything at all (5%) and takes 10 years to rise to a maximum of 40%.

The difference, as you can see, in both time and the rate of relief, is enormous!

6.31 NON-BUSINESS ASSET TAPER RELIEF

On the disposal of any asset which does not qualify as a 'business asset', the taxpayer is entitled to Taper Relief at the lower, or 'non-business' rate.

Hence, this lower rate will generally apply to most <u>residential</u> property investments.

One major exception to this is any property used in a business which qualifies as the commercial letting of 'furnished holiday accommodation' (see section 8.14).

Another exception arises in the case of any residential property let to an unconnected qualifying trading entity (see section 6.32) for use as accommodation for its employees.

Prior to 6th April 2004, the lower taper rate generally also applied to most other investment property. However, from that date, most non-residential property qualifies as a 'business asset'.

This will benefit commercial property investors greatly. The new, wider, definition of business property is examined further in the next section.

The Non-Business Asset Taper Relief rate will also apply to a proportion of the gain where:

- The asset is used only partly for a qualifying business purpose, or
- The asset only qualified as a business asset during part of the period of ownership.

In applying the second point above, any period more than ten years before the date of disposal, or which falls prior to 6th April 1998, is ignored. Nevertheless, this point does arise in a great many situations and we will be looking further at the implications of this in section 6.35.

Rates of Non-Business Asset Taper Relief

The rates of relief have remained the same since its introduction on 6th April 1998, and are as follows:

- Assets held for less than three years: Nil
- Assets held for three years but less than four: 5%
- Assets held for four years but less than five: 10%
- Assets held for five years but less than six: 15%
- Assets held for six years but less than seven: 20%
- Assets held for seven years but less than eight: 25%
- Assets held for eight years but less than nine: 30%
- Assets held for nine years but less than ten: 35%
- Assets held for ten years or more: 40%

Assets held before 6th April 1998

The rates set out above have to be adapted in the case of assets already held when Taper Relief was first introduced on 6th April 1998. Two adjustments are required:

- Firstly, in applying the ownership periods set out above, any period of ownership prior to 6th April 1998 is disregarded, but
- To compensate for this, an additional year is counted in respect of any assets held before 17th March 1998.

Example ('George the Fourth')

You may remember from section 6.11 above that, after indexation relief, George had a gain of £171,902 on the sale of his house in July 2006. We now refer to this as the 'untapered gain'.

George has owned the house since July 1984. His total period of ownership is therefore 22 years. However, for Taper Relief purposes, George can only count the period since 6th April 1998. This gives him eight years of ownership for Taper Relief purposes.

But, as he owned the property before 17th March 1998, George gets an additional 'bonus' year, meaning that he is deemed to have owned the property for nine years for Taper Relief purposes.

Therefore, George gets Taper Relief at 35%. This amounts to £60,166, leaving him with a tapered gain of £111,736.

Note that the same rate of Taper Relief applies to the whole of George's gain. It makes no difference that some of his enhancement expenditure was incurred after 17th March 1998, all that matters is the date that he originally purchased the property.

It would have been different if George had made a completely new purchase, e.g. an adjacent strip of land. In that case, the Taper Relief would have to be worked out separately for the new asset. However, this does not apply here, as George had merely enhanced an existing asset.

As can be seen from our example, the rate of Taper Relief applying to the sale during 2006/2007 of any non-business asset acquired before 17th March 1998 is 35%.

6.32 BUSINESS ASSET TAPER RELIEF PRINCIPLES

As the name suggests, Business Asset Taper Relief applies to business assets.

Gordon Brown has had some difficulty in deciding what he considers to be a 'business asset'. He started out with one set of rules in 1998, expanded them quite significantly in April 2000, tinkered a little more in 2001 and changed them yet again with effect from 6th April 2004.

The latest changes are the most significant and most beneficial for property investors and mean that, from 6th April 2004, most non-residential property is likely to qualify as a 'business asset'.

Wealth Warning

Where an asset which only qualifies as a business asset with effect from 6th April 2004 was also held before that date, it will only be partly eligible for business asset taper relief. We will look at the impact of this in more detail in section 6.35.

With effect from 6th April 2004, any asset (including property) will be regarded as a business asset where it is used for the purposes of a trade carried on by a qualifying trading entity, i.e.:

- A sole trader,
- A trust,
- The estate of a deceased person,
- A qualifying company (see below), or
- A partnership, where at least one partner is an individual or a person falling under one of the other headings above.

The trading entity does not need to be in any way connected with the owner of the asset.

A company will be a 'qualifying company' for this purpose under any of the following circumstances:

a) Whenever the company is an **unquoted trading company**. (Broadly, this means that, in addition to qualifying as a trading company, the company must also not be listed on any recognised stock exchange.)

b) When the company is a **quoted trading company and the individual** claiming the taper relief (i.e. the property owner) is an **officer** or **employee** of that company or of another company that is a member of the same group of companies or which may reasonably be considered to be part of the same commercial association of companies.

c) When the company is a ***quoted trading company and the individual*** claiming the taper relief ***owns*** enough shares to enable ***at least 5%*** of the voting rights in the company to be exercised.

d) When ***the individual*** claiming the taper relief is an ***officer or employee*** of the company, or of another company as in (b) above, and ***does not have a 'material interest'*** in the company.

Broadly speaking, this means that the individual concerned, together with any 'connected persons' (see section 6.8) does not hold, and cannot control, more than 10% of any class of shares in the company.

Note that the qualifying company definition given here is also used to determine whether any shares or securities which an individual holds in that company qualify as business assets.

Summary: Position from 6th April 2004

In summary, almost any property you own which you either use yourself in a trading activity, or which you rent out and which your tenants use in a trade, will qualify as a business asset from 6th April 2004. As mentioned in section 6.31, this may sometimes even extend to residential property let to a trading entity.

The major exception arises where the tenant is a quoted company, unless you can fall under (b), (c) or (d) above.

Tax Tip

If you are letting a property to a quoted company, you will not generally qualify for business asset taper relief.

However, if you were an employee of that company, you would be entitled to business asset taper relief.

To be an 'employee' for this purpose, you could take on any job you like, and part-time work qualifies.

Don't think it's worth it? Take a look at the example below.

Example

Harry Grout is a commercial property investor. In May 2006, he buys a large retail property and lets it out to Sainways plc, a major supermarket chain.

In June 2009, Harry sells the property, realising a £1,000,000 capital gain. He is entitled to non-business asset taper relief of only 5%, leaving a tapered gain of £950,000 and giving Harry a Capital Gains Tax bill of £380,000.

John Barraclough is another commercial property investor who buys a large retail property in May 2006. John lets his property out to Tesda plc, another major supermarket chain. At the same time, he also takes a job with Tesda plc, three hours a week on a Saturday afternoon as a 'greeter'. (One of those people who says "hello, welcome to Tesda" just as you've walked in the door. I'm not sure of the point of these, but we'll soon see the point for John.)

John also sells his property at a gain of £1,000,000 in June 2009. He is entitled to business asset taper relief of 75%, leaving a tapered gain of only £250,000 and a Capital Gains Tax bill of just £100,000.

John probably didn't earn much as a 'greeter', but he saved £280,000 in Capital Gains Tax!

Note that John only needed to hold the property for two years to get his maximum taper relief. However, he needed to keep his job for as long as he held the property, or else he would have lost some of his taper relief.

Assets held before 6th April 2004

Before 6th April 2004, the definition of 'business assets' (other than shares and securities), for taper relief purposes, was broadly as follows:

a) Any asset used for the purposes of a trade carried on by the individual who owns it, or a partnership of which he or she is a member,

b) Any asset used for the purposes of a trade carried on by a qualifying company (or group of companies), or

c) Any asset used for the purposes of an office or employment held by the individual owning the asset whose employer carries on a trade.

The definition of a 'qualifying company' was the same during the period from 6th April 2000 to 5th April 2004 as set out under the new rules applying from 6th April 2004 onwards above.

Prior to 6th April 2000, the 'qualifying company' rules were much more difficult to satisfy. This will continue to be relevant to anyone disposing of a property which they held before that date and were letting to a company at that time.

The Relevance of Trading

As can be seen, the definition of 'business asset' is highly dependent on the question of what exactly constitutes a 'trade' or a 'trading company'. This is a new and rapidly developing area of tax law.

As far as companies are concerned, the general requirement is that at least 80% of the company's activities must constitute trading.

Sadly, the commercial letting of property is not considered to be a 'trade' for tax purposes.

This means that a company which lets out commercial property would not be a qualifying company for taper relief purposes, despite the fact that most such lettings, when made by an individual property owner, would now attract taper relief.

Unfortunately, the definition of a 'trade' for taper relief purposes is rather circular:

"A 'trade' means a trade, profession or vocation conducted on a commercial basis with a view to realisation of profits."

Apart from telling us that we can include professions (e.g. accountants) and vocations (e.g. doctors) and that we must be at least attempting to make a profit, this definition rather unhelpfully falls back on stating that a "trade is a trade"!

This, as explained in chapter two, is where Revenue & Customs will tend to fall back on trying to have their cake and eat it – deciding whether you have a trade when it suits them!

Most cases are obvious, of course, such as the proverbial sweet shop. In more doubtful cases, it is best to take professional advice.

Lastly, remember that furnished holiday lettings will qualify as business assets for taper relief purposes.

6.33   RATES OF BUSINESS ASSET TAPER RELIEF

For disposals made any time after 5th April 2002, the rates of business asset taper relief are:

- Assets held less than one year: Nil
- Assets held for one year, but less than two years: 50%
- Assets held for two years or more: 75%

Unlike the lower, Non-Business rate, there is no 'bonus year' for Business Asset Taper Relief.

6.34   MAXIMUM TAPER RELIEF ON INVESTMENT PROPERTY

To summarise, the maximum 75% rate of Taper Relief will be available on any property held for two years or more which:

- Is used in the owner's own trade,
- Is used in a qualifying furnished holiday letting business,
- Was purchased after 5th April 2000 and let to a qualifying company,

180

- Was purchased after 5th April 2004 and let to any qualifying trading entity.

In each case, the qualifying use (or a combination of qualifying uses) as described above must apply throughout the property's ownership.

This enables most new commercial property investments, most furnished holiday accommodation and even some residential property to be sold with a maximum effective Capital Gains Tax rate of just 10% after a mere two years.

Unfortunately, however, an office used to run a property investment business would not itself qualify.

A lot of commercial property purchased prior to 6th April 2004 will, however, be subject to what is known as 'tainted taper', meaning that the maximum 75% relief won't be available until 2014. We will look at this situation further in the next section.

6.35   TAINTED TAPER

Where any asset has been a business asset for only part of the relevant period of ownership, whether because of changes in the 'business asset' definition, or because of actual changes in use, it will be subject to what is known as 'Tainted Taper'. This involves getting the Business Asset Taper Relief rate on a proportion of the gain and the non-business asset rate on the remainder.

The relevant period of ownership for this purpose is the whole of the owner's period of ownership except for:

- Any period more than ten years prior to the disposal, and
- Any period prior to 6th April 1998.

An asset subject to tainted taper will not be eligible for the full rate of taper relief until it has qualified as a business asset for a full **ten years!**

To demonstrate the impact of 'tainted taper' in practice, let's look at an example:

Example

Reggie owns a retail unit which he rents out to an unconnected partnership business, "Perrin & Co.". Although Reggie has owned the property since January 1996, it only starts to qualify as a business asset from 6th April 2004.

On 6th April 2006, Reggie sells the property, realising a capital gain, after indexation relief, of £100,000.

As the taper regime started on 6th April 1998, Reggie is deemed to have held the property for eight years for taper relief purposes.

Of these eight years, the property only qualified as a business asset for two. Hence, 2/8ths of Reggie's gain qualifies for business asset taper relief at 75%.

The remaining 6/8ths of Reggie's gain is only eligible for non-business asset taper relief. The bonus year (see section 6.31) applies for this purpose, giving Reggie an effective nine years of non-business asset taper, or 35%.

Reggie's taper relief is thus calculated as follows:

Business asset taper relief:
£100,000 x 2/8 x 75% =   *£18,750*

Non-Business asset taper relief:
£100,000 x 6/8 x 35% =   *£26,250*

Total: *£45,000*

As we can see, in this example, the property owner ends up with an effective 'hybrid' taper relief rate of 45%. This rate will slowly improve, day by day, until reaching the full maximum rate of 75% on 6th April 2014.

Incidentally, it is also worth noting that Reggie starts to get **some** business asset taper relief immediately on 6th April 2004. It is not necessary for the property to have been a business asset for a year before he gets **any** business asset taper relief at all, it is only necessary that he has held the property for at least one year.

Partial 'Non-Business' Use

A similar situation arises where a part of the property is used for a non-qualifying purpose. Let's look at another example to illustrate this.

Example

Arkwright purchases an office building called Granville House on 6th April 2004. Granville House is subdivided into six office units, all of equal size.

Four of these units are let to qualifying businesses for taper relief purposes but the other two are let to quoted companies which do not qualify for taper relief purposes as far as Arkwright is concerned (i.e. he is not an employee of either of these companies and nor does he own 5% of the shares in either of them).

Two years later, Arkwright sells Granville House at a considerable gain.

Four-sixths of Arkwright's gain on Granville House will qualify for business asset taper relief of 75%.

The remaining 2/6ths will not qualify for any taper relief. (Non-business asset taper relief does not apply until an asset has been held for at least three years.)

Combating Tainted Taper

Tainted taper lasts for up to ten years. It will therefore often be worth considering taking steps to combat it.

A transfer of property with tainted taper to another individual person other than your spouse or registered civil partner, or into a trust, will re-start the taper relief clock and will often allow maximum taper relief to be obtained in two years instead of ten.

Unfortunately, however, most transfers directly to another individual other than your spouse or registered civil partner are likely to give rise to an immediate Capital Gains Tax liability.

Furthermore, from 10th December 2003, any transfers into a 'self-interested trust' may also potentially give rise to an immediate Capital Gains Tax liability. This applies whenever the transferor, their spouse or civil partner, or a dependent minor child of the transferor, is able to benefit from the transferee trust.

Such transfers are, however, still worth considering under the following circumstances:

a) Where the transferee is a discretionary trust with different beneficiaries (e.g. adult children of the transferor).

b) Where a disposal of the property would not currently give rise to any significant Capital Gains Tax liability (e.g. transferring your own former main residence prior to converting it into office premises).

c) Where the Capital Gains Tax liability arising now is far outweighed by the likely future savings (although this does, of course, carry a major element of risk).

The risk of Income Tax charges arising from 6th April 2005 under the new 'pre-owned asset regime' would also need to be considered.

6.36 TAPER RELIEF ON TRANSFERRED PROPERTY

Where a property is transferred from one spouse or registered civil partner to the other as a no gain/no loss transfer (see section 6.6), the transferor's period of ownership is thereafter included as part of the transferee's period of ownership for taper relief purposes.

This means that such transfers are ineffective as a means to re-start the taper relief clock, as discussed in the previous section.

It does, however, generally also mean that a transfer of a property from one spouse or registered civil partner to the other will not result in any loss of taper relief.

Furthermore, in the case of a property already held by one of the couple prior to 6th April 2004, a transfer of this nature may actually be highly beneficial.

When an asset is transferred to a spouse or registered civil partner and, prior to that transfer, it had already been used in a trade carried on by the transferee, the transferee is then able to treat the transferred asset as a business asset for the whole period during which it was being used in their own trade even though they personally did not own it at the time.

Example

Albert bought some small retail premises on 6th April 1998 and has rented them to his partner Victoria ever since. Victoria has been running a sweet shop from the premises owned by Albert throughout this period.

Victoria and Albert got married in 2005 and, in late 2006, she gives Albert the happy news that she is expecting.

The couple decide that Victoria should give up work to look after the baby and therefore plan to sell the shop early in the 2007/2008 tax year.

If Albert sells the property himself, he will only be entitled to the more generous business asset taper relief on the proportion of his period of ownership falling after 6th April 2004.

If, for example, this sale took place on 6th April 2007 then Albert would be able to claim business asset taper relief at 75% on just three ninths of his capital gain. He would be able to claim 35% non-business asset taper relief on the other six ninths of his gain.

If Albert transfers the shop to Victoria, however, then when she sells it, she will be entitled to the full 75% taper relief because the shop has always been used in her business.

On a gain of, say, £120,000, this would save the couple up to £12,800 in Capital Gains Tax.

Tax Tip

It will almost always be worth transferring a property to a spouse or registered civil partner when they are using it in their own trading business.

In addition to the possibility of improving the taper relief situation, the spouse or civil partner using the asset in their trading business would be eligible for Capital Gains Tax hold over relief and also rollover relief on replacement of business assets on a sale of the asset.

The asset would also generally be exempt from Inheritance Tax if held by the partner using it in their own trade.

6.37   THE ANNUAL EXEMPTION

Each individual taxpayer is entitled to an annual exemption for every tax year.

The annual exemption is available to exempt from Capital Gains Tax an amount of capital gains after all other reliefs have been claimed, including the compulsory set-off of capital losses arising in the same tax year.

Where capital losses are brought forward from a previous tax year, however, the set-off is limited to an amount which reduces the taxpayer's untapered capital gains in the current year to the level of the annual exemption.

Any unused annual exemption is simply lost. It cannot be carried forward. Although it cannot be guaranteed, the exemption generally rises each year in line with inflation.

Tax Tip

To make the most of your available annual exemptions, try to time your capital gains so that each disposal falls into a different tax year whenever possible.

The current annual exemption, for capital gains arising during the year ended 5th April 2007 is £8,800.

Example ('George the Fifth')

George has a capital gain of £111,736 in 2006/2007, after claiming all relevant reliefs, including Taper Relief. After setting off his annual exemption of £8,800, he will be left with a taxable gain of £102,936.

Note: in this example, and in the one in section 6.38 below, we have assumed that the annual exemption is fully available.

This will not always be the case and it should be remembered that the exemption applies to all of an individual's capital gains, net of capital losses, for a whole tax year, and not specifically to any single gain.

6.38   THE AMOUNT OF TAX PAYABLE

Having arrived at the taxable gain, it only remains to work out how much tax is actually payable.

Capital Gains Tax is calculated at the same rate as would have applied if the taxable gain had been an extra slice of interest income received by the taxpayer in the same tax year on top of all other income (including dividends and their related tax credits). (See section 3.3 and Appendix A for further details of tax rates and their application.)

Hence, if the taxpayer is already a higher rate taxpayer for Income Tax purposes, Capital Gains Tax will be paid at a flat rate of 40%.

For an individual with no taxable income whatsoever in the same tax year, the Capital Gains Tax would be calculated as follows (based on 2006/2007 rates):

- On the first £2,150:   10%
- On the next £31,150: 20% (the 'savings rate')
- On the remainder: 40%

Of course, many taxpayers are in a position somewhere between these two extremes. For these individuals, the amount of Capital Gains Tax payable is calculated by first using up what remains of their lower and basic rate tax bands (£33,300 in total) and then taxing any remaining amount at the higher rate, 40%.

Example ('George the Sixth')

After all available reliefs and exemptions, including his annual exemption, George has a taxable gain for 2006/2007 of £102,936. His gross income for 2006/2007 totals £12,000. After deducting his personal Income Tax allowance for 2006/2007 (£5,035) this leaves him with taxable income of £6,965.

George therefore pays Capital Gains Tax as follows:

- *Nil at 10% (his lower rate band has already been fully used up by income).*
- *£26,335 at 20% (the amount of his basic rate tax band still available after the amount used up by income - £33,300 LESS £6,965) = £5,267.*
- *£76,601 at 40% (the remainder of the gain - £102,936 LESS £26,335) = £30,640.*

Total Capital Gains Tax payable: £35,907.

6.39 WHEN IS CAPITAL GAINS TAX PAYABLE?

The total amount of Capital Gains Tax payable for each tax year is due and payable by 31st January following the end of the tax year. Hence, in the example in section 6.38 above, George's Capital Gains Tax liability of £35,907 for 2006/2007 is due by 31st January 2008.

Capital Gains Tax liabilities are excluded from the instalment system applying to Income Tax liabilities under self assessment (see section 3.4).

188

6.40 WHAT MUST I REPORT TO REVENUE & CUSTOMS?

The general rule is that disposals giving rise to proceeds exceeding four times the annual exemption, or which do give rise to an actual Capital Gains Tax liability, will need to be reported.

Disposals which are fully covered by the principal private residence exemption alone, however, continue to be exempted from reporting requirements. This includes cases where the 'last three years of ownership' rule applies to fully exempt the gain, but does not include cases where the taxpayer is additionally relying on the private letting exemption to ensure full relief from Capital Gains Tax.

The Return is due for submission by 31st January following the end of the relevant tax year (i.e. by the same date that any Capital Gains Tax liability is due). If you have a reportable property disposal, you will need to complete pages CG1 to CG8 of the tax return.

Pages CG1 to CG8 form the Capital Gains Supplement of the tax return. Download: www.hmrc.gov.uk/forms/sa108.pdf or call 0845 9000 404 to order a copy.

6.41 JOINTLY HELD ASSETS

Where two or more taxpayers hold assets jointly, they must each calculate their own Capital Gains Tax based on their own share of the net proceeds received less their own base cost.

Example

Let's take the same facts as the example used in section 6.38 above, except that George owns the house jointly with his wife, Charlotte. Charlotte's income for 2006/2007 is less than her personal Income Tax allowance (£5,035).

Up to the point of calculating the tapered gain, everything will be exactly the same, except that George and Charlotte will each have a gain of exactly half of the amount given for George. The major changes will come in the fact that each of them has their own annual exemption and each will be subject to different tax rates. This can be summarised as follows:

£

Net proceeds	184,475 (half of £368,950 – section 6.8)
Less:	
Base Cost	72,525 (half of £145,050 – section 6.9)
Indexation	25,999 (half of £51,998 – section 6.11)
Equals:	85,951
Less:	
Taper relief (35%, as before)	30,083
Equals:	55,868
Less:	
Annual Exemption	8,800
Equals:	47,068

Tax Payable

Based on the same facts as in 'George the Sixth' in section 6.38 above, George would pay Capital Gains Tax on his gain as follows:

- £26,335 at 20% (as before, the amount of his basic rate tax band still available after the amount used up by income - £33,300 LESS £6,965) = £5,267.
- £20,733 at 40% (the remainder of George's gain - £47,068 LESS £26,335) = £8,293.

George's Capital Gains Tax bill: £13,560.

Having no taxable income for the year, Charlotte will pay Capital Gains Tax as follows:

£2,150 at 10%	£215
£31,150 at 20%	£6,230
£13,768 at 40% (£47,068 LESS £33,300)	£5,507

Charlotte's Capital Gains Tax bill: £11,952.

It is well worth noting that the total Capital Gains Tax now payable by the couple, £25,512, is considerably less than the amount George had to pay when he owned the house in his sole name (£35,907 – see section 6.38 above).

Another important point to note when looking at jointly held property is that the £40,000 limit for Private Letting Relief (see section 6.14) applies to each individual taxpayer. Hence, up to a total of £80,000 can be exempted by that relief where a house is held jointly. We will examine the potential effect of this later in chapter eight.

6.42 CAPITAL LOSSES

Generally speaking, capital losses are computed in the same way as capital gains. However, there are a few significant differences in the treatment of capital losses, as follows:

- When dealing with the base cost of assets acquired before 31st March 1982 (section 6.10), the question of whether to use the March 1982 value or the original cost is determined according to whichever produces the lower loss. If one produces a loss and the other a gain, then a 'no gain/no loss' disposal results.

- There is an exception to the above rule in the case of a person who has elected that March 1982 values should always take precedence over original cost in the computation of all their capital gains or losses.

- Indexation relief (section 6.11) cannot augment or create a capital loss. Hence, where there is a capital loss before indexation relief, no indexation relief is given. In other cases, indexation relief must be limited to a maximum equivalent to the amount that would bring the gain after indexation relief down to nil.

- Taper relief does not apply to capital losses.

- Where a taxpayer has an overall net capital loss for the year, it is carried forward and set off against gains in future years BUT only to the extent necessary to reduce future gains before taper relief down to the annual exemption applying for that future year.

- Capital losses arising on any transactions with 'connected persons' (see section 6.8) may only be set off against gains arising on transactions between the same parties.

6.43   LEASES

The taxation treatment of leases has a long and chequered history. Here is a brief summary of the current situation.

Granting a long lease of more than 50 years' duration

This is a capital disposal, fully chargeable to Capital Gains Tax (subject to applicable reliefs). The Base Cost to be used has to be restricted under the 'part disposal' rules. In essence, what this means is that the Base Cost is divided between the part disposed of (i.e. the lease) and the part retained (the 'reversionary interest') in proportion to their relative values.

Example

Llewellyn owns the freehold of a commercial property in Cardiff. He grants a 60-year lease to Brian, a businessman from Belfast moving into the area. Brian pays a premium of £90,000 for the lease. The value of Llewellyn's reversionary interest is established as £10,000. The Base Cost to be used in calculating Llewellyn's capital gain on the grant of the lease is therefore 90% of his Base Cost for the property as a whole.

Granting a short lease of no more than 50 years' duration

As we saw in section 4.13, part of any lease premium obtained will be taxable as income. The remainder is a capital disposal and is dealt with in the same way as the grant of a long lease, as outlined above.

Assigning a long lease with no less than 50 years' duration remaining

This is simply a straightforward capital disposal. Any applicable reliefs may be claimed in the usual way.

Assigning a short lease with less than 50 years' duration remaining

This is treated entirely as a capital disposal. However, leases with less than 50 years remaining are treated as 'wasting assets'. The taxpayer is therefore required to reduce his Base Cost in accordance with the schedule set out in Appendix E. For example, for a lease with 20 years remaining, and which had more than 50 years remaining when first acquired, the Base Cost must be reduced to 72.77% of the original amount.

Where the lease had less than 50 years remaining when originally acquired (or granted), the necessary reduction in base cost is achieved by multiplying the original cost by the factor applying at the time of sale and dividing by the factor applying at the time of purchase.

Example

John takes out a ten year lease over a building and pays a premium of £10,000. Five years later, John assigns his lease to Roy at a premium of £6,000.

When calculating his capital gain, the amount which John may claim as his base cost is:

£10,000 x 26.722/46.695 = £5,723

Chapter 7

Other Taxes to Watch Out For

7.1   STAMP DUTY – INTRODUCTION

Stamp Duty is the oldest tax on the statute books. It was several centuries old already when Pitt the Younger introduced Income Tax in 1799. Even today, we are still governed (to a limited extent) by the Stamp Act 1891. From 1st December 2003, however, for transfers of real property (i.e. land and buildings, or any form of legal interest in them), Stamp Duty has been replaced by Stamp Duty Land Tax.

7.2   STAMP DUTY LAND TAX

The rates of Stamp Duty Land Tax applying to transfers of property are the same regardless of what type of property business the purchaser has and regardless of whether that purchaser is an individual, a trust, a partnership or a company.

Unfortunately, the introduction of the new tax has mainly preserved the dramatic increases in the rates of Stamp Duty that we have seen over the last few years. Stamp Duty has been at the forefront of Gordon Brown's strategy of 'stealth taxation', through which he has raised additional taxes in ways which largely go unnoticed in the media frenzy that surrounds the annual Budget process. The changeover to the Stamp Duty Land Tax regime has done nothing to alter this and, for larger transactions, the tax still represents a significant barrier to property investment.

The current rates of Stamp Duty Land Tax (other than in 'disadvantaged areas' – see below) are as follows:

- Residential property up to £125,000 – Zero.

- Non-residential property up to £150,000 – Zero.

- Residential property over £125,000 but not more than £250,000 – 1%.

- Non-residential property over £150,000 but not more than £250,000 – 1%.

- All property over £250,000 but not more than £500,000 – 3%.

- All property over £500,000 – 4%.

All of the amounts shown above refer to the consideration paid for the purchase – whether in cash or by any other means.

Like Stamp Duty, the Stamp Duty Land Tax payable is always rounded up to the nearest £5.

Whenever any rate less than the maximum 4% is to be applied, the purchaser is required to certify that the lower rate is properly applicable. A complex and very lengthy form has been introduced for this purpose!

Furthermore, it should also be noted that the rate of Stamp Duty Land Tax to be applied must be determined after taking account of any 'associated transactions' taking place.

It can readily be seen from the above table that a small alteration in the purchase price of a property can sometimes make an enormous difference to the amount of Stamp Duty Land Tax payable.

Example

Ian is just about to make an offer of £250,001 for a house in Edinburgh when he realises that the Stamp Duty Land Tax payable on this purchase, at 3%, would be £7,505. Horrified at this prospect, he amends the offer to £249,999, thus reducing the potential Stamp Duty Land Tax payable to £2,500 (1%).

This sort of change is, of course, perfectly acceptable, because the whole situation is taking place at 'arm's-length'.

However, where connected parties are involved, Revenue & Customs' Stamp Office is likely to scrutinise very closely any transactions where the consideration is only just under one of the limits set out above.

Leases

Stamp Duty Land Tax is also payable on leases (sometimes known as 'Lease Duty') and this represents one of the most significant changes from the old Stamp Duty regime. Although Stamp Duty was often payable on leases under the old regime, it had some rather odd quirks and was open to a good deal of abuse.

The Stamp Duty Land Tax payable on the granting of a lease is based on the 'Net Present Value' of all of the rent payable under the lease over its entire term. Where the net present value does not exceed £125,000 (for residential property) or £150,000 (for non-residential property), no Stamp Duty Land Tax will be payable. For new leases with a net present value exceeding these limits, Stamp Duty Land Tax is payable at a rate of 1% on the excess.

VAT is excluded from the rent payable under the lease for the purposes of Stamp Duty Land Tax calculations <u>unless</u> the landlord has already exercised the option to tax (this applies to commercial property only).

Example

Clive is about to take on a ten year lease over a house in Kent at an annual rent of £18,000.

The Stamp Duty Land Tax legislation provides that the net present value of a sum of money due within the next 12 months is equal to the sum due divided by a 'discount factor'. The applicable discount factor is currently 103.5%.

Hence, the 'Present Value' of Clive's first year's rent of £18,000 is £17,391 (i.e. £18,000 divided by 103.5%).

Similarly, the second year's rent, which is due a further 12 months later, must be 'discounted' again by the same amount, i.e. £17,391/103.5% = £16,803.

This process is continued for the entire ten year life of the lease and the net present values of all of the rental payments are then added together to give the total net present value for the whole lease. In this case, this works out at £149,699.

The Stamp Duty Land Tax payable by Clive is therefore just £250 (1% of £149,699 less £125,000, £24,699, rounded up to the nearest £5).

Note that it does not matter for the purposes of this calculation whether the rent is payable monthly, quarterly or annually, or whether it is payable in advance or in arrears. Net present value is, in each case, always calculated by reference to the total annual rental payable for each year of the lease.

The current 'discount factor' (103.5%) may be changed in the future, depending on a number of factors, including the prevailing rates of inflation and interest.

Lease Premiums

Lease **premiums** also attract Stamp Duty Land Tax at the same rates as given above for outright purchases. Additional special rules apply where there is also annual gross rent payable in excess of £600.

Disadvantaged Areas

There are 2,000 areas in the UK which have been specifically designated as 'Disadvantaged Areas'. This is done by reference to postcodes in England and Wales and by reference to Electoral Wards in Scotland. (My apologies to readers with properties in Northern Ireland – I don't know how it is done there.)

Residential properties within these areas are subject to the zero rate of Stamp Duty Land Tax on purchases where the consideration does not exceed £150,000.

Non-residential properties within these areas were fully exempt from Stamp Duty Land Tax until 16th March 2005. Sadly, however, this relief has now been withdrawn.

Application to all UK Property

Stamp Duty Land Tax is payable on all transfers of UK property in accordance with the above rules regardless of where the vendor or purchaser are resident and regardless of where the transfer documentation is drawn up.

7.3 STAMP DUTY ON SHARES

Before we leave the subject of Stamp Taxes, it is just worth briefly mentioning that the rate of Stamp Duty on purchases of shares and securities is still unchanged at a single uniform rate of only 0.5%.

This has led to many tax-avoidance strategies, designed to avoid the excessive rates applied to property transactions by making use of this more palatable rate. However, new legislation introduced over the last few years has effectively blocked most of the more popular methods.

Nevertheless, for those investing in property through a company, there remains the possibility of selling shares in that company at a much lower rate of Duty than would apply to the sale of individual properties within the company.

7.4 INHERITANCE TAX

Inheritance Tax is the direct descendant of Estate Duty and Capital Transfer Tax. It is quite ironic that Inheritance Tax should have such a long lineage because it is, of course, one's descendants who will suffer its effects.

Inheritance Tax is really a complete subject in its own right. For a full examination of the workings of this tax and the planning opportunities available to reduce its potential impact on your family see the Taxcafe.co.uk guide *How to Avoid Inheritance Tax.*

Nevertheless, death and taxes are, of course, the only two certainties in life and unless pre-emptive action is taken, sooner or later an Inheritance Tax liability will arise whenever a UK domiciled individual owns non-trading property worth more than the 'Nil Rate Band'. It is therefore worth us taking a brief look at the potential impact of this tax.

If you are UK domiciled then, on your death, Inheritance Tax will be levied at one single rate of 40% on the entire value of your estate, less certain exemptions. The first, and for most people perhaps the most important, exemption is the Nil Rate Band.

As the name suggests, this means that an Inheritance Tax rate of nil is applied to the first part of your estate, which falls within this band. From 6th April 2006, the Nil Rate Band stands at £285,000.

Example

Arthur has spent many years building up an investment property portfolio. At the time of his death in December 2006, his portfolio is worth £2,000,000. He has no other assets and no liabilities.

The first £285,000 of Arthur's estate is exempt from Inheritance Tax, as it is covered by the Nil Rate Band. The remaining £1,715,000, however, is charged to Inheritance Tax at 40%, giving rise to a tax charge of £686,000!

In certain circumstances, Inheritance Tax can also apply to transfers of assets (or cash) made during a person's lifetime. However, for most people, death is the only occasion when they (or, more accurately, their executors), are concerned with this tax.

Apart from the Nil Rate Band, there are a number of other Inheritance Tax exemptions and reliefs available. The most important of these is probably the fact that transfers to spouses or registered civil partners are wholly exempt.

There is a crucial exception to this exemption, however, where the inheriting spouse or civil partner is foreign domiciled and does not have 'deemed domicile' in the UK. In these cases, the exemption is restricted to a paltry £55,000.

Domicile

Inheritance Tax is payable on the worldwide assets of UK domiciled individuals. Foreign domiciled individuals are only subject to Inheritance Tax on assets situated in the UK, (unless they have 'deemed domicile' in the UK – see below).

Under general principles, most people acquire their father's domicile at birth and hence your domicile is usually your country of birth (or his, if you were living abroad at the time). You can change your domicile, but it is difficult. An intention to stay abroad permanently is required.

Deemed Domicile

Notwithstanding any of the above, anyone who has been resident in the UK for at least 17 out of the last 20 tax years is deemed to be UK domiciled for Inheritance Tax purposes (but not necessarily for other UK taxes).

In some cases, however, the deemed domicile rule may be over-ridden by a Double Tax Treaty between the UK and the taxpayer's country of origin.

The Implication of High Property Values

For the vast majority of people, the largest proportion of their estate will be property. Inheritance Tax was once viewed as a 'rich man's tax', but recent dramatic increases in property values mean that even modestly wealthy people will find that, without careful planning, their estate has a large potential Inheritance Tax liability.

7.5   VAT – INTRODUCTION

VAT, or Value Added Tax, to give it its proper name, is the 'new kid on the block' in UK taxation terms, having arrived on our shores from Europe on 1st April 1973.

Despite its youth, VAT is, quite probably, the UK's most hated tax and there are some nasty pitfalls awaiting the unwary property investor at the hands of this indirect form of taxation.

VAT is currently charged at three different rates in the UK; these are zero, 5% and 17.5%. All of these rates may be encountered by property businesses.

You may recall me stating in section 2.2 that the type of property held by a business did not affect how that business was treated for Income Tax and Capital Gains Tax purposes.

For VAT, however, it does become important to distinguish between residential property and commercial property.

7.6   VAT ON RESIDENTIAL PROPERTY

Residential Property Letting

Generally speaking, a property investment business, engaged primarily in residential property letting, does not need to be registered for VAT. (Nor, indeed, most likely, would it be able to.)

The letting of residential property is an exempt supply for VAT purposes. VAT is therefore not chargeable on rent, although, of course, VAT cannot be recovered on expenses and the landlord should therefore claim VAT-inclusive costs for Income Tax and Capital Gains Tax purposes.

Beware, however, that the provision of ancillary services (e.g. cleaning or gardening) may sometimes be Standard-Rated, and hence subject to VAT at 17.5%, if the value of annual supplies of these services exceeds the VAT registration threshold, (£61,000 from 1st April 2006).

Some landlords making ancillary supplies of this nature prefer to register for VAT, even if they have not reached the registration threshold, as this means that they are able to recover some of the VAT on their expenses.

Residential Property Development

Sales of newly constructed residential property are zero-rated for VAT purposes. This means that the developer can recover all of the VAT on their construction costs without having to charge VAT on the sale of the property. (In theory, VAT is charged, but at a rate of zero.)

This treatment is extended to the sale of a property which has just been converted from a non-residential property into a residential property (*e.g. converting a barn into a house*).

It is also extended to 'substantially reconstructed protected buildings'. In essence, this means the sale of a listed building following the carrying out of major alterations. Such alterations do, of course, require approval from the authorities.

Property developers carrying out construction work under any of these headings are therefore able to register for VAT and then recover the VAT on the vast majority of their business expenses.

Other Residential Property Sales

Other sales of residential property are generally an exempt supply meaning, once again, that the taxpayer making the sale is unable to recover any of the VAT on his or her expenses.

This means that VAT cannot be recovered by most residential property investors and most residential property dealers.

Furthermore, property developers who merely renovate or alter existing residential property prior to onward sale are also generally unable to recover VAT on their costs. Where, however, the work qualifies as a 'conversion', as described below, they may at least be able to reduce the amount of VAT payable.

Conversions

A reduced VAT rate of 5% is available in respect of any building work carried out on a residential property where the work results in a change to the number of dwellings in the property.

For example, this would apply to the conversion of:

- One house into several flats.
- Two or more flats into a single house.
- Two semi-detached houses into a single detached house.

202

The reduced rate also applies to conversions of commercial property into residential use.

Approved alterations to listed properties are eligible for zero-rating.

Property investors or developers carrying out projects of this nature should try to ensure that they only pay the appropriate lower VAT rate from the outset, as it is difficult to recover any excess paid in error.

7.7   VAT ON COMMERCIAL PROPERTY

Commercial Property Letting

For commercial property, there is an 'option to tax'. In other words, the landlord may choose, for each property and on a property-by-property basis, whether or not the rent should be an exempt supply for VAT purposes.

If the 'option to tax' is exercised, the rent on the property becomes Standard Rated (at 17.5%) for VAT purposes. The landlord may then recover VAT on all of the expenses relating to that property. Ancillary services are again likely to be Standard Rated if supplies exceed the £61,000 registration threshold, regardless of whether you have opted to tax the rent itself.

Charging VAT on your commercial property rent is usually known as 'exercising the option to tax', although, technically, the proper term, as sometimes used by Revenue & Customs, is 'exercising the option to waive exemption from the requirement to charge tax'. Either way, it means the same thing.

Tax Tip

If the potential tenants of a commercial property are all, or mostly, likely to be VAT-registered businesses themselves, it will generally make sense to exercise the 'option to tax' on the property in order to recover the VAT on expenses incurred.

If your tenants themselves have a VAT-registered and fully taxable (for VAT purposes) business, then everyone's happy. The problem comes where your tenants cannot recover some or all of the VAT which you are charging them. And remember that you cannot change your option on a property once it has been exercised (well, not for 30 years anyway). Hence, if you opt to charge VAT to a fully taxable tenant, you will still need to charge VAT to the next tenant in the same property, even if they cannot recover it.

Sometimes, though, with non-taxable (for VAT) tenants, where you have not yet exercised your option to tax, you can refrain from doing so and negotiate a higher rent to compensate you for your loss of VAT recovery on your own costs.

Example

Norman owns an office building and hasn't yet opted to tax the rents. He has monthly costs of £200 plus VAT (i.e. £235 gross) and expects a monthly rent of £1,000. If Norman opts to tax he will recover £35 a month from Revenue & Customs and make a monthly profit of £800.

However, Lenny, the prospective tenant, is not registered for VAT. If Norman opts to tax the property, Lenny's rent will effectively be 17.5% higher, i.e. £1,175 per month.

So, as a better alternative, Norman and Lenny agree that Norman will not opt to tax the building but will, instead, charge Lenny £1,050 a month rent. Now Norman is making a monthly profit of £815 (£1,050 minus £235) and Lenny's rent is effectively £125 less than it would have been. Norman and Lenny both win and HM Revenue & Customs loses.

Commercial Property Sales & Purchases

Where the 'option to tax' has previously been exercised by the owner of a commercial property, their sale of that property will again be Standard Rated and this has major implications for such transactions.

Sales of new or uncompleted commercial property are also Standard Rated for VAT purposes.

Wealth Warning

Where VAT must be charged on a commercial property sale, the Stamp Duty Land Tax arising must be calculated on the basis of the gross, VAT-inclusive price.

This can lead to an effective combined VAT and Stamp Duty Land Tax rate of up to 22.2%!

This represents a pretty hefty cost if the purchaser is not VAT registered, probably enough to prevent the sale from taking place in some cases.

Imagine a large insurance company buying a new office block in central London – the combined VAT and Stamp Duty Land Tax cost would be astronomical!

Where a property investor incurs VAT on the purchase of a commercial property, the only way to recover that VAT will be for the investor to exercise the 'option to tax' on the property. In this way, the Government generally forces everyone to maintain the taxable status of the building for VAT purposes.

If a VAT registered property developer incurs VAT on the purchase of a commercial property, they can recover the VAT in the same way as on any other purchase of goods or services for use in the business. This initial recovery is not dependent on exercising the 'option to tax', as the developer has a taxable business for VAT purposes, but ...

Wealth Warning

If VAT has been recovered on the purchase of a commercial property, a sale of that property without first exercising the option to tax would be an exempt supply.

If that property were trading stock, this would result in the loss of all the VAT initially reclaimed on its purchase and on any development, renovation or conversion work carried out on it. Some of the VAT recovered on general overhead costs would probably also become repayable.

Furthermore, when more than £250,000 has been spent on the purchase or improvement of a property for use as the business's own trading premises, a sale of that property within ten years without first exercising the option to tax would also trigger a VAT liability.

7.8 VAT ON PROPERTY MANAGEMENT

Property management services are Standard Rated for VAT and hence a property management business will need to be registered for VAT if its annual supplies (i.e. sales) exceed the £61,000 registration threshold. The taxpayer may still register voluntarily even if the level of sales is below the threshold.

Whether the properties under management are residential or commercial makes no difference for this purpose.

Naturally, a property management business which is registered for VAT can recover the VAT on most of its business expenses. There are, however, a few exceptions where VAT cannot be wholly recovered, as we shall see in the next section.

7.9 INTERACTION OF VAT WITH OTHER TAXES

Any business which is registered for VAT should generally include only the net (i.e. excluding VAT) amounts of income and expenditure in its accounts for Income Tax purposes. Where VAT recovery is barred or restricted, however, the additional cost arising should be treated as part of the relevant expense.

Expenses subject to restrictions on the recovery of VAT include:

- Business entertaining.
- Purchases of motor cars.
- Provision of private fuel for proprietors or staff.

As you can see, many of the expenses subject to a VAT recovery restriction are also subject to some form of restriction for Income Tax purposes.

A non-registered business should always include the VAT in its business expenditure for Income Tax purposes.

Similar principles apply for Capital Gains Tax and Corporation Tax purposes.

7.10 NATIONAL INSURANCE CONTRIBUTIONS

In most cases, rental income is not classed as 'earnings' and is not therefore subject to National Insurance Contributions.

In a few instances, individual taxpayers with income from furnished holiday lettings have been charged for Class 2 National Insurance Contributions. The Class 2 rate is, however, only £2.10 per week for 2006/2007.

All forms of letting income are specifically exempted from the rather more significant Class 4 National Insurance Contributions. Taxpayers with property trading income, however, are fully subject to both Class 2 and Class 4 National Insurance Contributions and this is covered in detail in section 5.5.

Non-trading taxpayers can, of course, pay voluntary Class 3 National Insurance Contributions of £7.55 per week in order to secure state retirement benefits, etc, if they so wish.

Naturally, if you should employ anyone to help you in your property business, then their salary will be subject to both employer's and employee's Class 1 National Insurance Contributions (at 11% and 12.8% respectively). If you provide them with any taxable Benefits-in-Kind, you will additionally be liable for Class 1A National Insurance Contributions (again at 12.8%).

Capital Gains

National Insurance Contributions are never payable on capital gains.

Remember, however, that if you are classed as a property developer or a property trader, your profit on property sales will be taxed as trading income and hence will be subject to National Insurance Contributions.

7.11 PLANNING GAIN SUPPLEMENT

In December 2005, the Government published a consultation document proposing a new tax, 'Planning Gain Supplement'.

As the name suggests, it is proposed that this new tax will be applied when a property developer makes a gain owing to the granting of planning permission.

The planning gain will be calculated when full planning consent is given for a development project. The taxable planning gain will be the difference between the current use value of the land and the value of the land with planning permission.

Although it is proposed that the tax be calculated when full planning permission is granted, it will only become payable when actual development commences. The proposed regulations will make it unlawful for any person to commence development until the Planning Gain Supplement has been paid. In this way, the developer will be forced to 'volunteer' as the person responsible for payment of the tax.

No official proposed rate for the new tax has yet been announced but there is speculation that it may be around 20%.

At present, it is proposed that Planning Gain Supplement will apply to all developments, residential or commercial and whether on greenfield or brownfield sites. A lower rate of tax for brownfield site developments is, however, under consideration.

Some consideration is also being given to the possibility of an exemption for smaller developments, although no concrete proposals on this point have emerged as yet.

It is proposed that the new tax will be deductible as a business expense in the calculation of other tax liabilities. Let's have a look at how we currently believe this will work in practice:

Example

Richard, a self-employed property developer, has a conditional contract to buy an acre of land from his cousin Philip for £1,000,000, subject to detailed planning permission. The land is currently used for farming and its current use value is just £5,000.

In early 2009, Richard obtains detailed planning consent for a development of eight houses on the site. The land alone is now valued at £1,005,000.

Hence, before proceeding with his development, Richard will have to pay Planning Gain Supplement of £200,000.

Richard then proceeds with the development and eventually realises a gross profit of £400,000 on the project.

Richard may deduct the Planning Gain Supplement from his profit but must still pay Income Tax at 40% and National Insurance Contributions at 1% on his net profit of £200,000. (I'm assuming here that Richard already has enough other income to push him into higher rate tax.)

Richard's total tax bill on this project is thus:

	£
Planning Gain Supplement	*200,000*
Income Tax	*80,000*
National Insurance	*2,000*
Total	*282,000*

That amounts to a total effective tax rate of 70.5%!

The new tax is, of course, merely a proposal at the moment and we are told that it will not be implemented before 2008, at the earliest.

Planning for Planning Gain Supplement

With details of the new tax still very sketchy, it is hard to know what planning can be done for the new tax.

The most important point for property developers must surely be to build a Planning Gain Supplement clause into all land purchase contracts, so that the price payable for the land can be adjusted to take account of any Planning Gain Supplement which may become payable.

It is tempting to suggest that it also makes sense to try to get detailed planning permission pushed through before the new tax comes into force.

This would probably make sense for some very small developments, such as a home-owner building a second house in their own garden.

For larger developments, however, there is the issue that the new Planning Gain Supplement will partly replace some of the current planning consent obligations levied by local authorities (known as Section 106 Agreements in England or Section 75 Agreements in Scotland). This may potentially mean that an attempt to push a development through the planning process before Planning Gain Supplement comes into force could actually prove more costly.

Another possible way to reduce the impact of Planning Gain Supplement might be to try to increase the land's current use value before planning consent is granted. The danger, however, is that this may increase the planning value of the site even more and thus actually increase the amount of Planning Gain Supplement payable.

A Silver Lining?

There is a strong chance that the introduction of the Planning Gain Supplement will have an inflationary effect on new house prices.

This, in turn, must lead to a further increase in value for current housing stock, which can only be good news for property investors with an existing portfolio.

Chapter 8

Advanced Tax Planning

8.1 INTRODUCTION TO TAX PLANNING

In the previous chapters we have looked at the mechanics of the UK tax system as it applies to the individual property investor. A great many planning ideas and principles have already emerged and doubtless, by now, some readers will have begun to form ideas of their own.

In this chapter we will take a look at some further useful planning strategies for property investors. These strategies relate in the main to those investors who continue to hold their property investments personally.

In many cases, the best tax-planning results will be obtained through the use of a combination of different techniques, rather than merely following any single one. Each situation is different and the optimum solution only comes through a detailed analysis of all the relevant facts.

Tax planning should therefore never be undertaken without full knowledge of the facts of the case and the exact circumstances of the individuals and other legal entities involved.

For this reason, the techniques laid out in this chapter, which are by no means exhaustive, are intended only to give you some idea of the tax savings which can be achieved through careful planning.

If and when you come to undertake any tax-planning measures of your own you should seek professional advice from someone fully acquainted with your own situation. The author cannot accept any responsibility for any action taken, or any decision made to refrain from action, by any readers of this guide.

So, that's the health warning, now for the interesting stuff....

8.2 PLANNING FOR THE FUTURE

The Future of the Principal Private Residence Exemption

A few days before Gordon Brown's 2005 Budget, rumours began to circulate of a possible abolition of the principal private residence exemption after the May 2005 General Election. Twelve months later, these rumours thankfully appear to have proved totally unfounded.

Personally, I always felt that a total abolition of the exemption was extremely unlikely.

We may, nevertheless, at some future stage see some 'tightening up' of some of its more generous aspects. Abolition or reduction of the additional three-year period of exemption at the end of a taxpayer's ownership would seem like a strong possibility.

Guiding Principles

As with all tax planning, we can only follow these guiding principles:

- Hope for the best,
- Plan for the worst,
- Review your position constantly, and
- Expect the unexpected!

8.3 THE BENEFITS OF JOINT OWNERSHIP

In many cases, owning property jointly with one or more other people can be highly beneficial for tax purposes. In this section, we will look at joint ownership benefits which are available to anyone.

In the next section, we will concentrate purely on the additional planning available only to married couples and registered civil partnerships.

A number of important tax reliefs and tax bands are available on a 'per person' basis, these include:

- The personal allowance
- The annual exemption
- Private letting relief
- The lower rate tax band
- The basic rate tax band
- The small earnings exception for Class 2 National Insurance Contributions
- The nil rate band for Inheritance Tax

As a consequence of this, the value of these allowances, bands and reliefs can effectively be doubled in the case of many properties held jointly by two people. (Or tripled for three joint owners, etc.)

How Much Is At Stake?

Sticking with two joint owners and using 2006/2007 tax rates, the maximum tax savings which joint ownership can generate are as follows:

- £10,395 on most capital gains.
- £26,395 on capital gains where private letting relief is available.
- £8,266 in Income Tax on rental income **annually**
- £8,669 in Income Tax and National Insurance Contributions on trading profits **annually**
- £114,000 in Inheritance Tax

Wealth Warning

Not every tax relief or band is given on a 'per person' basis. Exceptions to be wary of include:

- All Corporation Tax rate bands
- All Stamp Duty Land Tax bands
- The VAT registration threshold
- Landlord's energy-saving allowance for insulation expenditure

Additionally, in the case of the upper earnings limit for National Insurance Contributions, the fact that this works on a 'per person' basis will actually work against joint owners in a trading situation. (Though this is usually outweighed by Income Tax savings.)

Non-Equal Splits

When considering the benefits of joint ownership, remember always that it is possible to have any split of beneficial ownership which you desire, as long as the correct form of joint ownership is in place (see section 2.13).

In this context, it is worth mentioning that a joint tenancy can be changed fairly easily into a tenancy in common. This change is not treated as a disposal for Capital Gains Tax purposes unless, of course, at the same time there is also a change to a non-equal split of beneficial ownership.

Get It Right First Time

Where the prospective joint owners are not a married couple or a registered civil partnership, it is very difficult to transfer any share in the property across to the other person without incurring Capital Gains Tax or other charges.

Hence, in all other situations it is generally essential to get your ownership structure right from the outset.

However, as we will see later in this chapter, not being legally 'hitched' has its advantages too!

Optimising Rental Income Shares

Joint owners who are not a legally married couple or registered civil partnership may agree to share rental income in different proportions to their legal ownership of the property (perhaps because one of the investors is carrying out the management of the jointly held portfolio). The Income Tax treatment should follow the agreed profit-sharing arrangements. It is wise to document your profit-sharing agreement in order to avoid any dispute, however.

8.4   USING YOUR SPOUSE OR CIVIL PARTNER

Putting property into joint names with your spouse or registered civil partner can generate considerable tax savings, just like any other joint owners, as we have seen in the previous section.

In some cases, an outright transfer of the whole property to your spouse or registered civil partner may even be more beneficial.

The major difference between those who have legally 'tied the knot', by marriage or registered civil partnership, and the rest of us, however, is the fact that the transfer itself is free from tax and will not normally result in any loss of existing reliefs, such as principal private residence exemption (but see further below).

The example in section 6.41 above (George and Charlotte), already demonstrates the potential Capital Gains Tax savings. However, it is normally immaterial whether the property was in joint ownership throughout, or was only transferred into joint ownership at a later date, prior to the ultimate sale. The effect on the couple's final tax liabilities usually remains exactly the same.

Furthermore, where there is scope to claim the private letting exemption, it is possible to double the maximum amount of relief available (from £40,000 to £80,000) by putting the property into joint names prior to sale.

Three key provisos must be made here however:

a) The spouse or partner must be beneficially entitled to his/her share of the sale proceeds. Any attempt to prevent this could make the transfer invalid for tax purposes.

b) An interim transfer of property into joint names prior to sale must take place early enough to ensure that the transferee spouse or partner genuinely has beneficial title to their share. If it is left until the ultimate sale is a contractual certainty, it may be too late to be effective for tax purposes.

c) Revenue & Customs' interpretation of the law is that a spouse or registered civil partner will not be entitled to any principal private residence relief or private letting relief on their portion of a capital gain if the property in question was NEVER their only or main residence during the couple's ownership.

I am not sure that I agree with Revenue & Customs' interpretation at (c) above, but it would perhaps be foolish to plan your affairs on any other basis.

Example

Caleb has lived in his house in Liverpool for many years as his main residence. In September 2006 he moves out to be closer to his partner David in London and begins to rent the property out.

In March 2007, Caleb and David become registered civil partners and David decides to put his Liverpudlian property into joint names in order to save some Income Tax.

In June 2008, Caleb decides to sell the house in Liverpool.

Caleb will be fully exempted by principal private residence relief on his share of the capital gain.

David, however, would be fully taxable on his share as the property was never his only or main residence.

There are one or two ways in which Caleb and David might get around this dilemma.

The easiest method might simply be to transfer the property back into Caleb's sole ownership.

Alternatively, they might perhaps consider both moving back into the property for some reasonable period prior to the sale, so that it could qualify as David's main residence for principal private residence purposes.

Under the second scenario, David would then be entitled to the same level of principal private residence relief and private letting

216

relief as Caleb, even though he didn't live there all of the time that Caleb did.

Timing

Where a transfer to a spouse or registered civil partner prior to sale is planned, the following guidelines may assist in making it effective for tax purposes. Bear in mind always, though, that the transferee must have beneficial ownership for the transfer to work as intended.

- It is preferable to do the transfer as soon as possible.

- Ideally, it should be done before the property is put on the market.

- A transfer at any time after there is a contract for sale to a third party is quite likely to be ineffective in providing the transferee with the requisite beneficial ownership.

But Joint Ownership Is Not Always Beneficial

It should be noted that a transfer into joint names prior to sale is not always beneficial. Sometimes, it is preferable to have the property in the sole name of one spouse or partner at the time of sale. This may arise, for example, if:

- One spouse or partner is a higher rate taxpayer, whilst the other has little or no income,

- One spouse or partner's annual exemption for Capital Gains Tax will be fully or partly utilised on other capital gains in the same year, whilst the other's annual exemption remains fully available, or

- One spouse or partner has capital losses available to set off against the gain on the property.

If the best spouse or partner to hold the property at the time of the sale is not the one that already holds it then a pre-sale transfer could generate considerable savings. The same provisos as set out above apply equally here.

In summary, when a sale is in prospect, it is well worth assessing whether a transfer into joint ownership, or to the other spouse or civil partner outright, might result in a significant Capital Gains Tax saving. Always remember, however, that whoever has legal title to the property at the time of the sale is entitled to the proceeds!

Lastly, it is also worth remembering that joint ownership does not have to mean equal shares and any other allocation is also possible.

8.5   HAVE YOUR CAKE AND EAT IT

Income Tax savings can also be generated by transferring an investment property into either joint names with your spouse or registered civil partner, or into the sole name of the spouse or registered civil partner with the lower overall income. In the right circumstances, moving income from one spouse or civil partner to another in this way can save over £8,000 in Income Tax *each year* (based on 2006/2007 tax rates).

However, as explained in section 8.4 above, this form of tax planning is not effective unless beneficial title in the property is genuinely transferred. But not everyone trusts their spouse or civil partner enough to simply hand over the title to their property!

For Income Tax purposes, at least, there is a way to solve this dilemma. Where property is held jointly by husband and wife or by registered civil partners, there is an automatic presumption, for Income Tax purposes, that the income arises in equal shares. This 50/50 split will continue to be applied unless and until the couple jointly elect for the income to be split in accordance with the true beneficial title in the property.

Hence, where a property owner who is married or in a registered civil partnership wants to save Income Tax on their rental profits without giving up too much of their title to the property, what they should do is:

- Transfer the property into joint names with their spouse or partner.
- Retain 99% of the beneficial ownership and transfer only 1% to their spouse or partner.

AND

- Simply never elect for the income to be split in accordance with the true beneficial title.

Conversely

Conversely, of course, there will be cases where the actual beneficial ownership split is preferable for tax purposes. In these cases, the election to split the income on an actual basis should usually be made.

Beware though that, once made, this election is irreversible.

8.6   MARRIAGE, DIVORCE AND CIVIL PARTNERSHIPS

Getting married or entering into a registered civil partnership alters your tax status dramatically.

One major aspect of this for property investors is the fact that, from that date onwards, the couple can only have one main residence between them for principal private residence relief purposes.

On this occasion, there are some important points to bear in mind:

i)   If more than one private residence is available to you as a couple, you should elect which one is to be your main residence (see section 6.23). In these circumstances, the election must be done within two years of the date of marriage or registration.

ii)   You will normally have at least three years during which the residence which is no longer regarded as a main residence continues to be exempt under the principal private residence exemption.

In most cases, where each member of the couple had their own main residence prior to the marriage or civil partnership, the best way to maximise your overall tax reliefs would be to do the following *after* you marry or register the partnership:

   i)   Put both of your former main residences into joint names.

   ii) Both live in each property as your main residence (together) at some period, or

   iii) If both properties continue to be your private residences (i.e. not let out, etc), use main residence elections to ensure that each property has main residence status for you both at some time.

Divorce and Separation

Once you get separated or divorced your married status for tax purposes ends.

'Separated' in this context means either legally separated under the terms of a court order or separated in circumstances which are likely to be permanent.

The good news is that, once again, you will be able to have your own individual main residence for principal private residence relief purposes.

Alternatively, however, if you have not claimed any principal private residence relief on a main residence elsewhere in the interim, your former marital home will continue to be exempt as long as your ex-spouse or ex-civil partner continues to use it as their main residence.

8.7   WHY 'LET TO BUY' BEATS 'BUY TO LET'

From a tax perspective, 'Let to Buy' scores heavily over 'Buy to Let', simply because both properties will attract the principal private residence exemption.

Where a taxpayer lets out their existing home in order to fund the purchase of a new property, we call this 'Let to Buy'. This technique is becoming increasingly popular for a number of reasons and one of them is the potential Capital Gains Tax saving.

Example – Buy to Let

Gregor bought his current home in 1991 for £50,000 and in 2006 it is worth £200,000.

Eventually, in 2016, he sells the house for £400,000. Naturally, it is fully exempt from Capital Gains Tax as it has been his main residence throughout his ownership.

Gregor also buys a 'Buy-to-Let' property for £200,000 in 2006. This property is also sold for £400,000 in 2016.

After Taper Relief at 40% and his annual exemption for 2016/2017 of £11,800 (say), Gregor has a taxable gain of £108,200 and a Capital Gains Tax bill of £43,280.

Example – Let to Buy

The situation is exactly as before except that, on acquisition of the second property in 2006, Gregor moves out of his former home, begins to rent it out and adopts the new property as his main residence.

Gregor's former home produces an overall gain of £350,000. Indexation relief on the property from 1991 to 1998 amounts to 19.8% and results in an indexed gain of £340,100.

18/25ths of this gain is exempted by principal private residence relief. This represents the 15 years of occupation of the property as Gregor's main residence plus his last three years out of a total period of ownership of 25 years. Gregor's private residence relief thus amounts to £244,872.

Gregor is also entitled to Private Letting Relief of £40,000, bringing his gain down to £55,228 before Taper Relief at 40% and his 2016/2017 annual exemption of £11,800 (say). The taxable gain is thus a mere £21,336, giving him a CGT bill of only £8,534.

In this example, Gregor thus saves £34,746 simply by moving house!

Added Benefits

In addition to Gregor's huge Capital Gains Tax saving, he could also save substantial amounts of Income Tax on his rental income by maximising the mortgage on his original home before he first lets it out. (See section 4.4.)

Gregor's Income Tax relief would be unaffected even if he used any additional borrowings for the deposit on his new home.

Gregor might even manage to avoid the need to take out any mortgage on his new home, thus confining any risk to his rental property alone.

8.8   CLIMBING THE LADDER

In chapter six we saw just how far the principal private residence exemption can be extended through its interaction with other reliefs.

This can be used to great effect to enable a taxpayer to build up a property portfolio virtually free of any Capital Gains Tax. The basic method is best explained by way of example.

Example

Malcolm buys a small flat (Flat A) in 2004. He moves in and it becomes his main residence. A year after buying the first flat, he buys another, larger, flat (Flat B). He does not immediately move into the new flat but spends a year renovating it. He moves into Flat B in 2006, just before the anniversary of its purchase and then starts renting out Flat A as private residential accommodation.

The story so far

Malcolm now has two flats, both of which will be fully exempted by the principal private residence exemption until at least 2009. The private letting exemption may also further extend Flat A's tax-free status until at least 2014 (depending on the ultimate sale price).

Example Continued

In 2008, Malcolm buys a house (House C). Again, he does not move in immediately but spends a year renovating the house before moving in just before the anniversary of its purchase.

He now starts renting out Flat B as private residential accommodation.

The story so far (2009)

Flat A may be exempt from any Capital Gains Tax until at least 2014, Flat B will be fully exempted until at least 2012 and quite possibly until 2019 and House C will be fully exempted until at least 2012, possibly 2016. All of this without even resorting to taper relief or the annual exemption.

You get the idea!

Eventually some of the earlier acquisitions will begin to be exposed to Capital Gains Tax. As illustrated in chapter six, however, this may take several years. When that point is reached, Malcolm can sell off the properties one at a time in order to make best use of his annual exemptions.

Potential Drawbacks

The first and most obvious potential problem is finance. However, with the rapid expansion in the 'buy-to-let' mortgage market, many people have successfully been able to follow a strategy similar to Malcolm's.

Secondly, Revenue & Customs have the power to overturn the principal private residence exemption if they perceive that the taxpayer is carrying on a trade of property development or is acquiring properties with no motive other than to realise a profit.

Hence, Malcolm's strategy does carry a degree of risk and may not succeed beyond the first few properties. The longer Malcolm retains the properties after his original renovation and occupation periods, however, the more this risk will diminish.

Relying On The Principal Private Residence Exemption

In this, as with any other planning scenario which places reliance on the principal private residence exemption, it is essential to ensure that the property or properties concerned genuinely become your private residence.

There is no 'hard and fast' rule as to how long you must reside in a property to establish it as your private residence for Capital Gains Tax purposes. It is the quality of occupation that counts, not the length. Hence, it is recommended that:

i)   You (and your spouse or partner and/or family, if applicable), move into the property for a substantial period.

ii) You ensure that all relevant institutions (banks, utilities, Revenue & Customs, etc) are notified that the property is your new, permanent, address.

iii) You inform family and friends that this address is your new permanent home.

iv) You furnish the property for permanent occupation.

v)   You register on the electoral roll for that address.

vi) You do not advertise the property for sale or rent until after the expiry of a substantial period.

It is not possible to provide a definitive view of what would constitute a 'substantial period'. What matters is that the property genuinely becomes your 'permanent home' for a period. In this context, 'permanent' means 'not temporary', i.e. intended to be your residence, rather than a temporary abode. You must move into the property with no clear plans for moving out again.

As a rough guide only, you should plan your affairs on the basis that you will be residing in the property for at least a year. However, as already stated, the question would ultimately be decided on quality of occupation, rather than length. Where you are looking to use the principal private residence exemption on a property you must embark upon occupying that property completely wholeheartedly; a mere 'sham' occupation will not suffice.

In some instances, you may be able to establish the desired result merely by electing for the property to be treated as your main residence (see section 6.23). However, it can only be your <u>main</u> residence if it is indeed your private residence and the safest way to ensure that a property is accepted as being your private residence, is to make it your main residence, or even your only residence, by following the measures set out above.

8.9   GENERAL ELECTIONS

As explained in section 6.23, where a taxpayer has two or more private residences it is possible to elect which is to be regarded as their main residence. In fact, it is more than <u>possible</u>, it is **highly advisable**, even when it seems obvious which property should be regarded as the main residence.

Example

Diana owns a house in London purchased in 2002 for £300,000. In July 2005, she buys a small cottage in Sussex for £100,000, to be used as her 'weekend retreat', although, in fact, she only manages to spend a few weekends a year there.

In early 2009, plans for a new motorway junction to be built only half a mile from Diana's cottage are announced. Simultaneously, the value of her property increases dramatically, whilst her own desire to use the place herself rapidly diminishes. A few months later, in July, she sells it for an astonishing £400,000.

Now, fortunately for Diana, her accountant had insisted that she make a main residence election in January 2006. At the time, she naturally elected that her London house was her main residence, since it seemed far more likely to produce a significant capital gain.

Because of this earlier election, however, Diana was able to make a new election in 2009, stipulating her Sussex cottage as her main residence. As a result, the cottage is covered by the principal private residence exemption for the last three years of Diana's ownership, thus exempting her from Capital Gains Tax on £225,000 out of her total gain of £300,000, a saving of up to £90,000!

Furthermore, her London house will only lose its principal private residence exempt status for a short period.

The moral of the story – always, always, always make the main residence election where applicable.

Tax Tip

A property only has to be classed as your main residence for **any** period, no matter how short, in order for your last three years of ownership to be exempted under the principal private residence exemption.

Hence, in order to minimise the impact on the principal private residence relief available to another property, it is only necessary to elect in favour of the new 'main residence' for a very short period.

In Diana's case, she could have preserved most of the principal private residence exemption on her London house by making another revised 'main residence' election in favour of that property a week after she had made the election in favour of her Sussex cottage.

Wealth Warning

Electing for an existing private residence to be your 'main residence' for just a week is fine.

Do not confuse this, however, with the need to establish the property as being your private residence in the first place (as explained in section 8.8 above), where a considerably longer period of occupation is recommended.

8.10   SOMETHING IN THE GARDEN

It's a common scenario: a taxpayer has a large garden so he or she sells part of it off for property development. (See section 6.16 above for general guidance on the limitations of the principal private residence exemption in these circumstances.)

There are the right ways to do this and there are other ways, which are very, very wrong.

The wrong ways

DO NOT:

- Sell your house first before selling the development plot.

- Fence the development plot off or otherwise separate it from the rest of your garden before selling it.

- Use the development plot for any purpose other than your own private residential occupation immediately prior to the sale.

- Allow the development plot to fall into disuse.

Each of these will result in the complete loss of your principal private residence exemption for the development plot. And, furthermore, do not assume that the plot is covered by the principal private residence exemption if the total area of your garden exceeds half a hectare.

The right ways

First, the simple way:

Carefully ensuring that you do not commit any of the cardinal sins described above, you simply sell off the plot of land. This sale will now enjoy the same principal private residence exemption as applies to your house itself, whether that be full or partial. (E.g., if 90% of a gain on your house would have been exempt, then 90% of the gain on the plot of land will be exempt.)

The other 'right way'

The only drawback to the simple way is that you do not get to participate in any of the profit on the development of the plot.

But, what if you hang on to the plot and develop it yourself? Yes, at first this looks like we've gone the wrong way, but not if you then proceed to move into the new property and adopt it as your main residence.

Your old house can safely be sold at any time up to three years after the date you move out and still be covered by the principal private residence exemption.

The new house should be fully covered by the principal private residence exemption as long as you moved in within a year of the date that development started.

As in section 8.8, there are some potential dangers here, but the exemption should be available if you genuinely adopt the new house as your new main residence.

8.11 STUDENT LOANS

Each individual adult, who is neither married nor in a registered civil partnership, is entitled to have their own main private residence which is exempt from Capital Gains Tax. Once your children reach the age of 18 therefore, it is possible to put some tax-free capital growth into their hands. (They do not actually have to be students by the way – it works just as well if they are in employment or even just living a life of leisure at your expense, as many teenagers seem to do!)

The method is fairly straightforward, all that you need to do is purchase a property in their name which they then move into and adopt as their main residence.

Financing can be achieved in a number of ways, but the important point is that they must have legal and beneficial title to the property. (Hence this technique should only be undertaken if you are prepared to pass wealth on to the children.)

The purchase of the property has possible Inheritance Tax implications but these are avoided simply by surviving for seven years.

Wealth Warning

You should also be careful not to make any use of the property yourself, since, if you have provided the funds for its purchase, any subsequent occupation by you, your spouse or your registered civil partner may give rise to an Income Tax charge under the 'pre-owned assets' regime.

8.12 MULTIPLE EXEMPTIONS

This technique looks fairly clumsy but can save some reasonably large amounts of Capital Gains Tax. It simply revolves around using a transfer of property into joint names with a friend or adult family member, and a short delay in the ultimate sale, to triple the number of annual exemptions available and double the potential to utilise the lower and basic rate tax bands.

The method also works for unmarried (and unregistered) couples.

Again, it is best illustrated by way of an example. All figures quoted in this example are based on 2006/2007 tax rates and on the assumption that a half share in a property as 'tenants in common' is worth 90% of half of the value of the whole property.

This last assumption may be disputed, but the same effect can be achieved without it if prices are rising sufficiently rapidly.

Example

Edmund has a property which he has owned for many years and which he is looking to sell in the near future. The property is worth £200,000 and he anticipates making a capital gain of £150,000 after all available exemptions other than his annual exemption. He has only a modest level of income, below the level of his personal allowance. A straightforward sale now would nevertheless still give him a Capital Gains Tax liability of £49,605.

In March 2007, however, Edmund puts the property into joint names with his adult son, Edgar, as 'tenants in common'. This still gives Edmund a Capital Gains Tax liability, as he has made a disposal to a connected person and this must be treated as having taken place at market value.

However, Edmund has only disposed of a half share in the property, which, as 'tenants in common' is only worth 90% of half of what the whole property is worth, i.e. £90,000. This gives him a taxable gain of £65,000 and an immediate Capital Gains Tax liability of £15,605.

In the following tax year, Edmund and Edgar sell their jointly owned property. Edmund has another capital gain of £75,000, giving him a further Capital Gains Tax liability of £19,299. Most of Edgar's modest gain of £10,000 is covered by his 2007/2008 annual exemption, giving him a maximum Capital Gains Tax bill of only £360.

The total Capital Gains Tax payable by Edmund and Edgar amounts to £35,264 and a saving of £14,341 has therefore been achieved.

(The annual exemption for 2007/2008 has been estimated at £9,100 in this example.)

As in section 8.11 above, this technique may involve the passing on of wealth and again has possible Inheritance Tax implications. As with other methods described, it is also essential that beneficial title in the property is genuinely passed over.

8.13   MAIN RESIDENCES AS BUSINESS ASSETS

Principal private residence relief and business asset Taper Relief are calculated quite independently of each other.

Where both apply to the same property, this can produce some quite unexpected results.

Firstly, any principal private residence relief (and private letting relief, if applicable) is claimed in arriving at the untapered gain.

That untapered gain must then be apportioned between the business element and the non-business element. This may produce the result where the business element of a property is denied principal private residence relief (fair enough) and also the taper relief on the remaining gain is further restricted (which is ludicrous & tantamount to double taxation).

Example

Geoffrey has owned a large house for many years and which has been used as his main residence since purchase. Throughout his ownership, however, one quarter of the house has been used exclusively for business purposes.

In January 2007, Geoffrey sells the house and realises a capital gain of £500,000. Three quarters of the gain is exempted by principal private residence relief, leaving an unrelieved gain of £125,000.

Quite obviously, the unrelieved gain has arisen entirely due to Geoffrey's business use of part of the property. One might therefore have reasonably expected taper relief of 75% to be available.

Not so! The unrelieved gain must again be divided between the business and non-business elements of the original total gain.

Hence, Geoffrey only obtains business asset taper relief on £31,250, or 1/16th of his total gain.

The remaining unrelieved gain will only attract non-business taper relief at a maximum of 40%.

Much has been said about the unfairness of this in the tax press but, unfortunately, to précis the response from Dawn Primarolo, Paymaster General to the Treasury, it's "just tough".

Tax Tip

Revenue & Customs' own Capital Gains manual (paragraph CG64662) states that any restriction of principal private residence relief should be done on a just and reasonable basis.

Applying the 'just and reasonable' criterion to the above example, one could surely argue that the part of the gain not exempted by principal private residence relief must be entirely related to the business part of the property and therefore eligible for the full 75% taper relief rate.

It must be worth a try?

Turning the Tables

Nevertheless, as is so often the case in tax planning, there is perhaps scope to turn the tables and use this ridiculous interpretation of the legislation to the taxpayer's advantage.

Example

Carl buys a cottage in the small town of Melrose in the Scottish Borders and uses it as his main residence for one year. He then rents it out for two years before finally selling it six years after purchase and realising a capital gain of £300,000 (it's a big cottage).

Carl is eligible for principal private residence relief on 4/6ths of his gain (one year as main residence plus last three years out of a total period of ownership of six years), i.e. £200,000, plus he is entitled to private letting relief of £40,000, leaving him with an untapered gain of £60,000.

Taper relief for a non-business asset held for six years is 20%, thus giving Carl a tapered gain of £48,000.

Alternatively, however, Carl might have used the cottage as his office premises for the last three years of his ownership. Provided that this did not involve any significant structural alterations to the property, this will not affect his principal private residence exemption or his private letting relief.

It will, however, mean that 3/6ths of his £60,000 untapered gain will attract business asset taper relief at 75% (instead of 20%), thus reducing his tapered gain to only £31,500 and potentially saving him up to £6,600 in Capital Gains Tax.

8.14 FURNISHED HOLIDAY LETTINGS

Furnished holiday lettings are nothing less than wonderful!

Properties which qualify as furnished holiday lettings enjoy the best of all worlds. They continue to be treated as investment properties whenever that is the more beneficial treatment but get treated like a trade whenever most trading reliefs are up for grabs.

They can sometimes qualify as private residential accommodation and yet still get so many of the advantages generally reserved for commercial property.

Getting one of your properties to qualify as furnished holiday accommodation is the property tax equivalent of winning the lottery!

In essence, UK properties qualifying as 'furnished holiday lettings' enjoy a special tax regime, which includes many of the tax advantages usually only accorded to trading properties. At the same time, however, the profits derived from furnished holiday lettings are still treated as rental income.

The taxation benefits of qualifying furnished holiday lettings include the following:

- Business asset taper relief.
- Rollover relief on replacement of business assets.
- Holdover relief for gifts.
- Capital allowances for furniture, fixtures and fittings.
- Losses may be set off against other income of the same tax year or the previous one.
- Despite its 'trading-style' advantages, National Insurance Contributions should not usually be payable in respect of income from furnished holiday accommodation (but see section 7.10).
- A non-UK resident investing in UK furnished holiday accommodation would usually continue to be exempt from Capital Gains Tax.

Income arising purely from the provision of furnished holiday accommodation continues to be an exempt supply for VAT purposes. Ancillary services such as cleaning, etc, may, however, be standard-rated. See section 7.6 for further details.

A furnished holiday letting business may also be exempt from Inheritance Tax where the lettings are short-term and the owner (or his or her employees) was substantially involved with the holidaymakers' activities.

The available reliefs extend to any property used in a furnished holiday letting business. This will include not only the holiday accommodation itself but also any office premises from which the business is run.

Qualification

The qualification requirements for a property to be regarded as a furnished holiday letting are as follows:

i) The property must be situated in the UK.
ii) The property must be furnished (again, this would generally be expected to be to at least the minimum level which an occupier would usually expect).
iii) It must be let out on a commercial basis with a view to the realisation of profits.
iv) It must be available for commercial letting to the public generally for at least 140 days in a 12-month period.
v) It must be so let for at least 70 such days.
vi) The property must not normally be in the same occupation for more than 31 consecutive days at any time during a period of at least seven months out of the same 12-month period as that referred to in (iv) above.

The 12-month period referred to in (iv) and (vi) above is normally the tax year. On a claim by a taxpayer with more than one furnished holiday letting property, a system of averaging may be used to determine whether they meet test (v) above.

Whilst the property need not be in a recognised holiday area, the lettings should strictly be to holidaymakers and tourists in order to qualify.

Where a property qualifies, as set out above, then it generally qualifies for the whole of each qualifying tax year, subject to special rules for the years in which holiday letting commences or ceases.

234

Where, however, there is some other use of the property during the year, the Capital Gains Tax reliefs described above will be restricted accordingly.

Nevertheless, it remains possible for the taxpayer and their family to use the property privately as a second home during the 'off season' and still fit within the rules described above.

However, the overall position must still fit in with rule (iii) above and hence, in practice, the property must be made available for letting to third parties for a sufficiently large proportion of the year to give its owners a realistic expectation of profits.

The result of failing to meet this test would be the loss of furnished holiday letting status and hence the consequent loss of all the additional reliefs which that status provides.

Tax Tip

Preparing a credible business plan when you first acquire the property would provide valuable supporting evidence that you had a reasonable expectation of profit.

A documented annual review of the plan will also be useful, as the 'profit expectation' test must be met every year.

Note, however, that a business plan will not help you if it clearly bears no resemblance to your actual behaviour in respect of the property.

Interaction with Other Reliefs

A property which qualifies as furnished holiday accommodation and which has also qualified as the owner's main residence at some time during their ownership, will also be eligible for private letting relief.

This could produce a quite remarkable combination of tax reliefs.

Example

In section 6.22 we met Bonnie who had a small cottage on Skye which, for twelve years, she had rented out as furnished holiday accommodation for 48 weeks each year and occupied herself for the remaining four weeks. The property also qualified as Bonnie's main residence (perhaps by election).

When, in 2018, Bonnie realised a capital gain of £104,000 on her sale of the property, we saw that she obtained principal private residence relief of £32,000. But it doesn't end there!

Bonnie would also be entitled to private letting relief of £32,000 (equal to her principal private residence relief), thus reducing her gain to just £40,000.

Bonnie would then be entitled to business asset taper relief at 75% on 48/52nds on this gain. Her total taper relief would thus be:

£40,000 x 48/52 x 75% =	*£27,693*
£40,000 x 4/52 x 40% =	*£1,231*
Total:	*£28,924*

Leaving her with a tapered gain of just £10,076, which is very likely to be covered by her 2018/2019 annual exemption.

Note, in this example, that Bonnie's business asset taper relief is restricted due to her private use of the property for four weeks per year.

A similar restriction would apply if she attempted to claim rollover relief on a replacement of the property or holdover relief on a gift of it.

Note also that these restrictions apply whenever the owner makes any private use of the property, whether it qualifies as their main residence or not.

8.15 TAX-FREE HOLIDAY HOMES

There is a fairly easy way to shelter the entire capital gain on a qualifying furnished holiday letting property.

If the property has never been used for any other purpose then the entire capital gain arising on a gift of the property can be held over where a joint election is made by the transferor and the transferee.

If the transferee then adopts the property as their main residence then any capital gain arising when they sell it, including the original held over gain, will be fully exempt.

Example

Bonnie also has a flat in Edinburgh, which she has let out as furnished holiday accommodation for many years and has never used for any other purpose. The flat now stands at a substantial capital gain.

Bonnie can, however, gift the flat to her adult daughter, Flora, and jointly elect with her to hold over the capital gain arising.

Flora can then make occasional (but regular) personal use of the property as a holiday home and can elect for it to be regarded as her main residence for Capital Gains Tax purposes.

Potentially, Flora's election in favour of the flat could be for as little as one week, thus preserving most of the Capital Gains Tax exempt status on her own home.

The flat may then be sold at any time within three years of the date of Bonnie's gift and will be totally exempt from Capital Gains Tax.

It is probably advisable that Flora does not let out the flat for a reasonable period (say a year) and that period must include the period during which she has elected the property as her main residence.

Bonnie should avoid any personal use of the flat after her gift to Flora, as this could give rise to an Income Tax charge.

8.16   ENTERPRISE INVESTMENT SCHEME SHARES

Capital Gains Tax liabilities may be deferred by reinvesting some or all of the underlying untapered capital gain in Enterprise Investment Scheme shares. To obtain relief, the investment must take place within the period beginning a year before, and ending three years after, the date of the disposal which gave rise to the gain.

Enterprise Investment Scheme shares are not eligible for Income Tax relief (see below) when the investor is connected with the company issuing the shares. However, this does not prevent reinvestment relief for Capital Gains Tax purposes from applying. Hence, a taxpayer could potentially defer Capital Gains Tax on his property gains by investing in his own trading company!

Unfortunately, however, companies engaged in any form of property business are generally ineligible to issue Enterprise Investment Scheme shares. (But see the Taxcafe.co.uk guide *Using a Property Company to Save Tax* for some pointers on how to use an Enterprise Investment Scheme company to make property investments.)

Alternatively, products are now available which enable taxpayers to utilise a 'portfolio' approach when investing in these intrinsically risky investments. This does not totally eliminate the risk, but it certainly improves the odds!

Income Tax Relief and Other Points

Qualifying investments in Enterprise Investment Scheme shares issued by an unconnected company also carry an Income Tax credit of up to 20% of the amount invested. Hence, combining the Income Tax credit with the potential for Capital Gains Tax deferral outlined above gives a potential for total tax savings of up to 60% of the amount invested!

Enterprise Investment Scheme shares must be Ordinary Shares, as defined in tax legislation, must be issued wholly for cash and must be held for at least three years (sometimes longer).

The issuing company must also continue to carry on a 'qualifying trade' (broadly one which is not property-based) throughout this period. All tax relief given on the initial investment will be withdrawn if any of these conditions are breached.

Any capital gain arising on the sale of Enterprise Investment Scheme shares which did initially qualify for Income Tax relief, as described above, is exempt from Capital Gains Tax. This exemption is also lost if the Income Tax relief is withdrawn.

Note that it is only the capital gain on the Enterprise Investment Scheme shares themselves which may be exempt. Gains held over on reinvestment into Enterprise Investment Scheme shares will become chargeable to Capital Gains Tax on a sale of those shares at any time. When a deferred gain becomes chargeable, the same rate of taper relief is given as that which would have applied on the occasion of the original gain.

From 6th April 2006, an annual limit of £400,000 applies to the amount invested in Enterprise Investment Scheme shares which is eligible for Income Tax relief.

Tax Tip

With careful timing, Enterprise Investment Scheme shares could be used to defer capital gains of up to £2,000,000, whilst still obtaining total Income Tax savings of £400,000 over a five-year period.

Whilst there is no limit on the amount which can be invested annually in Enterprise Investment Scheme shares for Capital Gains Tax deferral purposes, it should be borne in mind that the Income Tax savings and Capital Gains Tax exemption on the shares themselves are permanent (unless certain rules regarding the period of ownership and other matters are broken).

Hence, sticking within the annual investment limit of £400,000 for Income Tax purposes, where possible, is likely to be highly beneficial.

Example

Dawson anticipates making a taxable capital gain (before taper relief) of £2,000,000 on 1ˢᵗ May 2007.

He could defer all of his potential Capital Gains Tax liability by reinvesting his gain in Enterprise Investment Scheme shares at any time between 1ˢᵗ May 2006 and 1ˢᵗ May 2010. However, it is only by timing his investments very carefully that he will be able to obtain the maximum Income Tax saving of £400,000 also.

To do this, Dawson needs to time his Enterprise Investment Scheme share purchases as follows:

- *£400,000 between 1ˢᵗ May 2006 and 5ᵗʰ April 2007*
- *£400,000 during each of the tax years ended 5ᵗʰ April 2008, 2009 and 2010*
- *£400,000 between 6ᵗʰ April and 1ˢᵗ May 2010*

If Dawson had simply made his whole £2,000,000 Enterprise Investment Scheme share investment in 2007/2008, he would have achieved the same Capital Gains Tax deferral relief, but would have managed an Income Tax saving of only £80,000, rather than the maximum £400,000.

Furthermore, all being well, Dawson should also be fully exempt from Capital Gains Tax on any increases in the value of his Enterprise Investment Scheme shares.

8.17   SWEET SHOP COMPANIES

After the last section, you may be wondering what use Enterprise Investment Scheme shares are for property investors.

Well, this is where what I call the 'sweet shop principle' comes in.

The idea is that you simply find a very simple and low risk business, like a sweet shop, which requires business premises.

Then you set up 'Sweet Shop Company Limited' to run the shop. This company issues Enterprise Investment Scheme shares to you in exchange for the cash which has come from a capital gain which you wish to defer. The company then uses this cash to buy its retail premises.

In this way, you are effectively able to roll over any capital gain into the purchase of the business premises, via the medium of the sweet shop company. This is probably the least risky way to secure a Capital Gains Tax deferral with Enterprise Investment Scheme shares.

It doesn't necessarily have to be a sweet shop, but it must not be any of the types of trade or business which are specifically excluded in the legislation and, as I explained in the last section, this covers most types of property business. Even hotels and guest houses are excluded.

8.18 EMIGRATION

Taxpayers facing substantial potential Capital Gains Tax liabilities often avoid them by emigrating. However, merely going on a world cruise for a year will not usually be sufficient, as it is necessary to become non-UK ordinarily resident, as well as non-UK resident.

This is a complex field of tax planning, which really requires a separate guide on its own. However, the key points worth noting are:

- Emigration must generally be permanent, or at least long-term (usually at least five complete UK tax years).

- Disposals should be deferred until non-residence has been achieved.

- Limited return visits to the UK are permitted.

- Returning prematurely to the UK, to resume permanent residence here, may result in substantial Capital Gains Tax liabilities.

- It is essential to ensure that there is no risk of inadvertently becoming liable for some form of capital taxation elsewhere. (There is no point in 'jumping out of the frying pan and into the fire!')

Until recently, shorter periods of absence abroad were sometimes sufficient to avoid UK Capital Gains Tax by making use of the terms of a Double Tax Treaty between the UK and the new country of residence (e.g. Belgium). Unfortunately, however, it would appear that this strategy no longer works for new emigrants after 16th March 2005.

Emigration to avoid UK tax is generally a strategy which is only worth contemplating when the stakes are high. Naturally, therefore, detailed professional advice is always advisable.

The following example, however, illustrates the broad outline of what is involved.

Example

Lea has been a highly successful UK property investor for many years. By early 2007, she has potential Capital Gains Tax liabilities on her UK investment property portfolio of over £2,000,000.

She therefore decides to emigrate and, on 3rd April 2007 she flies to New Zealand where she settles down to a new life.

During the 2007/2008 tax year, Lea sells all her UK properties, but is exempt from Capital Gains Tax as a non-resident.

Eventually, however, she decides that she wants to return home and, on 8th April 2012, she comes back to the UK to live.

As Lea was non-resident for over five complete UK tax years, she should be exempt from Capital Gains Tax on all her property sales.

Notes to the Example

i) I picked New Zealand because I happen to know that there is no Capital Gains Tax there. Nevertheless, it is always essential to take detailed local professional advice in the destination country.

ii) When a taxpayer emigrates, they may often be regarded as non-resident immediately on the day of departure. This is not something which I would like to rely on and I would always recommend that the sales giving rise to capital gains are deferred until the next tax year after the tax year of departure.

iii) If Lea had returned to the UK to live on or before 5th April 2012, all of her property disposals in 2007/2008 would have become liable to UK Capital Gains Tax. The gains would then be treated as if they had arisen in the tax year in which Lea returned to the UK. I guess you can put up with a lot of homesickness for £2,000,000.

Return Visits

Limited return visits to the UK will not prevent the emigrant from retaining their non-resident status. The general rules on return visits are:

- They must not exceed 182 days in any one UK tax year.
- They must average less than 91 days per year.

A 'day' in the UK is not counted for this purpose unless you stay here overnight.

8.19   PENSION RELIEF

On 6th April 2006, known as 'A Day', the UK pensions regime underwent a radical transformation.

Under the new regime, taxpayers may contribute up to £215,000 to qualifying pension schemes in the 2006/2007 tax year.

Unfortunately, however, the amount of gross contributions qualifying for tax relief is limited to the lower of:

a) £3,600, or
b) The taxpayer's total 'earnings' for the tax year.

The problem for property investors is that rental income and capital gains are not classed as 'earnings' for this purpose.

This will leave a property investor with no employment or self-employed trading income able to obtain tax relief on a maximum of £3,600 of gross pension contributions per annum.

Basic rate tax relief at 22% continues to be given at source, so that actual payments of £2,808, or £234 per month, equate to gross contributions of £3,600. Higher rate tax relief, where applicable, is then given through the self assessment tax system.

We will return to some of the other implications of 'A Day' in chapter nine.

8.20 FLAT CONVERSION ALLOWANCES

In an effort to regenerate some of the UK's urban centres, the Government has provided a special tax incentive known as 'Flat Conversion Allowances'.

Broadly speaking, what this allowance does is to enable you to make an immediate claim against your taxable income for the costs of converting qualifying properties back into residential flats.

Furthermore, as long as you keep these flats for a sufficient length of time after completing the conversion work, the allowance will never be clawed back, meaning that Gordon Brown & Co. will, for once, have actually made a contribution in return for their silent partnership stake in your property business!

To qualify for the allowance, the flats must be in a property which was built before 1980 and has no more than five floors in total. The ground floor must be in business use, such as a shop, café, office or doctor's surgery, and the upper storeys must originally have been constructed primarily for residential occupation.

Additionally, in the year before conversion takes place, the storeys above the ground floor must have been used only for storage purposes or been unoccupied.

In other words, the allowance is given for converting former residential property which is now in business use, or vacant, back into residential property.

Let's look at an example of how the allowance might work in practice.

Example

Gordon has a large portfolio of rented properties, giving him net annual rental income of £100,000. As he is a higher rate taxpayer, his income tax bill on his rental income is thus £40,000. In June 2006, Gordon buys a run-down three storey property on Kirkcaldy High Street.

Despite having once been the site where Adam Smith wrote his 'Wealth of Nations', the ground floor is now leased to a rather poor quality fast-food retailer.

However, Gordon is more interested in the upper storeys which are currently unoccupied and in a state of disrepair. He spends £60,000 converting these storeys into a number of small flats which he then lets out.

Not only does Gordon now have a valuable property and a stream of rental income, but he will also be able to slash his tax bill this year by £24,000!

As long as he continues to own the flats for a further seven years after the conversion, this money will never be clawed back.

The only drawback (there has to be one, doesn't there?) is that Gordon cannot claim this same expenditure in his Capital Gains Tax computation when he eventually sells the flats. Even this still leaves a major benefit for Gordon, since he is getting the certainty of tax relief now at 40% at the expense of merely potential future relief, which, due to the impact of taper relief, may only be worth 24% at best (if he holds the flats for ten years or more).

There are some restrictions on the type of flat which you can create out of the conversion. Basically, they have to be small and not particularly luxurious.

The type of expenditure which can be claimed is also restricted and excludes, in particular, the original cost of the property prior to conversion, the cost of any extensions to the property and the cost of furnishing the flats.

Still, on the whole, this is a pretty useful allowance. So, who wants to go to the shops?

8.21 THE TENDER TRAP: THE BENEFITS AND PITFALLS OF RE-MORTGAGING

"What, no tax at all, that's amazing! Well, thanks a lot, that's wonderful news."

This is the kind of reaction I often get when people ask me about the tax consequences of re-mortgaging their properties.

The situation is a pretty common one. You have a property which you bought some years ago and which has risen significantly in value since then. Rather than sell the property, you can realise the 'profit' from this growth in value by re-mortgaging and thus obtain the cash value of your equity by different means.

However, whilst this might initially seem to be a very good way of avoiding tax on the growth in the capital value of your investment properties, there are some long-term dangers inherent in this strategy which could ultimately prove to be your downfall if you are not prepared for them.

The contrast between the initial tax-saving benefits of re-mortgaging and the potential ultimate pitfalls of the strategy is what leads me to call this scenario 'The Tender Trap'. It's tender because of its initial apparent benefits, but it can prove to be a costly trap from which it is difficult to escape.

More about the trap later, though. To begin with, let's look at the short-term benefits of the re-mortgaging strategy.

In the short term, this method works extremely well from a tax point of view. Potentially, in fact, realising equity value through re-mortgaging can produce benefits under each of the three main taxes which affect property investors – Capital Gains Tax, Income Tax and Inheritance Tax. To illustrate these benefits, let's look at an example.

Example Part 1

Steve has a buy-to-let property in Essex which has grown significantly in value since he bought it for £25,000 in November 2000. In fact, by June 2006 the property's current market value is £85,000.

However, Steve feels that property values in Essex are unlikely to show any further significant increase in the foreseeable future and he now wishes to invest in some new developments in Leeds.

In order to pursue his new investment opportunity in Leeds, Steve will need to 'cash in' his equity in his Essex property. Initially he considers selling the Essex property, but he is horrified to learn that he would have a Capital Gains Tax bill of £20,400. (He has already utilised his annual exemption elsewhere, but does get taper relief at 15%.) After repaying his original mortgage of £20,000, Steve would be left with only £44,600 to invest in Leeds.

Instead of selling the Essex property, therefore, Steve decides to re-mortgage it. His new mortgage is at 85% of current value, £72,250. Hence, after repaying his original mortgage, Steve has freed up £52,250 of equity value in cash. He therefore has an additional £7,650 (or 17.2%) more cash available for his new investment than he would have done if he had sold the Essex property. And, what's more, he still has the rental income from his original property.

Benefit 1: Capital Gains Tax

Capital Gains Tax can generally only be charged where there is a disposal of an asset. If you sell a property, you have made a disposal and hence, usually, there will be Capital Gains Tax to pay.

On the other hand, however, when you re-mortgage a property, you have not actually made any disposal, as you still own the property. Hence, although you will have realised some of your capital, you cannot be charged any Capital Gains Tax.

Although, in our example, Steve did this for investment purposes, this Capital Gains Tax benefit remains equally true whatever your reason for re-mortgaging a property.

Example, Part 2

Steve uses the £52,250 which he generated by re-mortgaging his Essex property as a deposit on a buy-to-let development in Leeds.

However, when he is completing his next Tax Return, Steve is uncertain what to do about the mortgage interest he is now paying on the Essex property. Fortunately, his friend Matthew (a Chartered Accountant) is able to point him in the right direction.

Matthew explains that the portion of the interest which relates to the original £20,000 loan (i.e. 20,000/72,250ths or 27.7%) should continue to be claimed against the rental income from the Essex property and the remainder (52,250/72,250ths or 72.3%) can be claimed against rental income from the Leeds properties.

"In fact," Matthew explains, "you could even have claimed the interest on the new part of the borrowings if you had re-mortgaged your own home instead because it's where you spend the money that matters, not where it came from."

Benefit 2: Income Tax

Where the funds generated by re-mortgaging an existing property are used to purchase new investment properties, the interest on the new borrowings can be claimed against the income from the new properties. This remains true even if the re-mortgaged property itself is the borrower's own home. The interest relief remains available as long as the funds are invested for business purposes.

Sometimes, however, the borrower will re-mortgage a property for other reasons – perhaps simply to provide living expenses. Whilst this will still produce the Capital Gains Tax benefit described above, there will be no Income Tax relief for the interest on the new borrowings in this instance.

Example, Part 3

For the next ten years, Steve continues to re-mortgage his existing properties and invest his realised capital growth in new buy-to-let developments.

By September 2016, he has 12 properties in Essex, Leeds and Newcastle worth a total of £2,500,000. His borrowings at this stage amount to £1,400,000 in total, giving him a total net equity value in his property portfolio of £1,100,000.

Steve happens to bump into his old friend Matthew, who he hasn't seen in years, and tells him how well his property portfolio has grown. "That's great", says Matthew. "Have you done anything about the Inheritance Tax though?"

Once again, Steve is horrified to discover that he has a huge potential tax bill on his properties – this time Inheritance Tax of £440,000. "Well, I'm wealthy enough now," he thinks. "I'll stop investing in new properties, live off the existing ones and give as much as I can away to my family."

For the next ten years, Steve continues to re-mortgage his properties up to 85% of their market value and he spends or gives away the proceeds. By 2026, his portfolio is worth £5,000,000, but he has total borrowings of £4,250,000, leaving him with a net equity value in his portfolio of only £750,000 and thus reducing his potential Inheritance Tax bill to only £300,000.

Benefit 3: Inheritance Tax

Re-mortgaging your properties as much as possible is an effective way to limit the net value of your estate for Inheritance Tax purposes. Rather than selling properties, which creates Capital Gains Tax liabilities, this enables you to give away some of the value of your assets, hopefully tax free (as long as you survive for seven years after making the gift).

Of course, to save Inheritance Tax, you will need to spend or give away the proceeds of re-mortgaging your properties, so this technique does not allow you to claim any Income Tax relief on the new borrowings.

Following this method may also put a severe strain on your cashflow. One of the ways to alleviate this would be to use some of the funds realised through re-mortgaging to purchase annuities, thus keeping the value of your estate down for Inheritance Tax purposes, whilst still providing you with an income during your lifetime.

Naturally, you need to be able to afford to spend or give this money away and still be able to pay the interest on your ever-increasing borrowings, so this strategy is not for everyone!

The Trap

So far, we've looked at the 'tender' part of the re-mortgaging strategy, namely the potential tax benefits. Now we turn to the trap.

The problem in essence is that Capital Gains Tax is based on the difference between sales proceeds and purchase cost. Hence, in order to calculate the capital gain arising when you sell a property, you deduct the original cost of the property from your sale proceeds.

What you do not deduct in your capital gains calculation is the outstanding amount of the mortgage over the property.

Naturally, if you have used additional borrowings to make improvements to the property, then these costs may also be deducted from sale proceeds.

However, where your additional borrowings have been spent, given away, or used to invest in other properties, you will have a liability to the lender without a corresponding deduction in your capital gains calculation. This is what creates the trap and we will go back to our friend Steve to see it in action.

Example, Part 4

In 2027, Steve runs into some financial difficulty and decides that he needs to sell one of his properties. The rental yield of his original Essex property has been pretty poor lately, so he sells this property for £360,000.

His borrowings against this property now amount to £306,000, so he realises net proceeds of only £54,000 (even before any sale expenses).

However, as Steve's original cost for the property was only £25,000, he realises a capital gain of £335,000. As he's held the property for over ten years, he is entitled to taper relief of 40%, reducing his gain to £201,000.

Nevertheless, as a higher rate taxpayer, he is still left with a Capital Gains Tax bill of £80,400. (Once again, he has used up his annual exemption elsewhere.)

After tax, Steve's sale of the Essex property has actually generated an overall net cost of £26,400!

In fact, if Steve were to sell his entire £5,000,000 portfolio, he would need to find an extra £104,000 to pay his tax bill!

Escaping The Trap

Steve's story is a lesson to us all. It's only an example, I know, but I have met property investors who are in a very similar position, or who will be if they keep on the way they're going.

Escaping the trap is possible, but does require some drastic action. The first option is to hang on to the properties until you die. This resolves the Capital Gains Tax problem and, as we have seen, the level of borrowings keeps the Inheritance Tax bill down.

If Steve had died before selling his properties, the portfolio would have yielded a net sum of £450,000 for his family after Inheritance Tax, rather than creating an overall cost of £104,000. This is because Capital Gains Tax is not charged on death. Furthermore, for future Capital Gains Tax purposes, the deceased's beneficiaries are treated as having acquired the properties at their market value at the time of death.

This is all very well, but what if you can't afford to keep the properties. This could happen for a variety of reasons, rental yields could fall, interest rates could rise. Additionally, as you get older, you may need to employ more help to maintain the portfolio and this will impact on your overall cashflow.

On the other hand, though, if you have insufficient other wealth beyond your property portfolio, you may be unable to fund the Capital Gains Tax bill arising if you do sell!

You could end up not being able to afford to keep the properties, nor able to afford to sell them!

In a case like Steve's, I would probably recommend emigration as his best chance to escape the tender trap. If he went abroad before selling the properties and then stayed away for at least five whole tax years, he would be exempt from UK Capital Gains Tax. Still quite drastic, but not as bad as the previous option.

'Safe Haven' Borrowings

Better still though, it is advisable to avoid getting into Steve's type of situation in the first place. To do this, the re-mortgaging strategy should be limited to a 'safe haven' level.

For properties held for less than three years, the 'safe haven' for your borrowing is 'original cost plus 60% of any increase in value'. On each anniversary of the property's purchase from the third anniversary to the tenth anniversary, the percentage of 'increase in value' which may safely be borrowed goes up by two percentage points. Eventually, for properties held for ten years or more, the 'safe haven' becomes 'original cost plus 76% of any increase in value'.

Keeping mortgage levels down to these 'safe haven' levels should ensure that you will have sufficient net funds arising on a sale of the property to be able to pay your Capital Gains Tax bill.

To err on the side of caution, though, I would also advocate reducing the resultant 'safe haven' figure by a further 5% to safeguard against a downturn in property values or any other nasty surprises.

Example

Russell has a flat in Glasgow which he bought seven years ago for £50,000. It is now worth £125,000, an increase in value of £75,000.

Russell's safe haven borrowing is his original cost, plus 70% of the
increase in value – this totals £102,500.

To be cautious, however, we reduce this by 5% - suggesting a 'safe'
figure for Russell's new mortgage of £97,375.

In Conclusion

Using a re-mortgaging strategy to build your property portfolio has
tremendous potential Capital Gains Tax and Income Tax benefits.
Realising your equity through additional borrowings is more tax
efficient than selling properties when you intend to reinvest the
proceeds in your portfolio.

Re-mortgaging can also be used to reduce the value of your net
estate for Inheritance Tax purposes.

However, a trap awaits the unwary and can, in the most extreme
cases, put the taxpayer in a quite untenable position.

Sticking to 'safe haven' levels of borrowing should ensure that you
don't fall into this trap.

8.22   NON-DOMICILED INVESTORS

As explained in the previous chapters, a UK resident but non-UK
domiciled taxpayer is generally only liable for UK tax on income
from, or capital gains on, foreign properties if these sums are
remitted back to the UK.

Very simply, therefore, if you are non-UK domiciled, you have the
opportunity to invest in property outside the UK and pay as much
or as little UK tax as you choose!

Remember also that the 'deemed domicile' after 17 years of
residence in the UK (see section 7.4) applies only for Inheritance
Tax purposes.

If you are non-UK domiciled under basic principles, your ability to
invest abroad free of UK Income Tax and Capital Gains Tax (as
long as you keep the funds offshore) should continue regardless of
how long you may have lived in the UK.

This gives rise to two very important tax planning points.

Firstly, if you are lucky enough to be non-UK domiciled, you should confirm this fact by completing the appropriate parts of the 'Non-Resident' supplementary pages to your tax return. (Despite its name, this supplement also covers taxpayers who are UK resident but non-UK domiciled.)

It is wise to do this as soon as possible, even if you have no foreign-source income or gains yet.

Following this, you may be sent a form 'DOM 1' to complete in order to confirm your non-domiciled status. The key point here is to confirm that you do not intend to remain in the UK permanently, i.e. until your death. Any lesser period, such as 'until retirement' or 'until my husband passes away' is, however, acceptable, even if this is still likely to be the majority of your remaining life.

Secondly, whenever you do have any income or gains from foreign property, you should try to keep it offshore.

Keeping funds offshore still permits you to do any of the following:

- Invest funds in the Isle of Man or Channel Islands.
- Hold funds denominated in sterling, but kept offshore.
- Spend the money whilst travelling abroad on business or even on holiday.
- Move the funds to a different country outside the UK (but watch out for any local exchange control restrictions).
- Invest in new foreign properties.

Wealth Warning

When doing any of the above, you must take care that the funds never flow via the UK, including any UK bank account.

What About Existing Capital Held Offshore?

Existing capital held offshore before you became UK resident may be brought into the UK without generating any tax charges.

Tax Tip

Have the interest on any such capital paid into a separate account.

You can then safely bring the 'capital' back to the UK, without being taxed on a remittance of your offshore interest income to the UK.

8.23 USING LEASE PREMIUMS TO GENERATE TAX-FREE RECEIPTS

As we saw in section 6.43, the granting at a premium of a lease of between two and fifty years' duration gives rise to a capital receipt equal to 2% of that premium for each whole year that the lease exceeds one year. For example, 12% of the premium charged for a seven-year lease will be treated as a capital disposal. Clever investors might consider this a good way to use their annual Capital Gains Tax exemption.

Example

Bob owns a small workshop which Terry wants to lease for 20 years. If Bob charges a premium of £23,000, 38% of this (£8,740) will be treated as a capital disposal. If Bob has no other gains this year, his 2006/2007 annual exemption of £8,800 will cover any capital gain, meaning that £8,740 of the premium is received tax free.

Bob and Terry then simply negotiate a level of rent which takes suitable account of the premium Bob has paid.

To keep this example simple, I have ignored any base cost which Bob has in the workshop. (See section 6.43 for more details.)

8.24 COMMERCIAL DEVELOPMENTS IN DISADVANTAGED AREAS

A new 'Business Premises Renovation Allowance' is to be introduced to provide immediate 100% tax relief for the cost of renovating or converting disused commercial property in disadvantaged areas to bring it back into business use. (These are the same 'disadvantaged areas' discussed in section 7.2.)

The new 'business use' need not be the same as the building's original use and can include offices and shops.

The start date for this new relief is not yet known, as it requires 'State Aid' clearance from the European Union.

8.25 ROLLOVER RELIEF

The capital gain arising on the sale of a property used in your own trading or furnished holiday letting business may be rolled over into the purchase of a new trading or qualifying furnished holiday letting property within the period beginning one year before, and ending three years after, the date of disposal of the original property.

This effectively defers any Capital Gains Tax liability on the original property until such time as the new property is sold.

Full relief is available only if the old property was used exclusively for 'trading purposes' throughout your ownership, or at least since 31st March 1982, if it was acquired earlier.

Furthermore, for rollover relief purposes, it is the sale **proceeds** of the old property which must be reinvested and not merely the capital gain arising. Any shortfall in the amount reinvested is deducted from the amount of gain eligible for rollover.

The use of a property for 'furnished holiday accommodation', as defined in section 8.14, however, counts as 'trading purposes' for the purposes of rollover relief.

If there is less than full trading use of the property then an appropriate proportion of the gain arising may be rolled over.

Example

Stavros sells an office building in June 2006 for £400,000, realising a capital gain of £100,000.

Stavros has owned the building since June 1996 and, up until June 2001, he rented all of it out to tenants. From June 2001 until the date of sale, however, Stavros used two thirds of the building as his own premises from which he ran a property development trading business.

Stavros is therefore eligible to roll over £33,333 (£100,000 x 5/10 x 2/3) of his capital gain into the purchase of new trading premises or furnished holiday accommodation. The eligible amount has been restricted both by reference to the proportion of time in Stavros' ownership that the property was used for trading purposes and also by reference to the proportion of the property used for trading purposes.

In August 2008, Stavros buys two cottages in Cornwall for £120,000 and begins to let them out as furnished holiday accommodation.

He is therefore able to claim rollover relief of £20,000.

He cannot claim the full £33,333 which was eligible for rollover, because he has not reinvested the whole qualifying portion of his sale proceeds (£400,000 x 5/10 x 2/3 = £133,333).

Important Points To Note

1. The new qualifying property does not need to be in the same trade or even the same kind of trade and it can also be qualifying furnished holiday accommodation.

2. There is no minimum period for which the new property needs to be used for trading purposes. (Although it must be acquired with the intention of using it for trading purposes.) In our example, Stavros could run the holiday cottages for, say, two seasons and then change to normal, long-term letting. His Capital Gains Tax rollover relief would not be clawed back, although he would have reduced base costs on the cottages when he eventually came to sell them.

Tax Tip

Where you have a capital gain eligible for rollover relief, it is only necessary to use the replacement property for trading purposes for a limited period.

As explained below, this could include initially running the new property as a guest house before later reverting to long-term letting.

What Kinds of Investment Properties Can Qualify?

Rollover relief can also apply where:

i) Any commercial property is purchased by an authority with compulsory purchase powers.

ii) Any residential property is purchased by a tenant exercising a legal right to acquire the freehold reversion or a new leasehold interest (e.g. under the Leasehold Reform Act 1967).

Other than these instances, however, rollover relief is only likely to be available to property investors for:

- Furnished holiday accommodation.
- The trading premises of a property development, property dealing or property management business.
- A property where the owner is providing significant additional services.

The latter case would generally require a level of services akin to a guest house, although the owner need not reside there themselves.

Other Assets

Rollover relief is not restricted to property and could also apply where the old asset and/or the new asset are one of the following:

- Fixed plant and machinery
- Goodwill*

- Ships, aircraft and hovercraft
- Satellites, space stations and spacecraft
- Milk and potato quotas*
- Ewe and suckler cow premium quotas*

In each case both old and new assets must again be used for trading purposes, as explained above. The assets marked * above are not eligible for rollover relief claims by companies.

8.26   YEAR END TAX PLANNING

Rental Income

As explained in chapter four, for individuals or partnerships with rental profits, it is compulsory to draw up accounts for the tax year, rather than for any other accounting period. Hence, for these property businesses, 5th April is twice as important since, not only is it the end of the tax year, but it is also the end of their accounting period.

Where I refer in this section to 'your year end', those with property rental businesses should read this as meaning 5th April.

Property Trades

As we saw in chapter five, those with property trades may choose their own accounting date.

Where I refer in this section to 'your year end', those with property trades should read this as meaning their own accounting date, rather than the tax year end.

The Tax Year End

Where I refer to 'the tax year end' this means 5th April whatever kind of business you have!

Timing Is Everything

For most property businesses, the 'accruals' basis will apply, meaning that income and expenditure must be recognised when it arises, or is incurred, rather than when it is received or paid.

Expenses may therefore be recognised as they are incurred. Hence, wherever you are expecting to need to make some business expenditure in the near future, it may make sense to ensure that it takes place by your year end, in order to get tax relief in an earlier year, rather than having to wait another 12 months.

Obviously, this does not mean it is worth incurring expenditure just for the sake of it. It is seldom wise to make uncommercial decisions purely for tax reasons!

What it does mean, however, is that it can often be worth accelerating some of the expenditure, which is going to be taking place in any case, so that it falls into an earlier accounting year.

Landlords on The Cash Basis

For any smaller landlords still operating on the cash basis, the tax-planning objective is to accelerate the actual <u>payment</u> of any necessary property expenditure to before the tax year end on 5th April.

Such landlords might also do well to consider setting the due dates for rent receivable so that it falls shortly after the tax year end (although care needs to be exercised as this concessionary accounting basis may be withdrawn if it does not produce a reasonable result).

Capital Allowances

Where capital allowances are available, the full allowance is usually given for the year in which the expenditure is incurred. Where expenditure is eligible for capital allowances, therefore, consider making your purchase by your year end.

Cars

Some capital allowances may be available on a car which you use in your property business. The allowance is usually restricted by reference to the private use of the car, but nevertheless it is worth noting that:

- A balancing allowance is usually available on the sale of an old car previously used in your property business, and
- A full year's allowance will be given on any new car brought into use in the business by your year end.

Hence, both sales of old cars and purchases of new cars before your year end will often save tax where the vehicles are used in your property business.

A few words of caution about capital allowances

a) Sales of old cars can sometimes give rise to a balancing charge instead of a balancing allowance (although the latter is far more common).

b) Assets bought on Hire Purchase must actually be brought into use in the business by your year end. Merely purchasing them by that date is not enough.

c) Assets bought on credit terms where payment is due four months or more after the purchase may not produce an immediate right to capital allowances.

d) Cars, office equipment and other assets purchased partly for your own private use can only attract allowances if genuinely used in the business. As already stated, an element of private use will lead to a reduction in the allowances available.

Furnished Lettings: Renewals and Replacements

As explained in chapter four, capital allowances are not available on furniture, fixtures or fittings in furnished residential lettings. The landlord may, however, claim either the 10% wear and tear allowance or renewals and replacements expenditure.

Anyone who is on the renewals and replacements basis should consider whether they need to make any replacement expenditure in the near future. If so, it is again worth accelerating such expenditure to before your year end.

Employees' Bonuses

If you have any employees in your property business, it may be worth considering whether you wish to pay any of them a bonus before your year end. Such a bonus would be tax deductible in your business, although, naturally you do need to actually pay it to them and you also need to consider any National Insurance Contributions liabilities which may arise.

Hence, bonuses are only worth thinking about from a tax-planning point of view if either:

a) You are going to pay them anyway, or
b) The employee is your spouse, partner or another adult family member.

However, where (a) or (b) do apply, a bonus can be recognised (or 'accrued') in your property business's accounts for the year, and thus obtain tax relief as long as:

- The bonus is in respect of the employee's work for your property business during the year, and
- The bonus is actually paid to the employee within nine months after your year end.

Hence, although PAYE and National Insurance Contributions liabilities will often arise, they can often be deferred until well into the next year.

Those with a spouse, partner or other adult family member working in their business should also be sure to maximise the use of personal allowances by ensuring that these employees receive sufficient salary or wages by the tax year end to utilise their personal allowances.

8.27 BED AND BREAKFASTING FOR PROPERTY INVESTORS

Firstly, I am not, in this section, talking about running guest houses. We looked at that in sections 2.11 and 8.25.

What we are concerned with here is the Capital Gains Tax planning strategy known as 'Bed and Breakfasting'.

To do this you need a good 'friend' or a trust. Your 'friend' cannot be your spouse or registered civil partner but partners in an unmarried, or unregistered, couple will do just fine.

The idea is simply to make use of your annual Capital Gains Tax exemption by transferring an investment property to your 'friend' or a trust in which you yourself are the main beneficiary.

The transfer triggers a taxable capital gain. This is used to provide 'value' for your annual Capital Gains Tax exemption if you are not using it elsewhere.

Is It Worth It?

Using up an otherwise wasted annual exemption could ultimately save you up to £3,520 in Capital Gains Tax.

However, finding a property which has gone up in value by exactly the amount of the annual exemption may not be easy with the result that you may end up actually paying some tax on the transfer.

Furthermore, there are also inevitably bound to be legal fees and other costs involved.

On balance, this is probably only worthwhile where a subsequent sale of the property to a third party in the near future is anticipated.

Chapter 9

Planning With More Complex Structures

9.1 USING A PROPERTY COMPANY TO SAVE TAX

In recent years, many UK property investors have been drawn towards the idea of running their property business through a limited company.

This is due, in part, to the highly favourable Corporation Tax regime, including the 'nil rate' of Corporation Tax introduced on 1st April 2002, which generally applied to the first £10,000 of a company's profits.

Sadly, that 'nil rate' was withdrawn with effect from 1st April 2006.

Nevertheless, despite the loss of the highly favourable 'nil rate' band, companies continue to enjoy a Corporation Tax regime which taxes both income and gains at rates which are almost always more beneficial than the corresponding Income Tax and Capital Gains Tax rates payable by an individual on the same level of income, thus providing the opportunity to make huge annual tax savings on rental profits.

Conversely, however, a company does not have as many reliefs available under the capital gains regime and is not entitled to principal private residence relief, taper relief or an annual exemption.

Furthermore, there is a significant 'catch' which lies in the fact that further tax costs will often arise when extracting profits or sale proceeds from the company.

All of these conflicting factors combine to make the decision whether or not to use a company a highly complex issue. Nevertheless, despite its complexity, it is well worth the effort of undertaking a detailed examination of your own particular circumstances to see whether you have scope to make the

264

substantial tax savings which are available under the right set of conditions.

A detailed examination of the tax benefits and pitfalls of using a company to invest in property is contained in the Taxcafe.co.uk Guide *Using a Property Company to Save Tax*.

In this guide, we show how, using the favourable Corporation Tax regime, a property investor can achieve a significantly higher income than a personal investor. Copies of this guide can be obtained directly from our website.

9.2 PARTNERSHIPS

Most of the tax rules outlined throughout this guide will apply equally to partnerships, including limited liability partnerships and any individuals who are members of a corporate or limited partnership.

In many ways, a property partnership simply combines joint ownership with a more sophisticated profit sharing agreement.

However, a partnership is considerably more flexible, as, subject to the terms of the partnership agreement, partners may join, leave or change their profit share at any time.

Some of the legal background to property partnerships was covered in section 2.13.

Since the year 2000, a new legal entity has been available throughout the UK – a Limited Liability Partnership, or 'LLP' for short. Like a Scottish partnership, an LLP is a legal person and may own property directly.

Each partner is taxed on his or her share of rental income, trading profits or capital gains, as allocated according to the partnership agreement.

One major drawback to property investment partnerships, however, is the danger of incurring Stamp Duty Land Tax charges at frequent intervals. Since 22nd July 2004, Stamp Duty Land Tax has been payable whenever a partner:

a) Introduces property into a partnership,
b) Takes property out of a partnership, or
c) Reduces his profit share.

In the case of a reduction in profit share, there must be some consideration given for the transaction concerned (cold comfort, as there often will be, even if only accounted for via the partners' capital accounts – which is enough to trigger the charge).

Furthermore, from 17th March 2005, Stamp Duty Land Tax may also be charged on partners withdrawing funds from a partnership within three years of introducing property into that same partnership.

Example Part 1

Dave has been in a property investment partnership with four friends, Dozy, Beaky, Mick and Tich, for several years. The five friends each have a 20% profit share. Dave would now like to retire and wishes to leave the partnership. The partners agree that, by way of consideration for giving up his partnership share, Dave should take the property known as 'Dee Towers' with him. Dee Towers is worth £1,000,000.

Dave already had a 20% share in Dee Towers through the partnership so he is treated as acquiring an 80% share, worth £800,000, when he leaves the partnership. He will therefore face a Stamp Duty Land Tax charge of £32,000! (4% x £800,000)

Example Part 2

A short time later, Mick inherits £1,000,000 from his great aunt Shirley. He decides that he would like to invest this in the partnership. At the same time, Tich has decided that he would like to retire and wishes to sell his partnership share. Mick therefore buys Tich's 25% partnership share for £1,000,000, thus increasing his own share from 25% to 50%.

Immediately prior to Mick's new investment, the partnership had a property portfolio with a total gross value of £20,000,000 and borrowings of £16,000,000. Whilst the partnership's net assets are only £4,000,000, the Stamp Duty Land Tax charge is based on its property portfolio's gross value.

Mick has increased his profit share from 25% to 50%. He is therefore treated as having acquired a 25% interest in property worth £20,000,000. Hence, Mick will be faced with a Stamp Duty Land Tax bill of £200,000! (25% of £20,000,000 charged at 4%.)

By and large, therefore, anyone using a property investment partnership should try to get their profit shares right in the first place and do their utmost to avoid changing them at a later stage.

Note, however, that a straightforward cash investment into the partnership will not incur any Stamp Duty Land Tax charge. Hence, if Mick had simply put £1,000,000 into the partnership, rather than buying out Tich's share, he could have avoided the Stamp Duty Land Tax charge whilst still increasing his profit share.

Note also that the amount which Mick paid for Tich's share has no bearing on the amount of Stamp Duty Land Tax payable which is based, instead on the gross value of the partnership's property portfolio.

It is worth contrasting this with the position which would have existed if the five friends had set up a property investment company instead.

Subject to some anti-avoidance rules, the shares in a property investment company can change hands for a Stamp Duty charge of only 0.5%, which represents a considerable saving compared to the rather draconian 4% applying to property investment partnerships as we have already seen. Furthermore, the charge on company shares would be based on the actual consideration paid for those shares and not on the gross value of the underlying properties.

Example Revisited

As above, Mick is investing £1,000,000 in a property investment business which owns a property portfolio with a gross value of £20,000,000 but has net assets of only £4,000,000. This time, however, he is purchasing shares in a property investment company. His Stamp Duty liability will therefore be only £5,000. (Compared with Stamp Duty Land Tax of £200,000 previously.)

The lesson here is clear – if you and your colleagues are likely to want to change profit shares with any degree of frequency whatsoever, a company is likely to be much better than a partnership.

Wealth Warning

Revenue & Customs interpret the Stamp Duty Land Tax rules for partnerships as applying not only to property held by the partnership, but also to property held by an individual partner for use in the partnership business.

Other Partnerships Holding Property

At present, the same Stamp Duty Land Tax charges apply to any partnership holding property.

From Royal Assent to the 2006 Finance Bill (probably around July 2006), however, these charges will no longer apply to partnerships whose main activity is a trade other than that of dealing in or developing property.

Sadly, this relaxation is of absolutely no use whatsoever to the vast majority of property partnerships!

9.3 PROPERTY SYNDICATES AND SPECIAL PURPOSE VEHICLES

The term 'syndicate' is a very loose one. When you join a property syndicate, you may, in fact, be investing through any one of a number of structures (or 'Special Purpose Vehicles' as they are often called), including those which I have already outlined above, Unit Trusts (either UK or Offshore) or a much more loosely defined Joint Venture agreement.

The best that I can say is that you should find out exactly how your syndicate is structured and take your own independent legal and tax advice on it. As with any other kind of investment, you need to be very careful who you trust with your money!

Syndicates structured as property investment companies can provide opportunities to make tax efficient investments benefiting from business asset taper relief or the Enterprise Investment Scheme (see section 8.16). More details on syndicates structured as a company are contained in the Taxcafe.co.uk guide *Using a Property Company to Save Tax*.

9.4   PENSION SCHEMES

The last few years have seen a great deal of excitement with the imminent approach of 'A Day' (6th April 2006) promising a major overhaul of the entire UK pensions regime.

Up until just four months before 'A Day' much of this excitement centred around the anticipation that our own Personal Pension Schemes would be able to invest in residential property.

As most people will know, however, on 5th December 2005, Gordon Brown announced a prohibition on Self-Invested Personal Pension Schemes (often known as SIPPs) investing directly in residential property.

Self-Invested Personal Pension Schemes may, however, still invest in:

- Commercial property
- Real Estate Investment Trusts
- Property Unit Trusts
- Dedicated student halls of residence (but not individual student flats).
- Hotels.
- Residential care homes.
- Residential property syndicates of 11 or more people.

The last heading is probably the closest that investors are going to be able to get to the original ideal of investing their pension funds directly into a residential property portfolio.

The Self-Invested Personal Pension Scheme will be regarded as investing in the syndicate rather than the property and this means that the syndicate will be able to borrow up to 85% of the value of its property investments – a vast improvement on the 50% of net value rule applying to the Self-Invested Personal Pension Scheme itself.

No syndicate member may hold 10% or more of the syndicate and personal use of any syndicate property by any member of the syndicate is strictly prohibited.

The last details of the new pensions regime are still emerging and the exact rules will not become final until around July 2006, but at least it looks like there is still some room for residential property investment by Self-Invested Personal Pension Schemes after all.

Self-Invested Personal Pension Schemes can also invest in Real Estate Investment Trusts or Property Unit Trusts and this provides another indirect method for investing pension funds into residential property.

Investment through a Self-Invested Personal Pension Scheme can provide some great advantages, as income and gains within the Pension Scheme are tax free. The difficulty for many property investors, however, as we saw in section 8.19, is that, without 'earnings', your tax-efficient contributions to the Self-Invested Personal Pension Scheme are limited to a paltry £3,600 per tax year.

9.5   REAL ESTATE INVESTMENT TRUSTS

Real Estate Investment Trusts are to be introduced on 1st January 2007. The key features include:

- Rental income and capital gains derived from investment properties will be exempt from tax within the Real Estate Investment Trust.
- Dividends paid out by the Real Estate Investment Trust will be treated as property income (i.e. like rent) in the hands of the investor. [This means tax payable of 22% for basic rate taxpayers receiving the dividends, instead of 0%; and 40% for higher rate taxpayers, instead of an effective 25%.]
- At least 90% of the Real Estate Investment Trust's tax exempt profits must be paid out as dividends each year.
- The Real Estate Investment Trust must be UK Resident and listed on a recognised stock exchange.
- No single investor may hold 10% or more of the Real Estate Investment Trust's shares.

- At least 75% of the Real Estate Investment Trust's assets must be investment property.
- At least 75% of the Real Estate Investment Trust's income must be rental income.
- The Real Estate Investment Trust's ratio of interest payable to rental income must be less than 1.25:1

Real Estate Investment Trusts may invest in both commercial and residential property.

Existing companies which qualify as set out above and which wish to convert to Real Estate Investment Trust status can do so on payment of an entry charge equal to 2% of the market value of the company's investment properties.

Sadly, despite the rule that dividend income received from a Real Estate Investment Trust must be treated like rental income in the investor's hands, it appears that it will not be possible to set off any losses which the investor is making on their own UK property portfolio against their Real Estate Investment Trust income. This denies anyone with UK property losses the opportunity to get tax-free income from Real Estate Investment Trust investments.

9.6   OTHER WAYS TO INVEST IN PROPERTY

Up to 100% of an Authorised Investment Fund can now be invested in property.

Investments in 'Authorised Collective Schemes' which invest in property may now be included within both ISA's (Individual Savings Accounts) and Child Trust Funds.

Appendix A

Tax Rates and Allowances
2004/2005 to 2006/2007

	Rates	Bands, allowances, etc.		
		2004/200	2005/2006	2006/2007
		£	£	£
Income Tax				
Personal allowance		4,745	4,895	5,035
Starting rate	10%	2,020	2,090	2,150
Basic rate	22%	29,380	30,310	31,150
Higher rate on over	40%	31,400	32,400	33,300
Normal higher rate threshold		36,145	37,295	38,335
National Insurance Contributions				
Class 1 – Primary	11%	- Earnings between lower & upper earning limits		
Class 4	8%	- Earnings between lower & upper earning limits		
Lower earnings limit		4,745	4,895	5,035
Upper earnings limit		31,720	32,760	33,540
Class 1 – Secondary	12.8%	- On earnings above lower earnings limit.		
Class 1 & Class 4	1%	- On earnings above upper earnings limit.		
Class 2 – per week		2.05	2.10	2.10
Small earnings exception		4,215	4,345	4,465
Class 3 – per week		7.15	7.35	7.55
Pension Contributions				
Pension scheme earnings cap		102,000	105,600	n/a
Annual allowance		n/a	n/a	215,000
Lifetime allowance		n/a	n/a	1,500,000
Capital Gains Tax				
Annual exemption:				
Individuals		8,200	8,500	8,800
Trusts		4,100	4,250	4,400
Inheritance Tax				
Nil Rate Band Threshold		263,000	275,000	285,000
Annual Exemption		3,000	3,000	3,000
Pensioners, etc.				
Age allowance: 65-74		6,830	7,090	7,280
Age allowance: 75 and over		6,950	7,220	7,420
MCA: born before 6/4/1935		5,725	5,905	6,065
MCA: 75 and over		5,795	5,975	6,135
MCA minimum		2,210	2,280	2,350
Income limit		18,900	19,500	20,100
Blind Person's Allowance		1,560	1,610	1,660

(The Married Couples Allowance, 'MCA', is given at a rate of 10%)

Appendix B

Indexation Relief Rates
(See section 6.11 for application)

Percentages applying to disposals made by individuals after 5 April 1998
of assets acquired (or enhancement expenditure incurred) during:

Month of expenditure	Index'n Rate	Month of expenditure	Index'n Rate
March 1982 or earlier	104.7%	July-85	70.7%
April-82	100.6%	August-85	70.3%
May-82	99.2%	September-85	70.4%
June-82	98.7%	October-85	70.1%
July-82	98.6%	November-85	69.5%
August-82	98.5%	December-85	69.3%
September-82	98.7%	January-86	68.9%
October-82	97.7%	February-86	68.3%
November-82	96.7%	March-86	68.1%
December-82	97.1%	April-86	66.5%
January-83	96.8%	May-86	66.2%
February-83	96.0%	June-86	66.3%
March-83	95.6%	July-86	66.7%
April-83	92.9%	August-86	67.1%
May-83	92.1%	September-86	65.4%
June-83	91.7%	October-86	65.2%
July-83	90.6%	November-86	63.8%
August-83	89.8%	December-86	63.2%
September-83	88.9%	January-87	62.6%
October-83	88.3%	February-87	62.0%
November-83	87.6%	March-87	61.6%
December-83	87.1%	April-87	59.7%
January-84	87.2%	May-87	59.6%
February-84	86.5%	June-87	59.6%
March-84	85.9%	July-87	59.7%
April-84	83.4%	August-87	59.3%
May-84	82.8%	September-87	58.8%
June-84	82.3%	October-87	58.0%
July-84	82.5%	November-87	57.3%
August-84	80.8%	December-87	57.4%
September-84	80.4%	January-88	57.4%
October-84	79.3%	February-88	56.8%
November-84	78.8%	March-88	56.2%
December-84	78.9%	April-88	54.5%
January-85	78.3%	May-88	53.1%
February-85	76.9%	June-88	52.5%
March-85	75.2%	July-88	52.4%
April-85	71.6%	August-88	50.7%
May-85	70.8%	September-88	50.0%
June-85	70.4%	October-88	48.5%

Appendix B (cont'd)

Month of expenditure	Index'n Rate	Month of expenditure	Index'n Rate
November-88	47.8%	September-92	16.6%
December-88	47.4%	October-92	16.2%
January-89	46.5%	November-92	16.4%
February-89	45.4%	December-92	16.8%
March-89	44.8%	January-93	17.9%
April-89	42.3%	February-93	17.1%
May-89	41.4%	March-93	16.7%
June-89	40.9%	April-93	15.6%
July-89	40.8%	May-93	15.2%
August-89	40.4%	June-93	15.3%
September-89	39.5%	July-93	15.6%
October-89	38.4%	August-93	15.1%
November-89	37.2%	September-93	14.6%
December-89	36.9%	October-93	14.7%
January-90	36.1%	November-93	14.8%
February-90	35.3%	December-93	14.6%
March-90	33.9%	January-94	15.1%
April-90	30.0%	February-94	14.4%
May-90	28.8%	March-94	14.1%
June-90	28.3%	April-94	12.8%
July-90	28.2%	May-94	12.4%
August-90	26.9%	June-94	12.4%
September-90	25.8%	July-94	12.9%
October-90	24.8%	August-94	12.4%
November-90	25.1%	September-94	12.1%
December-90	25.2%	October-94	12.0%
January-91	24.9%	November-94	11.9%
February-91	24.2%	December-94	11.4%
March-91	23.7%	January-95	11.4%
April-91	22.2%	February-95	10.7%
May-91	21.8%	March-95	10.2%
June-91	21.3%	April-95	9.1%
July-91	21.5%	May-95	8.7%
August-91	21.3%	June-95	8.5%
September-91	20.8%	July-95	9.1%
October-91	20.4%	August-95	8.5%
November-91	19.9%	September-95	8.0%
December-91	19.8%	October-95	8.5%
January-92	19.9%	November-95	8.5%
February-92	19.3%	December-95	7.9%
March-92	18.9%	January-96	8.3%
April-92	17.1%	February-96	7.8%
May-92	16.7%	March-96	7.3%
June-92	16.7%	April-96	6.6%
July-92	17.1%	May-96	6.3%
August-92	17.1%	June-96	6.3%

Appendix B (cont'd)

Month of expenditure Index'n Rate

Month of expenditure	Index'n Rate
July-96	6.7%
August-96	6.2%
September-96	5.7%
October-96	5.7%
November-96	5.7%
December-96	5.3%
January-97	5.3%
February-97	4.9%
March-97	4.6%
April-97	4.0%
May-97	3.6%
June-97	3.2%
July-97	3.2%
August-97	2.6%
September-97	2.1%
October-97	1.9%
November-97	1.9%
December-97	1.6%
January-98	1.9%
February-98	1.4%
March-98	1.1%
April 1998 or later	0.0%

Appendix C

The European Union &
The European Economic Area

The European Union

The 25 member states of the European Union are:

Austria	admitted 1st January 1995
Belgium	founding member
Cyprus	admitted 1st May 2004
Czech Republic	admitted 1st May 2004
Denmark	admitted 1st January 1973
Estonia	admitted 1st May 2004
Finland	admitted 1st January 1995
France	founding member
Germany	founding member
Greece	admitted 1st January 1981
Hungary	admitted 1st May 2004
Irish Republic	admitted 1st January 1973
Italy	founding member
Latvia	admitted 1st May 2004
Lithuania	admitted 1st May 2004
Luxembourg	founding member
Malta	admitted 1st May 2004
Netherlands	founding member
Poland	admitted 1st May 2004
Portugal	admitted 1st January 986
Slovakia	admitted 1st May 2004
Slovenia	admitted 1st May 2004
Spain	admitted 1st January 1986
Sweden	admitted 1st January 1995
United Kingdom	admitted 1st January 1973

Any rights which citizens of countries admitted on 1st May 2004 have under UK tax law will commence on that date.

The European Economic Area

The European Economic Area comprises the 25 member states of the European Union plus:

Iceland
Liechtenstein
Norway

Tax Return Supplements

Supplement	Download Document
Employment	www.hmrc.gov.uk/forms/sa101.pdf
Self-Employment	www.hmrc.gov.uk/forms/sa103.pdf
Partnership	www.hmrc.gov.uk/forms/sa104.pdf
Land & Property	www.hmrc.gov.uk/forms/sa105.pdf
Foreign	www.hmrc.gov.uk/forms/sa106.pdf
Trust Income	www.hmrc.gov.uk/forms/sa107.pdf
Capital Gains	www.hmrc.gov.uk/forms/sa108.pdf
Non-Residence	www.hmrc.gov.uk/forms/sa109.pdf

Alternatively, forms may also be obtained by calling the Revenue & Customs orderline: 0845 9000 404.

Short Leases
(See section 6.43.)

Proportion of the original cost of a lease of 50 or more years' duration allowed as a deduction for Capital Gains Tax purposes on a disposal of that lease.

Years Remaining	%	Years Remaining	%
50	100	25	81.100
49	99.657	24	79.622
48	99.289	23	78.055
47	98.902	22	76.399
46	98.490	21	74.635
45	98.059	20	72.770
44	97.595	19	70.791
43	97.107	18	68.697
42	96.593	17	66.470
41	96.041	16	64.116
40	95.457	15	61.617
39	94.842	14	58.971
38	94.189	13	56.167
37	93.497	12	53.191
36	92.761	11	50.038
35	91.981	10	46.695
34	91.156	9	43.154
33	90.280	8	39.399
32	89.354	7	35.414
31	88.371	6	31.195
30	87.330	5	26.722
29	86.226	4	21.983
28	85.053	3	16.959
27	83.816	2	11.629
26	82.496	1	5.983

Need Affordable & Expert Tax Planning Help?

Try Our Unique Question & Answer Service

The purpose of this guide is to provide you with detailed guidance on how to pay less tax on your property business.

Ultimately, you may want to take further action or obtain guidance personal to your circumstances.

Taxcafe.co.uk has a unique online tax service that provides access to highly qualified tax professionals at an affordable rate.

No matter how complex your question, we will provide you with some help through this service. The cost is just £69.95.

To find out more go to **www.taxcafe.co.uk** and click the Tax Questions button.

Pay Less Tax!

... with help from Taxcafe's unique tax guides and software

All products available online at www.taxcafe.co.uk

- ➤ **How to Avoid Property Tax** – Essential reading for property investors who want to know all the tips and tricks to follow to pay less tax on their property profits.

- ➤ **Using a Property Company to Save Tax** - How to massively increase your profits by using a property company... plus all the traps to avoid.

- ➤ **How to Avoid Inheritance Tax** – A-Z of inheritance tax planning, with clear explanations and numerous examples. Covers simple and sophisticated tax planning.

- ➤ **Tax Planning for Couples** – How married and unmarried couples can save thousands in income tax, capital gains tax, inheritance tax and national insurance using a variety of powerful tax planning techniques.

- ➤ **Non Resident & Offshore Tax Planning** – How to exploit non-resident tax status to reduce your tax bill, plus advice on using offshore trusts and companies.

- ➤ **The World's Best Tax Havens** – How to cut your taxes to zero and safeguard your financial freedom.

- ➤ **How to Avoid Stamp Duty** – Little known but perfectly legal trade secrets to reduce your stamp duty bill when buying or selling property.

- ➤ **Grow Rich with a Property ISA** – Find out how to invest in property tax free with an ISA.

- ➢ **Using a Company to Save Tax** – Everything you need to know about the tax benefits of using a company to run your business.

- ➢ **Bonus vs Dividend** – Shows how shareholder/directors of companies can save thousands in tax by choosing the optimal mix of bonus and dividend.

- ➢ **How to Avoid Tax on Your Stock Market Profits** – How to pay less capital gains tax, income tax and inheritance tax on your stock market investments and dealings.

- ➢ **Selling a Sole Trader Business** – A potential minefield with numerous traps to avoid but significant tax-saving opportunities.

- ➢ **How to Claim Tax Credits** – Even families with higher incomes can make successful tax credit claims. This guide shows how much you can claim and how to go about it.

- ➢ **Property Capital Gains Tax Calculator** – Unique software that performs complex capital gains tax calculations in seconds.

Disclaimer

1. Please note that this Tax Guide is intended as general guidance only for individual readers and does NOT constitute accountancy, tax, investment or other professional advice. Neither Taxcafe UK Limited nor the author can accept any responsibility or liability for loss which may arise from reliance on information contained in this Tax Guide.

2. Please note that tax legislation, the law and practices by government and regulatory authorities (e.g. Revenue & Customs) are constantly changing and the information contained in this Tax Guide is only correct as at the date of publication. We therefore recommend that for accountancy, tax, investment or other professional advice, you consult a suitably qualified accountant, tax specialist, independent financial adviser, or other professional adviser. Please also note that your personal circumstances may vary from the general examples given in this Tax Guide and your professional adviser will be able to give specific advice based on your personal circumstances.

3. This Tax Guide covers UK taxation only and any references to 'tax' or 'taxation' in this Tax Guide, unless the contrary is expressly stated, refer to UK taxation only. Please note that references to the 'UK' do not include the Channel Islands or the Isle of Man. Foreign tax implications are beyond the scope of this Tax Guide.

4. Whilst in an effort to be helpful, this Tax Guide may refer to general guidance on matters other than UK taxation, Taxcafe UK Limited is not expert in these matters and does not accept any responsibility or liability for loss which may arise from reliance on such information contained in this Tax Guide.

5. Please note that Taxcafe UK Limited has relied wholly on the expertise of the author in the preparation of the content of this Tax Guide. The author is not an employee of Taxcafe UK Limited but has been selected by Taxcafe UK Limited using reasonable care and skill to write the content of this Tax Guide.

Printed in the United Kingdom
by Lightning Source UK Ltd.
110092UKS00002B/52-1008